The Proudest Yankees of All

The Proudest Yankees of All
From the Bronx to Cooperstown

David Hickey and Kerry Keene

TAYLOR TRADE PUBLISHING
Lanham • New York • Oxford

Published by Taylor Trade Publishing
A Member of the Rowman & Littlefield Publishing Group
4501 Forbes Boulevard, Suite 200
Lanham, Maryland 20706

Distributed by National Book Network

Library of Congress Cataloging-in-Publication Data

Hickey, David, 1967–
    The proudest Yankees of all : from the Bronx to Cooperstown / David Hickey
and Kerry Keene.—1st Taylor Trade Pub. ed.
        p. cm.
    Includes bibliographical references and index.
    ISBN 0-58979-008-1 (alk. paper)
    1. New York Yankees (Baseball team)—History. 2. Baseball players—United States—
Biography. I. Keene, Kerry. II. Title.
GV875.N4 H53 2003
796.357'64'97471—dc21   2003002455

⊗™ The paper used in this publication meets the minimum requirements of
American National Standard for Information Sciences—Permanence of
Paper for Printed Library Materials, ANSI/NISO Z39.48–1992.
Manufactured in the United States of America.

Contents

For McKenna—who will always be daddy's baby girl.
   —David

For Pam—who was beside me every step of the way during the most difficult time of my life.
   —Kerry

Acknowledgments

Special thanks go out to Dick Thompson for once again providing access to his abundant collection of research materials. Thanks also go out to W. C. Burdick and Jeff Idelson of the National Baseball Hall of Fame and Museum, as well as the staff at the National Baseball Library; Joe Rocchio, Media Relations Department of the New York Yankees, as well as the Yankee organization; Lee MacPhail; Jill Langford and the staff at Rowman & Littlefield; Isaiah Arsenault and Zachary Keene.

Authors' Note

Each of the 39 chapters that make up this book serve as in-depth profiles of Yankee Hall of Famers. They are intended to be individual stories that stand on their own, not necessarily related to or dependent upon chapters that fall before or after. Many of these individuals were part of the Yankee organization at the same time, sharing many of the prominent happenings, such as World Series games, exclusive milestones, and noteworthy moments.

In an attempt to tell each man's story of their time with the Yankees as completely as desirable, particular events will be referred to numerous times throughout—each time, generally as it relates to that individual. It is the authors' hope that the reader will not find these instances unnecessarily repetitive.

Introduction

I n over 130 years of professional team sports in North America, there have literally been hundreds of franchises, yet there is only one that stands far above the rest in terms of stature, success, popularity, and recognizability.

The credentials possessed by the New York Yankee baseball team in its 100-year history are upon reflection near mind-boggling. After such a review, the only question to remain would be to determine which franchise might occupy second place. The sheer dominance achieved by the Yankee franchise is such that it would render virtually all others admiringly envious at the very least—insanely jealous at the very worst.

A recap of the team's successes on the field of play must begin with its phenomenal bottom-line figure of 26 World Championships. Going into the 2003 season, 27 percent of all World Series played since the inception of the modern day Fall Classic in 1903 have resulted in a Yankee victory. The franchise with the next-highest figure of Series championships, the St. Louis Cardinals, is lagging far behind with nine.

It is sobering to realize that the Cardinals would have to win the next 17 World Series in order to equal New York's lofty distinction. Since the team began its domination back in the 1920s, it has captured World Championships in eight different decades (1920s, 1930s, 1940s, 1950s, 1960s, 1970s, 1990s, and 2000s)—three more decades than any other team. In 1938, they became the first team to win three straight Series, then made it four the following year. Fourteen years later, the Yankees eclipsed their own mark by capturing their fifth straight crown in 1953. By this time, they had begun what was to be their most productive period (1949–1964), in which the Yankees took part in 14 of 16 consecutive World Series.

Though "winning it all" is ultimately the only truly acceptable conclusion to a successful season, it does bear mentioning that the Yankees have participated in well over one-third of all Fall Classics—a grand total of 37. There is a sign in the Yankee clubhouse that quotes General Douglas MacArthur: "There is no substitute for victory." The Yankees have taken this quote to heart far more than any other team.

Any sports franchise that is deemed "great" over a long period of time will surely have been made up of great personnel in various capacities that contribute each in their own way to the successes on the field of play. The New York Yankees would not merely be an example of this, they would absolutely epitomize the notion. Certainly no other organization could boast alumni who have attained the stature of a Ruth, Gehrig, DiMaggio, and Mantle, among the more prominent. When the concept of the National Baseball Hall of Fame was created in the mid-1930s and its first election was held in 1936, it was fitting that Babe Ruth would lead the way as the first Yankee representative. From that first election to this day nearly eight decades later, a total of 39 men have been elected to the Hall of Fame in the category in which they served the Yankees, be it as player, manager, or executive.

While the Cooperstown shrine is regarded as baseball's "Mecca," the Yankees' own Stadium is to many, every bit as hallowed. It is clearly the most revered of all athletic facilities. One favorite feature of the now 80-year-old ballpark is Monument Park, the area behind the outfield wall where plaques immortalize many of the team's greats. It is these "ghosts of Yankee past" that seem to watch over the team and help to further solidify the mystique that appears every bit as real as the unmistakable logo on the cap and jersey. As the players of today enter the Yankee clubhouse, they are greeted by a sign that features a quote from the great DiMaggio, which reads, "I just want to thank the good Lord for making me a Yankee."

As each of these 39 Yankee Hall of Famers are profiled on these pages, let us all try to hear in our minds their names announced by public address announcer Bob Shepherd as they gallantly stride out on the Yankee Stadium grass at a mythical Old-Timers Day for the ages.

The Birth of a Dynasty, 1902

t is somewhat ironic that the creation of the Yankee organization was prompted in part by the actions of legendary manager John McGraw, who went on to pilot the rival neighboring Giants for 30 years. McGraw had risen to prominence in the game as a star third baseman with the old Baltimore Orioles dynasty of the 1890s in the National League. When that team was disbanded after the 1899 season, McGraw landed with the St. Louis Cardinals.

In 1901, American League founder and president Ban Johnson had opted to place a new edition of Baltimore Orioles in that city to compete in the circuit's inaugural major league campaign. It was considered a coup for the new league when Johnson enticed McGraw to return to the scene of his former glory to act as player/manager of the Orioles. The presence of McGraw in the A.L. along with such noteworthy former National Leaguers as Cy Young, Nap Lajoie, and Jimmy Collins helped to elevate the A.L. to major league status in the eyes of the baseball public.

But it did not take long for two strong personalities like Johnson and McGraw to butt heads and engage in an increasingly bitter feud. Johnson was adamant that his American League was good clean baseball, free of the rowdiness that sometimes plagued the older, established National League. Johnson became disenchanted with McGraw quickly, criticizing him for his on-field demeanor and inability to get along with umpires which constantly resulted in controversy. Several times his behavior led to suspensions and fines. Johnson made it clear early on that he would back his umpires in such disputes.

The American and National Leagues were essentially at war from the beginning, and by late 1901 Johnson had publicly branded McGraw as a would-be traitor to the A.L. He never fully retracted the statement, and the relationship between the two men seemed irreconcilable from that point. The last straw may have come after McGraw was suspended yet again for refusing to leave the field when umpire Tommy Connolly threw him out of a game on June 28, 1902. The fiery manager claimed that the umpires were out to get him, and somewhat egotistically believed that the Orioles' lagging attendance was due in part to him being unavailable because of suspensions levied on him by Johnson. Noted longtime baseball writer Tim Murnane wrote that McGraw was wearing out his welcome with his antics.

Rumors had been rampant for some time that the A.L. would soon place a team in New York, with the Orioles or St. Louis Browns considered possibilities for relocation. Johnson had his eye on the city for some time, and with the N.L. aggressively negotiating with A.L. player setting up shop in New York was thought to be the A.L.'s best counterattack. Transferring the Baltimore team there before the 1902 season was apparently considered, but Johnson would not consent to it while McGraw still had a financial interest in the team. McGraw had been given a considerable amount of stock in the Orioles upon joining in 1901. In June 1902, he was claiming he was losing money and that baseball was doomed to fail in Baltimore. He attempted to take matters into his own hands by scheming with a New York businessman named Frank Farrell to buy a plot of land in Manhattan to build a park upon, then transfer the Orioles there. He felt that if he could accomplish this, he could make a run at putting the rival New York Giants out of business. McGraw soon discovered, however, that acquiring a suitable amount of land and building a major league, quality ballpark on it was an extremely expensive proposition.

Then, McGraw had a complete turnaround and began negotiating a deal with Giants owner Andrew Freedman, whereby he would take over as the team's manager and make his escape from the iron hand of his nemesis Ban Johnson. But McGraw and Freedman were attempting to do more than simply transfer one man—they were scheming to do great damage to the Baltimore Orioles and the league Johnson had built.

McGraw had several key accomplices in the plot: Freedman, who would be viewed as one of the most disliked owners baseball has ever seen; John T.

AMERICAN LEAGUE FOUNDER AND PRESIDENT BAN JOHNSON

Brush, owner of the Reds; and even Oriole team president John J. Mahon. At a meeting of Oriole executives on July 8, 1902, McGraw sold his stock in the team to president Mahon and was granted his unconditional release so that he could join the Giants as a player/manager. He reportedly signed a contract with New York for $10,000 per year. Also at this time, McGraw wanted to divest himself of his interest in a popular saloon known as the "Diamond Cafe" on North Howard St. in Baltimore, which he co-owned with Oriole teammate Wilbert Robinson. Like McGraw, catcher Robinson had starred with the Orioles in the 1890s and was in possession of a significant amount of stock in the new team. Also, like McGraw, Robinson would one day be elected to the Baseball Hall of Fame as a manager, having skippered the Brooklyn Dodgers for 18 seasons. It was likely no coincidence that when

Robinson sold his stock in order to buy out McGraw's share of the saloon, Mahon was there to purchase it, giving him controlling interest with 201 of the 400 total shares.

Then on July 16, a bombshell was dropped that set the wheels in motion for the American League's departure from Baltimore. Freedman and Brush purchased the 201 shares of Oriole stock from Mahon for a figure reported in various sources from between $21,000 and $50,000; the rival National League now had control of the Oriole franchise and its players. With Freedman having put up the majority of the capital in the transaction, he and Brush had an arrangement whereby the Giants would get first pick of the desired players while others would go to the Reds. Still others would be made available to the remaining N.L. teams. Four players were immediately released from Baltimore to the Giants; pitcher Joe "Iron Man" McGinnity, catcher Roger Bresnahan, first baseman Dan McGann, and pitcher Jack Cronin. Brush's Reds plucked outfielder Joe Kelley to take over as player/manager, and good hitting pitcher-turned-outfielder Cy Seymour. Kelley not only had starred with the old Orioles of the previous decade with McGraw and Robinson, he also happened to be the son-in-law of Mahon.

The Baltimore newspapers roasted McGraw and Mahon for the scheme that was intended to ruin baseball in Baltimore and devastate the American League. The Orioles were in shambles, and having been stripped of the majority of its players had to forfeit their game of July 17. Ban Johnson immediately came to Baltimore and assumed control of the franchise. He ordered Robinson to appear at a league meeting to explain his business association with McGraw, and after he was determined to not have played any role in the recent events, Johnson named the veteran catcher manager of the Orioles. Four other A.L. teams then contributed six players to the team in order to allow them to resume their schedule. Luckily for the team, Johnson personally held the lease on the Orioles park, which was located on the corner of York Road and 29th St. That prevented the National League from seizing that as well. All in all, Johnson admitted at this time that McGraw was the hardest man in the league to control, and he wasn't sorry to see him leave. Many across the league were also relieved to see him go. Even one N.L. owner, Pirates Barney Dreyfuss, denounced the scandalous nature of the incident, particularly Freedman's and Brush's role. Interestingly enough, Brush sold his interest in the Reds in early August 1902 and invested heavily in the Giants.

With McGraw now gone, the notion of transferring the Baltimore franchise to New York was now widely anticipated. Johnson didn't discourage the belief when he was quoted by *Sporting Life*'s July 19, 1902, issue: "The

American League has already won the fight in Boston, Philadelphia, Chicago, and St. Louis, and it remains to make the final stroke by putting a club in New York." Likely, the opportunity to compete for business with a McGraw-led team was appealing to Johnson as well. Several influential men in the Bronx had been working to get an American League team placed there. In making a case for the area, they argued that with a booming population along with increased trolley service, a team could succeed. Citizens of the Bronx were trying to persuade Johnson to locate a franchise in their borough, and even real estate people were attempting to convince the A.L. that suitable locations could be had. New York newspapers were editorializing on the need for an A.L. team, and even the *Philadelphia Public Ledger* weighed in on the topic:

> A good American League club in New York this year would have made money and had a wonderful moral effect upon the permanency of the American League. No one knows this better than President Johnson and his advisers. As events have shaped themselves, a winning American League team in the Metropolis would have made the populace baseball delirious.

Disillusioned Baltimore baseball fans were beginning to stay away, and by late July the Orioles were at the bottom of the league in attendance, averaging roughly 1,500 per game.

Meanwhile, a bitter war was being waged between the American and National Leagues. The N.L. was attempting to raid A.L. rosters to bring back players who had jumped leagues in the previous two years. Brush declared at an N.L. meeting in Boston in mid-August that there was room for only one major league, and that one would eventually dominate the other. He was reportedly attempting to lure four A.L. teams to join the N.L. to make up a 12-team league, with Baltimore being one of them. Brush, it should be noted, was also the chairman of the N.L.'s Executive Committee, which essentially gave him the same power as a league president. It was also reported that Pittsburgh might move to the A.L. and a brand new team would be created for New York to make a 10-team league. Not only was the Baltimore franchise's future in serious question, but the entire structure of major league baseball was seemingly at a crossroad.

New York baseball writer F. H. Koelsch wrote in late July, "The McGraw episode will result in some sensational changes this winter. An American League man 'in the know' says New York will surely have an American League club next year." Days later, Johnson himself spoke confidently of the situation, saying, "Would not New York look good in the American? And I can say right now that we can get a ball ground in that city. They said there was no location in this city, but we found one."

Though numerous sites would be reported by various sources as the home of a new ballpark, the situation would remain unresolved for some time. In the August 16, 1902, issue of *Sporting Life*, an item on the subject stated:

> It is said that the American League has secured grounds in New York in the Bronx at a distance requiring but three more minutes to reach than the National League grounds in that city.

Johnson went to New York and met with several unnamed men on August 25 to discuss placing a team there. In the days following that meeting it was reported, albeit it prematurely, that the A.L. had purchased land in New York at Cretona Park in the Bronx and that the Orioles would be transferred there. Regardless of the accuracy of the various reports, the possibility of an A.L. team in New York was the chief topic in baseball circles.

In early September, it was reported for the first time that Chicago White Sox manager Clark Griffith was a strong possibility to take over as leader of the proposed New York team. Griffith, one of the finer pitchers in the National League in the 1890s, had jumped to the White Sox in 1901 and led them to the league championship that first year while still taking his regular turn on the mound. Johnson, a close business associate and hunting partner of Charles Comiskey, apparently convinced the White Sox owner that a natural leader like Griffith would be just the right man to pilot a new team in the big city to success. Almost immediately, rumors surfaced that Griffith had set out signing players to contracts with New York, a team that technically did not exist, for the 1903 season. Two of the first names mentioned as having signed were Jack Chesbro, star right-handed hurler for the Pirates, and his staff mate, Jesse Tannehill. Even Joe Kelley, former Oriole and new manager of the Reds, claimed at this time that in his search for players to sign away from the A.L. he discovered many had made commitments to Griffith.

Back in Baltimore, the situation was growing increasingly hopeless as the season neared its end. The Orioles had come home from a road trip in early September in which they had lost 19 of 20 games, leaving them mired in last place. The city had lost interest in the team due to the likely move, and critics were suggesting that they should play their remaining home games on the road. Baltimore baseball writer Hugh Wynn wrote in a September 15 column: "If the American League can obtain a foothold in New York the Baltimore franchise will be transferred to Gotham. That has been virtually agreed upon." One noteworthy dissenter was one of the men who helped create the situation— John McGraw. He was very vocal in his belief that the idea of an A.L. team in New York was nothing more than a joke.

In late September while Ban Johnson was back in New York attempting to complete arrangements for the franchise shift, the Orioles were closing out their dismal season by losing their final seven games. On September 29 in what would end up being their last game as a team, they lost 9-5 to Boston before a loyal gathering of 138 Orioles fans.

Over the next several weeks, other sites in the Bronx and Manhattan were identified by various reporters as the future home of the team. In early November, Johnson stated, "We are going to New York without a doubt," but he was not ready to reveal the location of the park. John Brush, who had taken over the Giants officially in early October after reportedly paying Andrew Freedman $100,000, had joined McGraw in voicing his doubts that the A.L. would be able to complete the transfer to New York.

Both were openly willing to make wagers that there would be no A.L. team to compete with their Giants for the fan's attention in 1903.

There was a strong rumor circulating by October's end that Griffith had signed Brooklyn's outstanding hitting right fielder "Wee" Willie Keeler. A list of more than a dozen other noteworthy players were also reported to have signed at that time.

Griffith, it was said, would only be spending a short time at his Montana ranch that fall due to the amount of work he had to do in New York in connection with his new team. One New York newspaper speculated in mid-November that the team would be called the "Metropolitans" after the American Association team of the 1880s.

By the end of November, Johnson was still adamant that the situation would be worked out. He was quoted in the November 29, 1902, issue of *Sporting Life*:

> We will certainly put a club in New York next spring, and on Manhattan Island. I have been saying that for over a year now, but a good many people don't believe it yet. During this trip, the deal has been practically closed. We have the necessary leases, and there are only one or two minor details yet to wind up.

Johnson still felt the need to not reveal the location of the ballpark site, likely because he was aware that certain political factions might attempt to sabotage the deal. New York's famed Tammany Hall fraternal organization included many powerful politicians who wielded enormous influence over virtually all walks of life in the city.

By Christmas time, the situation had taken an official turn. At an American League meeting in Chicago on December 22, the Baltimore franchise, which had been taken over by a receiver, was formally declared vacated and awarded to New York, or more specifically the "New York American Base Ball and Amusement Company."

Wilbert Robinson was attempting to have an Eastern League franchise placed in Baltimore, and stockholder and former Oriole manager from the 1890s Ned Hanlon leased the park just vacated, with the same goal. Ultimately, the city of Baltimore would be granted the minor league team that it sought as the Eastern League transferred its Montreal franchise there in February 1903. Outside of its brief stint in the outlaw Federal League in 1914–1915, Baltimore would not achieve true major league status again until the St. Louis Browns transferred there in 1954.

As the calendar turned to 1903, Brooklyn papers reported that Willie Keeler officially announced that he had signed a two-year contract to play for the A.L. in New York. Keeler was a beloved figure in Brooklyn, where he had lived a good part of his life, but he explained that the difference in salary was significant, and that he had to think of himself. Former teammate Joe Kelley went on record at the time as saying he considered Keeler a better all-around player than Athletics' great second baseman Nap Lajoie, and believed he was the best in the game at that time.

A breakthrough in the bitter war between the two major leagues came at a meeting in Cincinnati on January 10, 1903. The leagues agreed once and for all to peacefully coexist, and proposed not to raid each others teams for players from that point on. Each team submitted a list of players they reserved, as the baseball world got its first official glimpse of those on the A.L.'s New York squad. The roster would in fact include Keeler, Chesbro, Tannehill, and Dave Fultz, among the more noteworthy.

Inexplicably, February rolled around and there appeared to still be no set plans for the location of the park. Speculation was rampant in the newspapers, with sites popping up on nearly a weekly basis. Johnson was convinced that Freedman and Brush were working very hard to put any obstacle they could in the way of the A.L. entering New York. Still more weeks passed, and on March 9 the *New York Tribune* wrote that Tammany Hall politicians were standing in the way of a deal being closed on a new park location. They were believed to not only want to be paid off, but also wanted stock in the team.

Finally, on March 13, with new manager Griffith set to take his team South to Atlanta for Spring Training not knowing yet where they would play their home games, the long anticipated announcement was made. Over the past several months there were a half-dozen locations considered, but now the plot of land that would soon become the ballpark that would be the home of the New York A.L. team was finally revealed to an anxious public. The exact location was in what was considered Washington Heights on a hill overlooking the Hudson River on Broadway, between 165th St. on the south and 168th St. on the north. Eleventh Ave. bordered the eastern side, with Fort Washington Road along the west side. It was written that the grandstand would have a "sweeping view of the Hudson and the Palisades and of the Westchester hills and Long Island Sound off to the East." The property at the time belonged to the New York Institute for the Blind and was to be leased to the team for a 10-year term. The lease for 1903 was said to be $6,000. A century later, Columbia-Presbyterian Medical Center occupies the site. Fort Washington Ave. (formerly "road") cuts through the middle of the medical center campus.

With less than seven weeks to go before the first game was scheduled to be played there, construction had to begin immediately. It was said that as many as 500 men were working on the project day and night in order to complete it by Opening Day. While the playing surface was being leveled, an 1817 U.S. penny was unearthed, as well as bullets and bayonets believed to be from a Revolutionary War battle that was fought on the site.

The day after the announcement of the new park site, a corporation called "The Greater New York Base Ball Association" filed papers at the state capital in Albany to operate the new team. The directors were listed as John R. Bushong, Samuel C. Worthen, Jerome H. Buck, Bernard T. Lynch, and Henry T. Randall. All were considered wealthy and prominent New Yorkers. Also at this time, New York native Joseph Gordon was appointed president of the team. Gordon had served as the city's superintendent of buildings previously, but also had a baseball background as president of the New York Metropolitans of the major league American Association back in the 1880s. The team also hired Joe Gavin away from Boston's A.L. team to act as business manager, and announced that an office had been opened in the Flatiron Building at Broadway and 23rd St. An official list of the team's stockholders was made public in late March, and aside from Gordon, who was said to have controlling interest, it included Frank J. Farrell, elected secretary-treasurer, Samuel A. Buyers, William H. Hurst, Thomas F. McAvoy, James, J. Wallace, and Louis J. Weil. John B. Day, Gordon's brother-in-law, was to assist him in running the team. All were said to be New York City residents.

HILLTOP PARK—THE PLACE NEW YORK'S AMERICAN LEAGUE FRANCHISE CALLED HOME FROM ITS BEGINNING IN 1903 THROUGH 1912. THEY THEN PLAYED THEIR HOME GAMES IN THE POLO GROUNDS UNTIL MOVING INTO THE NEWLY CONSTRUCTED YANKEE STADIUM IN 1923.

Ban Johnson was being hailed for his efforts in completing the transfer of the Baltimore team to New York City. The National League had attempted numerous methods by which they could block the move, but seriously underestimated Johnson's resolve to succeed. Chicago baseball writer W. A. Phelon Jr. wrote in late March:

> Ban is really a wonder. The National Leaguers found that out some time ago, and I fancy that the way he handled the ground proposition in New York makes him a bigger curio than anything ever exhibited in the museums of this wide world.

An editorial in *Sporting Life* at the time cited the A.L.'s entrance into New York as a move that placed them on equal footing with the N.L. and made their standing as a major league secure.

Johnson had believed wholeheartedly that Andrew Freedman and John Brush had been doing anything and everything in their power to prevent the move. Brush had gone so far as to say he would stake his life the A.L. could not enter New York. Johnson would later claim that Freedman had attempted bribery to have the city cut streets directly through the park before it was even completed. In fact, in early April such a move was a realistic possibility and was threatening to jeopardize the entire project.

A Washington Heights citizen's group had put together a petition in early April to have two new streets created that would divide that property and destroy the ballpark. The neighborhood's Board of Improvements subsequently voted the move down by the narrow margin of three to two on April 9, effectively ending the threat and allowing construction to continue. With everything now officially going forward, Gordon announced that he was willing to give a free season's pass to anyone who could suggest a suitable name for the new park. By mid-April he had settled on "New York American League Park," though it came to be more commonly referred to as "Hilltop Park." By this time, he had sold the first box seats to the Wasserman brothers, prominent local bankers. It was also in mid-April that the nickname "Highlanders" was suggested for the team due to the location of their home field, which was said to be the highest point in Manhattan. Another suggested variation was "Gordon Highlanders" in honor of their president, and it was written that the front of their uniform jerseys would feature the words "Greater New Yorks."

Spring Training was winding down in mid-April and Griffith's squad was beginning the trek north to open the season in Washington on April 22. The new manager was said to have instilled a wonderful degree of teamwork in a short time. This was especially noteworthy considering no two of the infield-ers or outfielders had played together the previous season. Ban Johnson cred-ited Griffith for having personally selected most of the players that had been signed for the team.

Just before the opener in D.C., the New York team stopped by the city they had abandoned several months prior to play two exhibition games against the new Baltimore Orioles Eastern League team. The contests were held on April 20 and 21 at the former A.L. park in the city, which was a mere two miles from the home of eight-year-old George Ruth. Ruth, of course, would one day wear the uniform of both teams.

As the Highlanders' inaugural campaign was set to commence, the gen-erally pro-N.L. New York American newspaper acknowledged that the com-petition between the two leagues in the city was positive for the game:

> The advent of the American League club into New York City has served to increase interest in the game in the metropolis rather than depreciate it, as many supposed it would. There is no denying the fact that the new club will start off with the best wishes of New York enthusiasts. The team on paper is sufficiently strong to attract attention anywhere and cannot well help standing high in the championship race from start to finish.

On Wednesday, April 23, 11,950 fans were in attendance at Washington's "American League Park" to witness former N.L. ace Jack Chesbro take the hill in the first official game in New York's American history. The team's left fielder Lefty Davis led off in the top of the first, but failed to reach base. Then the team's biggest offensive star, 5-foot 4-inch, 142-pound Willie Keeler, came to bat and proceeded to walk and subsequently score the first run in team history on a fielder's choice. It would be the only run they would score however, as their debut was spoiled by the Senators in the 3-1 loss. Along with being referred to in the newspaper box scores and recaps as "Highlanders," they were sometimes called the "Gordon Highlanders," or even "Invaders." They were also often generically referred to as "Americans," as many other A.L. teams were during that period. Team nicknames tended to be largely unofficial in the early twentieth century, sometimes depending merely upon the whims of the sportswriters and editors. The "Yankee" name is believed to have first appeared in print in 1904, and did not become official until 1913.

On the day of the team's second game, the *New York Tribune* broke an exclu-sive story concerning the team ownership situation. It was announced that for-mer N.Y.P.D. chief Bill Devery was reported to be the principal financial backer.

THE INAUGURAL EDITION OF NEW YORK'S AMERICAN LEAGUE FRANCHISE.

The article stated that according to an unnamed reliable source, Devery's name was connected to the ownership group publicly for the first time. The former police chief had been heavily involved in real estate ventures for some time, and an estimate of his investment in the A.L. team was said to be $100,000. As a result, the *Tribune* would add a couple of new nicknames to the team, referring to them in the April 24 edition as "Deveryites" and "New York's Finest." History would show that Frank Farrell and "Big Bill" Devery were the team's primary owners until Colonel Jacob Ruppert purchased it in 1915.

Back in Manhattan with one week to go before the home opener, finishing the new park in time seemed almost hopeless. It took a tireless effort with workers hammering away from dawn 'til dusk, but finally, come April 30, the only section left unfinished was the grandstand, not yet being covered by a roof. The contractors had succeeded with not a day to spare in transforming a rock-filled hill into a major league ballpark. That sunny Wednesday afternoon the park was decorated with a variety of flags snapping in the gentle breeze and draped around the grandstand. Each of the 16,293 spectators was given a small American flag upon entering the park, which they waved as the players marched onto the field accompanied by patriotic tunes performed by Bayne's 69th Regiment Band. Ban Johnson performed the duty of throwing out the ceremonial first pitch, and American League history within the confines of New York City was about to begin. Johnson was said to be smiling broadly, undoubtedly extremely satisfied with what he had accomplished. As for the sartorial appearance of the newly outfitted squad, the *New York Times* reported the following day:

> The Greater New Yorks were resplendent in their new white uniforms and caps of white flannel and black facings, topped off with natty maroon-colored coats.

With that, the Highlanders, behind the masterly pitching of Jack Chesbro, pleased their new fans with a 6-2 victory over the Washington Senators. It was Willie Keeler, who in his first at-bat in the opening frame got the team's first hit and scored its first run at their new park. Two weeks later, *Sporting Life* wrote, "Billy Keeler is the idol of New York fans, and why not? One of the grandest ballplayers the game has ever produced is 'Wee Willie.'"

Keeler was indeed New York's batting star in the inaugural campaign, leading the team in batting average, hits, runs scored, and stolen bases. Chesbro led the pitching staff with a 21-15 record, and even manager Griffith was still taking his regular turn in the rotation, still regarded as a quality pitcher. Though New York managed to only finish in fourth place with a 72-62 record, Griffith was praised for doing so well with a team made up from scratch.

Though the most famous member in the history of the franchise would not pull on the pinstripes for another 17 years, the likes of Griffith, Keeler, and Chesbro would supply a Hall of Fame presence right from the very beginning.

In mid-May 1903, the *New York Evening Sun* summed up the perception of what the presence of the new team meant to the game:

> The coming of the American League into New York City has done more
> to boom base ball, not only locally, but all over the country than even
> Ban Johnson and his staunchest followers ever dreamed of.

And very few could dream of the unequaled heights the new team would attain not only in baseball, but the world of sports in general over the next 100 years.

DAVID MARK WINFIELD

SAN DIEGO, N.L., 1973-1980, NEW YORK, A.L., 1981-1990
CALIFORNIA, A.L., 1990-1991, TORONTO, A.L., 1992
MINNESOTA, A.L., 1993-1994, CLEVELAND, A.L., 1995

A COMPLETE PLAYER WHO INTIMIDATED THE OPPOSITION WITH HIS
IMMENSE STATURE, POWER, AGGRESSIVE BASERUNNING AND DOMINANT
DEFENSE. ADVANCED DIRECTLY FROM COLLEGE TO THE MAJOR LEAGUES, THE
12-TIME ALL-STAR COMPILED 3,110 HITS, 465 HOME RUNS, 1,833 RBI AND A
.283 CAREER AVERAGE. THE MULTITALENTED OUTFIELDER, RENOWNED FOR
LONG STRIDES AND A ROCKET ARM, EARNED SEVEN GOLD GLOVE AWARDS.
AMONG ALL-TIME LEADERS IN HITS, RBI, GAMES, DOUBLES, EXTRA BASE HITS,
TOTAL BASES AND PUTOUTS. HIS 11TH INNING, TWO-OUT DOUBLE IN GAME SIX
CLINCHED TORONTO'S 1992 WORLD SERIES TITLE.

Dave Winfield

(Elected 2001)

From the day he was born, October 3, 1951, Dave Winfield would already have a connection to New York baseball. The day that the future Hall of Famer came into the world the New York Giants' Bobby Thomson hit his famous "shot heard 'round the world" home run against the Brooklyn Dodgers that catapulted his team into the World Series with the New York Yankees.

Fifty years later Winfield made another permanent connection in New York by accepting a bronze plaque that would forever be displayed in the village of Cooperstown.

The multitalented athlete attended his home state University of Minnesota, where he starred in both baseball and basketball. Though the Baltimore Orioles had drafted him out of high school in 1969, he opted to attend college instead. After graduating from Minnesota in 1973, the 6-foot 6-inch Winfield had the unique distinction of being drafted by four professional teams; the San Diego Padres, the NBA's Atlanta Hawks, the Utah Stars of the ABA, and the NFL's Minnesota Vikings, despite the fact that he had not played football in college.

It was on the baseball team at Minnesota where Winfield distinguished himself most. In his senior year he went 13-1 as a pitcher, hit over .400 as an outfielder, and was selected as MVP of that year's College World Series. When he was drafted that June by the Padres he chose baseball as the game he would pursue, and two days after signing with San Diego he was in uniform for them playing center field. He would never spend a day in the minor leagues.

In his first full season in 1974, Winfield posted a solid 20 home runs and 75 RBIs for an abysmal San Diego team that had very nearly relocated to Washington, D.C. For the duration of the decade of the 1970s, he toiled in relative obscurity for the Padres, yet it was clear to observers that he was a perennial

All-Star in the making. He was displaying five-tool ability, routinely posting excellent performances in all phases of the game. Winfield had an exceptional season in 1979, leading the National League with 118 RBIs, belting 34 home runs, batting .308, and stealing 15 bases.

After the 1980 season, the seventh time in Winfield's eight years with the team that the Padres had finished below .500, he decided it was time to look for greener pastures. He filed for free agency on October 22, 1980, and entered what was known as the re-entry draft. By the free agency rules of the time, a draft was held whereby a maximum of 13 teams could draft a free agent player, and only those teams had the right to negotiate with him. The Yankees, by virtue of having the best record in baseball that year had last pick in the draft. Wanting New York to have a chance at him, Winfield wrote letters to a few teams requesting that they not draft him so that he would still be available when the Yankees turn to pick came around. In the end, 10 teams selected him, but only the Mets, Indians, and Yankees made serious offers.

Reportedly, the Mets had offered $12 million over eight years in early December of 1980, but Winfield was put off when they withdrew certain additional provisions that had originally been included. He then seemed to narrow his focus to the Yankees, figuring that he had a better chance of winning a pennant, as well as much better protection in the batting order.

Finally on December 15, 1980, with the aid of agent Al Frohman, Winfield and George Steinbrenner reached an agreement that made him the highest-paid player in the history of team sports. The 10-year contract carried a potential value of $23 million and included a $1 million signing bonus. The first year's salary was said to be about $1.4 million, which would be subject to a cost of living increase that could be up to a maximum of 10 percent each year throughout the life of the contract. The deal represented a substantial raise for the 29-year-old Winfield, who had made $350,000 per year in each of his last four years with San Diego.

With Big Dave now officially a Yankee, some saw a potential clash of egos between him and Reggie Jackson, both of whom were right fielders. Jackson, who attended the press conference at which Winfield's signing was announced, stated that day, "I hit 40 home runs and I think the manager can find a spot for me. And when you have a guy making the numbers Dave is and putting the numbers on the board Dave is, they'll work it out." The Yankees' new manager Gene Michael did not have a definite answer at that time, but acknowledged that Winfield's versatility would give him a few options.

When one reporter asked him about the possibility of being booed if he didn't perform up to expectations he joked, "There's plenty of cotton at the drug store."

Come Opening Day, April 9, 1981, Winfield was occupying left field at the Stadium while Reggie had retained his familiar right field position. Wearing number 31 on his new pinstriped uniform, he impressed Yankee fans in that game with his ability to get on base. He singled twice and walked twice in five plate appearances. By mid-May, he was maintaining an outstanding .345 batting average.

Unfortunately, the season came to a grinding halt on June 12 as the players went on strike. At that point in the season, Winfield was hitting .324, and had stolen six bases without being caught. When the players and owners settled their differences, they held the All-Star Game on August 9 to kick off baseball's return. Winfield was voted to the team by the fans and played the entire game in center field.

In the abbreviated season, Winfield appeared in 105 of the 107 games the Yankees played. He batted .294, and his 13 home runs were only two behind the 15 hit by Jackson and Graig Nettles for the team lead. Winfield's 68 RBIs were tops on the Yankees, but the 55 games lost to the strike in all likelihood cost him what would have been his second 100-RBI season. In addition, his 11 stolen bases, his exceptional glove, and strong throwing arm left most with the impression that he was the best all-around player on the team.

The Yankees finished with 97 wins and were heading into the playoffs, but under rather unusual circumstances. Because of the seven-week strike, the season had been divided into two halves. Winners of the first half would engage in a playoff with the winner of the second half for the right to play in the League Championship Series. The Yankees had won the first half and faced the Milwaukee Brewers in a best of five series.

Winfield had three hits in Game Two and two hits in Game Three. Tied at two games apiece, the Yankees had a 7-3 lead in the ninth inning of the deciding game. The Brewers' Don Money came up with the bases loaded and hit what would have been a game-tying grand slam if Winfield had not reached over the wall to make the catch, preserving the win in the clincher.

The Yankees went on to sweep the Athletics in the League Championship Series, with Winfield being credited with the game-winning RBI in Game Two. Unfortunately, he slumped in the World Series as New York was able to beat the Dodgers only twice, losing in six games.

Winfield reported to Spring Training camp in Ft. Lauderdale on February 17, and shortly after walking into the clubhouse he shaved off the full beard that he had been growing. He told reporters, "I don't ever remember seeing Babe Ruth or Mickey Mantle with a beard, so I thought I'd fall in line."

With Jackson gone to the Angels via free agency after the 1981 season, Winfield now took center stage as the Yankees number one power threat. He came through with a performance in 1982 that would justify that standing, slugging the ball better than he ever had in his career. Winfield's 37 home runs were topped only by Jackson and Gorman Thomas's 39; his .560 slugging percentage was second only to Robin Yount's .578; and his 106 RBIs were 38 more than the next-most-productive Yankee. He showed off his terrific right arm by leading the A.L. with 17 outfield assists, and won the first of five Gold Glove Awards he would win while with New York.

But it was a rather unstable season that saw the Yankees employ three different managers, five pitching coaches, three batting instructors, and a constant shuttle back and forth from Triple A Columbus. They could do no better than fifth in the A.L. East.

Billy Martin took over the following season and the team improved from 79 wins to 91. Winfield was again the team's big offensive weapon. He contributed 32 home runs and 116 RBIs, leading New York in those categories as well as hits, runs, and triples. He was also a participant in one of the most infamous games of the year, the George Brett "pine tar" incident on July 24. Two weeks later Winfield was in the middle of something equally bizarre. On August 4, 1983, at Exhibition Stadium in Toronto, hoards of seagulls were flying around the field during the game. When Winfield was tossing the ball to warm up before one inning with Don Baylor, a large seagull was on the ground near Baylor. Winfield meant to bounce the ball near it to scare it off, but the ball bounced up and hit it in the head, killing it. The crowd started to boo, and a complaint was filed. The Royal Canadian Mounted Police came to arrest Winfield after the game for cruelty to animals. He deeply regretted the incident, and charges were eventually dropped.

In July in the All-Star Game held at Comiskey Park, where it had began 50 years before, Winfield had gone three for three with two runs and an RBI in the A.L.'s 13-3 pounding of the N.L.

A couple of changes marked Winfield's 1984 season. First, new manager Yogi Berra switched him to right field after having played left almost exclusively since he came to New York. With the exception of the occasional game as designated hitter, he spent the rest of his Yankee days in right.

Second, Winfield consciously shortened his swing in an attempt to improve his hitting. As a result, he drastically improved his ability to hit for high average. On June 25, he had his third five-hit game of the month, tying a record held by Ty Cobb. He engaged in a friendly battle for the batting title with young teammate Don Mattingly, losing on the final day of the season, .343 to .340. Winfield's .340 average was 56 points higher than his lifetime batting average going into the 1984 season. He once again paced the Yankees in runs scored with 106 and RBIs with 100.

Billy Martin returned as Yankee manager 16 games into the 1985 season and the team made a serious run at the division title. In the end, they fell only two games behind Toronto, finishing in second place with 79 wins. Although Big Dave's batting average dropped down to .275, he still provided solid production with 26 homers, 114 RBIs, and 105 runs scored. With his long strides, he also stole 19 bases, his high in a Yankee uniform. His most noteworthy theft was a steal of home on September 7 to beat Oakland. Winfield's salary in 1985 reached $1.8 million, the highest in all of the game, befitting his stature and all-around ability.

The next year under rookie manager Lou Piniella, Winfield's former teammate, the Yankees remained in the race until the final week of the season. Winning 90 games, they finished 4½ games behind rival Boston. Though he was turning 35, Winfield was still able to hit 24 homers and drive in 104 runs. Showing his versatility, he was used by Piniella at third base twice, the only times in his career he played the position.

In 1987, Winfield won the seventh and final Gold Glove of his major league career. The 156 games he played would be his highest total in all his time with New York. Still an integral part of the Yankee offense, he slugged 27 home runs, his highest figure since 1983, and drove in 97 runs.

Martin rejoined the Yanks in the middle of 1988 for what would be his final managerial job. It was also the final year that Winfield would be selected as a member of the American League All-Star team. He went on to lead the Yankees in RBIs with 107, and his 25 home runs were just two shy of designated hitter Jack Clark's team lead of 27. It could not be known at the time, but Winfield had played his last full season in a Yankee uniform. Shortly after reporting to Spring Training in 1989 he began having trouble with back spasms, and would undergo surgery on his lower back in March. He was originally expected to miss only three months of playing time, but ended up missing the entire season. He was set to resume playing in the spring of 1990.

After appearing in just 20 games that season, the Yankees traded Winfield to the California Angels on May 11 in exchange for pitcher Mike Witt. His relationship with owner Steinbrenner had become strained, and management was uncertain of his ability to return to his former level after his injury at nearly 39 years old. In the following years he also had stints with Toronto, Minnesota, and Cleveland. It was with his home state Twins on September 16, 1993, that he became a member of the 3,000-hit club. He had also hit his 450th home run the month before.

By the time his 22-season career had concluded in 1995, Winfield had amassed exclusive figures in many different statistical categories: 465 home runs, 1,833 RBIs, 3,110 hits, 540 doubles, 1,669 runs, and 223 stolen bases. Factoring in his terrific glove work and accurate throwing arm, he can rightly be regarded as a shining example of a truly outstanding all-around player. When his name appeared on the Hall of Fame ballot for the first time in December of 2000, Winfield received an impressive 85 percent of the vote.

In early August 2001, as he stood at the podium and accepted his bronze plaque, Winfield showed his appreciation by saying: "To George Steinbrenner, I want to thank you for bringing me to the New York Yankees. . . . This is an experience that changed my life forever, in a positive way. Yogi Berra, Whitey Ford, Joe DiMaggio, Mickey Mantle, all the guys, just to be in the same family with guys like that, it's a dream come true."

Two-and-a-half weeks later, on August 18, Winfield was honored at Yankee Stadium. He told the crowd during the ceremony, "I knew when I put on those pinstripes for the first time it's a moment I'll never forget and it's a moment that changed my life." Hall of Famer Dave Winfield had officially now traveled, as part of his baseball journey, from the Bronx to Cooperstown, and would stand for all time as one of the noteworthy representatives of Yankee excellence.

LELAND STANFORD MACPHAIL JR.

ONE OF THE LEADING EXECUTIVES IN BASEBALL HISTORY, HIS
NAME IS SYNONYMOUS WITH INTEGRITY AND SPORTSMANSHIP.
AS FARM DIRECTOR AND PLAYER PERSONNEL DIRECTOR OF
THE YANKEES (1949-58), HELPED BUILD A SYSTEM WHICH
YIELDED SEVEN WORLD CHAMPIONSHIPS. AS ORIOLES
GENERAL MANAGER (1959-65), HELPED LAY THE GROUNDWORK
FOR ONE OF THE GAME'S MOST CONSISTENTLY SUCCESSFUL
FRANCHISES; AND HE LATER REJOINED THE YANKEES IN THE
SAME CAPACITY. SERVED ADMIRABLY AS AMERICAN LEAGUE
PRESIDENT (1974-1983) BEFORE CONCLUDING HIS 45-YEAR
CAREER AS PRESIDENT OF THE PLAYER RELATIONS
COMMITTEE. HE AND HIS FATHER LARRY FORM THE FIRST
FATHER SON TANDEM IN THE HALL OF FAME.

Lee MacPhail
(Elected 1998)

While he may have been brought into the Yankee organization during the time his father Larry was co-owner of the team, Lee MacPhail more than made his own way in serving them as an executive for a combined total of 19 years. And though he may be best known for his 10-year stint as president of the American League, it was the several positions he held for the Yankees that helped to pave his way to Cooperstown.

Lee began his long and distinguished career as a baseball executive back in 1941 at 23 years old, just two years out of Swarthmore College near Philadelphia. His father tried to discourage him from entering baseball, insisting there were more worthwhile careers for a young college graduate, but Lee had made up his mind. Running the Brooklyn Dodgers at the time, Larry arranged for him to become the business manager of the Reading, Pennsylvania, minor league team in the Dodger organization. From there, Branch Rickey offered him the job as general manager of Toronto, a top-level minor league team in the International League. MacPhail spent the 1942 season there, but resigned in the aftermath of the bombing of Pearl Harbor to enlist in the Navy. After taking his physical, he was rejected due to a racing pulse, and ended up working for the Dodgers in the summer of 1943. He traveled a bit, setting up tryout camps in the Midwest, and also filled in for the team's traveling secretary for a time. The following spring, MacPhail was able to pass his military physical and entered the Navy in the spring of 1944.

By 1945, Larry MacPhail had put together a group that included Dan Topping and Del Webb and purchased the Yankees from Jacob Ruppert's estate. The purchase also included the team's minor league Kansas City franchise, and Lee's father offered him the job of running the team when he got out of the service. He accepted and took over in June of 1946. In a short time,

Lee would see several future noteworthy Yankees wear the Kansas City uniform including Hank Bauer, Cliff Mapes, and Jerry Coleman.

Lee had the opportunity to attend the 1947 World Series in which the Yankees beat Brooklyn. Contacted in September of 2002, just shy of his 85th birthday, Lee recalled the chaos that ensued at the team's victory party. "My father got drunk and got into a fight with George Weiss and Dan Topping. Weiss [Yankees minor league director] had previously talked to me about coming to New York to work with the big-league team, but he thought it would be best now to keep that on hold for a while until everything died down."

Very shortly after, the elder MacPhail sold his interest in the Yankees to Topping and Webb, and Lee returned to Kansas City to prepare for the 1948 season. At this juncture, had Lee not already shown himself to be conscientious and hardworking, his career with the Yankees would likely have ended with his father's. Lee was in fact very different in many ways from his famous father. Larry had a tendency to be abrasive and controversial, while Lee was soft-spoken, low key, and likely never made an enemy in his entire career.

Aside from many players who would contribute to future Yankee success, MacPhail added a couple other noteworthy players to the Kansas City roster that off-season, including catcher Ralph Houk and third baseman Al Rosen on option from Cleveland.

Immediately following the 1948 season Weiss, now the GM, asked Lee to come to New York to take over the position as Yankee farm director, which he quickly accepted. He would now be responsible for all Yankee farm teams as well as the scouting nationwide.

MacPhail stated 54 years later that he is proud to have been present when scout Tom Greenwade signed a 17-year-old Mickey Mantle to his first professional contract.

In the years immediately following the debut of Jackie Robinson and the integration of baseball, there was increasing pressure on the Yankees to add black players to the team. In 1950 MacPhail struck a deal with the Negro League's Kansas City Monarchs whereby they could rent the Yankee minor leaguer's park in return for the Yankees having first crack at any of their players. This eventually led to them signing Elston Howard, who went on to make his debut as the first black to play for the Yankees and a valuable member of several championship teams.

In 1952 MacPhail and Yankee scout Joe Devine created the idea of holding a development camp in the fall after the end of the season, where the organization's top prospects would be invited and given instruction by knowledgeable baseball men such as Casey Stengel, Frank Crosetti, Bill Dickey, and Harry

Craft. The concept started to catch on with other organizations, and ultimately gave birth to the Arizona Fall League.

MacPhail was promoted to vice-president and director of player personnel in 1955. He was now much more involved with the big league team, and essentially served as an assistant to Weiss. He dealt with many player signings, and often even acted as a buffer between Weiss and uniformed personnel.

In 1955 when Kansas City had been elevated to major league status, the Yankees transferred their top farm team to Denver. MacPhail had hired Ralph Houk to manage there, and he would eventually succeed Stengel in 1961 and take the Yankees to three straight World Series.

Seeing the Yankees come back from a three-games-to-one deficit to beat the Milwaukee Braves in the 1958 World Series provided MacPhail with one of his biggest thrills in his time with the Yankees. Lee had helped bring numerous players on that team through the organization in the previous years. But after the Series, the Baltimore Orioles offered MacPhail the job as their general manager. When Lee approached Yankee co-owner Dan Topping and informed him of the offer, he was told that general manager Weiss would probably remain in the position for the foreseeable future and gave MacPhail his blessing. Lee really didn't want to leave the Yankee organization, but with little hope of being the Yankees' GM, he didn't feel he should pass on the opportunity.

He took the position, and by 1960 the title of team president had been added. He and manager Paul Richards decided to go with a youth movement that year, and the young team actually made a run at the pennant and finished second that season to the Yankees. In his time with Baltimore he made many shrewd acquisitions, including Jim Gentile, Luis Aparicio, Curt Blefary, and Paul Blair, to name a few. His trade for Frank Robinson in December of 1965 is regarded as a masterstroke. He also reached back to his early Yankee days to hire Hank Bauer to manage the team in 1964.

When baseball commissioner Ford Frick resigned after the 1965 season, some recommended Lee as his replacement, which indicates the esteem in which he was held. John Fetzer of the Tigers and John Galbreath of the Pirates had been appointed by fellow major league owners to help select a successor to Frick. The two-man committee selected retired Air Force general William Eckert, but knew that he would require a truly knowledgeable assistant well-versed in baseball matters to help him become acclimated to the job. They saw MacPhail as just the right man. With a title of executive administrator to the commissioner, Lee committed himself to the position for one year, and would be free at the end of 1966 to pursue other opportunities. When the Orioles won the World Series of 1966, MacPhail was filled with a sense of satisfaction, as he was largely responsible for having assembled the vast majority of the team. *The Sporting News* voted him as the Executive of the Year for the combination of his contribution to the Orioles and his service to baseball in the commissioner's office.

The Yankees had called MacPhail during the 1966 season to ask if he would consider becoming their general manager. He responded that he would be interested in discussing it after the season. Finally in late 1966, eight years after he had left the Yankees for the first time, he was named as the team's executive vice-president and general manager. He now occupied the position held by his father two decades before.

At the press conference to announce his hiring, MacPhail admitted that he believed the Yankees were a few years away from serious contention. They had finished in last place in 1966, and with free agency not available for another decade, the team would have to rebuild with shrewd moves. Aside from keeping a few older veterans such as Mantle and Whitey Ford, MacPhail was set to institute a youth movement. Lee was also pleased to be working with manager Ralph Houk, one of his former players.

One of his first moves was to send an injury-plagued, unhappy Roger Maris to St. Louis, and MacPhail later said that the Cardinals were the only team that would take him. Lee also helped to convince Mantle that first base would be a better place at this point in his career. Ford had to retire by midseason of 1967, and Clete Boyer and Elston Howard were also traded. The face of the Yankees was growing younger, and they were about to begin the long climb back up the standings.

Under MacPhail's direction, the team in 1970 won 93 games, finishing second in the A.L. East to Baltimore. Lee had earlier convinced Thurman Munson to sign while in college, and he was now firmly entrenched as the Yankees starting catcher. Young lefty Ron Guidry, another MacPhail draftee, was just beginning his journey through the system at this time. Other significant acquisitions he made that contributed to future Yankee success included getting reliever Sparky Lyle from Boston for Danny Cater in January of 1972, and solving the third base problem for years to come by acquiring Graig Nettles later that same year for a handful of lesser players who were not in the Yankees' plans. Trading 38-year-old reliever Lindy McDaniel to Kansas City in December of 1973 for Lou Piniella was also a coup.

When the Yankees were approached in 1972 about the possibility of moving to a new stadium in New Jersey, MacPhail was adamant that it should not even be considered. He became actively involved in the refurbishing of Yankee Stadium, and was extremely pleased with the results upon its reopening in 1976.

By 1973, longtime American League president Joe Cronin had made the decision to retire. MacPhail was considered a top candidate as his replacement, and ultimately was elected to the post on October 24, 1973. He resigned from the Yankees and took office as A.L. president on January 1, 1974. He would serve the league in that capacity through 1983.

When the Yankees went to the World Series three years in a row from 1976 through 1978, MacPhail would have had every reason to feel a big part of the success. He was directly responsible for the presence of numerous members of those teams, yet Lee was far too modest to have ever made such a claim.

From the late 1940s through the 1970s, MacPhail had a far greater impact on the New York Yankees than he is generally credited. He was rewarded for his outstanding contributions for his life in the game as a baseball executive with his election to the Hall of Fame in 1998, joining his father Larry and becoming the first and only father–son combination in the Hall of Fame.

PHILIP HENRY NIEKRO

MILWAUKEE, N.L., 1964-1965
ATLANTA, N.L., 1966-1983, 1987
NEW YORK, A.L., 1984-1985
CLEVELAND, A.L., 1986-1987
TORONTO, A.L., 1987

PREEMINENT KNUCKLEBALL PITCHER WHOSE OUT-PITCH BAFFLED
HITTERS AND LED TO 3,342 STRIKEOUTS, 8th ON ALL-TIME LIST.
CAREER RECORD OF 318-274 WITH A 3.35 ERA PLACED HIM 14th
IN VICTORIES WITH WINNING PERCENTAGE SIGNIFICANTLY
HIGHER THAN THOSE TEAMS FOR WHOM HE PITCHED. TIED
WITH CY YOUNG FOR MOST SEASONS, 200 OR MORE INNINGS
PITCHED (19) AND LED LEAGUE FOUR TIMES IN THAT DEPARTMENT.
NO-HIT SAN DIEGO AUGUST 5, 1973. WON FIVE GOLD GLOVES
AND NAMED TO FIVE ALL-STAR TEAMS.

Phil Niekro

(Elected 1997)

Most of Phil Niekro's accomplishments are a direct result of his ability to throw a knuckleball. Therefore it's ironic to think that when he was trying for win number 300 he never threw one until the final batter, who he then struck out on three of the fluttering pitches.

Phil Niekro was born on April 1, 1939, in Blaine, Ohio, where he was a boyhood friend of Celtics great John Havilcek. His father, who had been a pitcher in the industrial leagues, played a joke on Phil when he was about 10 years old. While playing catch with his son, the elder Niekro threw him a knuckleball. Although Phil didn't catch the ball the pitch fascinated him and he asked his father to teach it to him. By the time he was entering high school he had mastered the knuckleball and it was his father who couldn't catch it.

A mainstay for the Atlanta Braves, Niekro pitched a phenomenal 24 seasons in major league baseball. A three-time 20-game winner, Niekro's durability allowed him to win 318 games in his career. Considering he mostly pitched for bad teams this is quite a remarkable feat. His two appearances in postseason, 1969 and 1982, coincided with two of his best seasons. He was 23-13 in 1969 and 17-4 in 1982 with a league-leading winning percentage of .810. Both years he led his team in wins en route to the League Championship Series. Unfortunately for Niekro and the Braves they never advanced to the World Series, as they lost to the eventual World Champs both times. In 1979, Niekro won a remarkable 21 games for a team that could only muster 66 wins. On August 5, 1973, Phil no-hit the Padres to record the first no-hitter by the Braves franchise in Atlanta.

Niekro's loyalty to the Atlanta Braves won him the admiration of the Atlanta fans. He was a great contributor to charitable groups during his career, and in 1979 he was awarded the Lou Gehrig Award for his exemplary character. When Phil signed a two-year deal with the Yankees on January 5, 1984, most Atlanta fans were glad to see him go. Not because they didn't like him, but because they were glad to see him going to a contending team.

In 1984 the Yankees were trying to get back to the playoffs. They hadn't been there since the 1981 World Series, which they lost to the Los Angeles Dodgers four games to two. After Goose Gossage didn't re-sign with the team, the Yankees signed the veteran Niekro. The team then moved Dave Righetti to the bullpen to make room for Niekro in the starting rotation.

At the age of 45, Niekro shined as he went 16-8 and led the team in wins and his 3.09 ERA was good enough for fourth in the league. Niekro became the oldest player ever to win 16 games.

On June 18, Niekro threw a three-hitter against the Tigers in Detroit. The Yankees won the game 2-1 as a Don Mattingly double in the fifth drove in the eventual game winner. On Independence Day 1984, Phil reached a milestone only achieved eight times before. In a shutout over the Texas Rangers, Niekro's five strikeouts were enough to push him over the top as he became the ninth pitcher in major league history to record 3,000 strikeouts.

Niekro was selected to his fifth and final All-Star Game in 1984 as he finished fourth in the league in ERA and fifth in winning percentage. Despite the middle-aged Niekro's efforts, the Yankees finished in third place 17 games behind the Tigers.

Although Niekro's statistics were compiled without much national attention, those in the know were very aware of his abilities. The Yankees shrewdly signed the 44-year-old veteran to a two-year deal in January 1984. Even though he was selected to five different All-Star teams, he only pitched a total of 1.1 innings in two of the games nine years apart, likely because most catchers were unfamiliar with his knuckler.

Things were much the same for Niekro in 1985 as he went 16-12. The 46 year old pitched 220 innings and finished second on the team in wins and innings pitched. Again, despite his best efforts the team fell short, finishing two games out as Toronto took the division. Even though the Yankees failed to capture the pennant in 1985, many noteworthy events occurred for Phil Niekro.

At Fenway Park on April 8 Niekro became the second-oldest player to ever start an opener. Only Jack Quinn was older who at the age of 47 started the season for the Brooklyn Dodgers in 1931.

On July 2, 1985, Phil's brother Joe won his 200th game in a Houston victory over the Padres. This enabled the Niekro brothers to join Gaylord and Jim Perry as the only brother combinations to win at least 200 games each. The

Niekros would eventually surpass the Perry brothers as the winningest brother pitching-duo of all time as they finished with 538 victories.

On October 6, the final day of the season, the Yankees shut out the Blue Jays 8-0. On the mound is the ageless Niekro, who allowed only four hits in the win. He became the oldest pitcher to ever throw a complete-game shutout and after five unsuccessful tries reached his career-defining 300th win, becoming the 13th player in major league history to do so.

It must have been the year of the dinosaur as three other players in their 40s also reached milestones. On August 4, both Tom Seaver and Rod Carew joined elite clubs. Seaver won his 300th game and Carew collected his 3,000th hit. On September 11, Pete Rose surpassed Ty Cobb to become the all-time hits leader.

Toward the end of spring training in 1986, the Yankees waived Niekro on March 28, four days shy of his 47th birthday. He was signed by the Indians six days later and finished out his career back in Atlanta in 1987. Niekro retired with 318 wins and 3,342 strikeouts.

On January 6, 1997, almost 13 years to the day he was signed by the Yankees, the Baseball Writer's Association of America elected Phil Niekro to the Hall of Fame.

On August 3, 1997, Niekro was inducted into the Baseball Hall of Fame alongside Tommy Lasorda, Nellie Fox, and Willie Wells.

PHILIP FRANCIS RIZZUTO
"SCOOTER"

NEW YORK, A.L., 1941-1942, 1946-1956

OVERCAME DIMINUTIVE SIZE (5'6", 150 LBS) TO
ANCHOR SUPERB YANKEE TEAMS WHICH WON 10
PENNANTS AND 8 WORLD SERIES DURING HIS 13
MAJOR LEAGUE SEASONS. OUTSTANDING SHORTSTOP
ON FIVE CONSECUTIVE WORLD CHAMPIONSHIP
CLUBS. SKILLED BUNTER AND ENTHUSIASTIC BASE
RUNNER WITH SOLID .273 LIFETIME BATTING
AVERAGE. ALL-STAR FIVE TIMES AND A.L. MVP IN
1950 WHEN HE PEAKED AT .324 WITH 200 HITS
AND A .439 SLUGGING PCT.

Phil Rizzuto

(Elected 1994)

At a young age, Phil Rizzuto had a tryout with both the New York Giants and the Brooklyn Dodgers. As they passed on the diminutive Rizzuto, Giants manager Bill Terry and Dodgers skipper Casey Stengel failed to realize they had just dismissed a future Hall of Fame shortstop. A player who the great Ty Cobb would describe as "pound for pound the best player alive . . . if it were not for Hans Wagner, who was a superman in every respect, I would make Rizzuto my all-time, All-Star shortstop."

Al Kunitz, who was Phil's coach at Richmond Hill High School, was unwilling to give up on Rizzuto. Kunitz knew how good Phil was despite his size and coaxed Paul Krichell, the famous Yankee scout, to attend a game Phil was playing in on Long Island. Phil not only played, he played well, and shortly thereafter he received an invitation to attend a tryout at Yankee Stadium.

Rizzuto fared better than he had in the past as the Yankees liked what they saw and intended on signing him. Phil signed for $75 a month and was assigned to Bassett, Virginia, in the Class D Bi-state League. Ed Barrow recalled that Rizzuto cost him less than 15 cents to get him; a dime for the postage on the invitation and a nickel for a cup of coffee he drank one day after a tryout. Rizzuto, whose father was a trolley conductor on the Myrtle Avenue line, was born and raised in New York. "Holy Cow!" What a thrill it must have been for the local kid to play for the hometown team. Not only to play for them, but also to play for them during what was their greatest period of dominance.

While playing in Bassett for the 1937 season, Phil hit .310 and led the team to the pennant. In 1938 he took Norfolk to a flag in the Piedmont League and in 1939 he batted .316 as he helped Kansas City win the American Association title.

After three successful minor league seasons, including being named the Minor League Player of the Year in 1940, Rizzuto was invited to spring training for the 1941 season. While at camp, Phil was the butt of many jokes due to his small stature. Joe DiMaggio, Lefty Gomez, and even Frank Crosetti, whose job was on the line, took a liking to Rizzuto. Although friendly with Phil, Gomez even had his fun on occasion. One day Lefty handed Rizzuto a stool and said, "Here, stand on this when you take a shower, that water will be ice cold by the time it reaches you down there."

Rizzuto won the shortstop job coming out of spring training, but after only six weeks he was benched in favor of Crosetti. After spending some time on the bench Phil returned to the lineup and proceeded to bat .307 in 133 games that season. The Yankees won the pennant by 17 games en route to the World Series. Rizzuto's rookie season was so impressive that Phil received MVP consideration and *Total Baseball* listed Phil as the Hypothetical Rookie of the Year for 1941.

In the World Series, the Yankees faced the Brooklyn Dodgers. Although the Yanks had played a Subway Series five times prior, this was the first time the train had stopped in Brooklyn. Although Rizzuto hit only .111 going 2 for 18, the Yankees won the Series four games to one as they captured their ninth World Championship.

In 1942, Rizzuto batted .284 in 144 games as he was named to his first of four All-Star teams. The Yankees once again won the pennant, this time by nine games over Boston. In the World Series Rizzuto, who had batted eighth in the 1941 Fall Classic, was batting first. The change was good for Phil as he batted .381 with a home run, two runs scored, and two stolen bases. In the Series Phil led the team in at-bats, hits, stolen bases, batting average, and slugging average. Unfortunately for Phil, his heroics went for naught as the Yankees dropped the Series. After winning the first game, St. Louis swept the next four to hand the Yankees their first Series loss since 1926, a string of eight consecutive championships.

When World War II came along, Rizzutto along with many others were called into service. Phil missed three seasons as he served from 1943 to 1945. While playing on the Navy team under the direction of Bill Dickey, Phil played third base. Alongside him, playing shortstop was his crosstown rival, Brooklyn's PeeWee Reese.

There has always been a debate as to who was better, Reese or Rizzuto, and with both playing in New York a natural rivalry was created. Statistically, Rizzuto's offensive numbers pale in comparison to Reese's. However, his two strongest attributes were his glove and his leadership, both impossible to measure. Ted Williams once said that Rizzuto made the difference in many Red Sox–Yankees pennant races. Joe DiMaggio said Phil "holds the team together" and Yankee pitcher Vic Raschi said, "My best pitch is anything the batter grounds, lines, or pops in the direction of Rizzuto." *The Sporting News* had no doubt, as it voted Phil its top major league shortstop from 1949 to 1952.

Rizzuto returned in 1946 and batted .257 in 126 games. During a game that year Phil was beaned by Nelson Potter of the St. Louis Browns, and for the rest of his career Rizzuto suffered from dizzy spells. The Yankees and Rizzuto finished in third place, 17 games behind the Red Sox. Upon his return in 1946, there was talk of a new Mexican League. Although other major league players had already signed, Phil turned down an offer of $100,000 to play three years without hesitation.

It didn't take long for the postwar Yankees to return to the top, winning the 1947 pennant by 12 games over the Tigers.

In a repeat of the 1941 Subway Series, the Yankees faced the Brooklyn Dodgers. Playing before a record World Series crowd of 73,365 at Yankee Stadium, the Bronx Bombers won Game One 5-3. In the game, Rizzuto went one for two with a single, a run scored and a walk. For the Series, Phil hit .308 with eight hits, three runs scored, two RBIs, four walks, and two stolen bases. Unlike the 1941 Fall Classic, which the Yankees won in five games, the Series went seven games. After dropping Game Six before another record World Series crowd of 74,065 in the Bronx the Yankees won Game Seven 5-2 to capture their 10th World Series Championship and first in four years.

The 1948 season came down to a three-way race between the Yankees, Red Sox, and Indians. The Yankees were eliminated on the next to last day of the season and finished 2.5 games out. Rizzuto finished with a .252 average in 128 games and his six home runs were the second-highest total of his career.

After finishing third in 1948, the Yankees made a manager change to start the 1949 season. Out was Bucky Harris and in was Casey Stengel. It was Stengel who as manager of the Brooklyn Dodgers passed on Rizzuto some 13 years earlier. Stengel had come a long way in his opinion of Rizzuto as he said, "When a little guy like Rizzuter beats out a big fellow he has to be terrific. He has to have everything." Upon seeing Rizzuto for the first time Mrs. Stengel replied, "You mean that little boy is going to play shortstop for you?" In response Casey said, "If he ain't my shortstop, I ain't going to be managing around here long."

The change turned out good for both the Yankees and Rizzuto, as they once again won the pennant and met the Dodgers in the World Series. Phil batted .275 in 152 games at short as the Yankees held off Boston by one game.

Although Rizzuto batted only .167 in the World Series, he played flawless defense as the Yankees rolled in five games to beat Brooklyn for the second time in three years. Phil's value to his team in such a close race was evident as he finished second in the MVP voting behind Boston's Ted Williams.

Rizzuto's career year came in 1950 as everything under the sun went his way. It all began on February 2 as Phil was the very first mystery guest on the famed TV show *What's My Line?* From there, Scooter went on to play 58 consecutive games without an error. He led the Yankees in batting average, on-base percentage, games, at-bats, runs scored, hits, doubles, walks, stolen bases, sacrifices, and hit by pitch. He finished first in the league in sacrifice hits, while finishing second in the league in runs, hits, and stolen bases. Phil also finished third in doubles, fifth in games and at-bats, sixth in batting average, seventh in on-base percentage, and ninth in walks. Rizzutto had career highs in batting average, slugging average, at-bats, hits, doubles, home runs, runs, walks, and games. Rizzuto speculated years later that part of the secret to his batting success that year was being given a Johnny Mize model bat by the Big Cat himself. Though the bat seemed oversized for the diminutive Scooter, he had great success with it and continued to use it throughout the season.

For all his hard work Phil was named to his second All-Star team and ran away with the American League MVP Award by over 100 votes. After the season Stengel was quoted as saying, "To me, Rizzuto is Mr. Shortstop."

On May 4 the Yankees lost at home 15-0 to tie a team record for most runs allowed in a shutout loss. In that game, the lone bright spot was Phil Rizzuto with three hits. On June 8 in an 11-4 Yankee win, Phil fumbled a grounder in the fifth to end his record string of 238 errorless chances. Riding the back of Rizzuto, the Yankees faced the Philadelphia Phillies in their second consecutive World Series.

Named the "Whiz Kids" because of the youth of its key players, the kids of Philadelphia were thoroughly taken to school by the precise excellence of the mature Yankees as they swept the Series four games to none. The closest the Phillies came to winning was in Game Three. With the score tied 2-2 in the bottom of the ninth there were two outs and one on base. Rizzuto singled to keep the rally alive and second baseman Jerry Coleman then singled in the winning run. Trailing three games to none, Philadelphia had little hope left for an upset.

In 1951 Rizzuto and the Yankees again won the pennant, this time by five games over Cleveland. Rizzuto and Berra starred as Casey Stengel platooned many of the other positions. The great Joe DiMaggio was winding up a fantastic career as he played his last season. Phil was selected to his second consecutive All-Star Game and third overall. This was the third consecutive World Series appearance for the Yankees and the fourth in five years.

Riding the wave from their pennant-winning home run, the Giants came into the Series full of confidence. They rode the wave in Game One as they beat the Yankees 5-1. After splitting the next two games, the Yankees won three straight to stop the wild ride of the Giants as New York won the Series four games to two. This was the third straight World Series Championship for the Yankees and their 14th overall. Rizzuto batted .320 with one home run in a Series-leading 25 at-bats and was named World Series MVP.

In 1952, Phil was selected to his fourth All-Star team and finished third in the league in triples as the Yankees captured their fourth consecutive pennant. An interesting event occurred on August 25 as the Yankees were no-hit by Virgil Trucks of the Detroit Tigers. In the third inning, Rizzuto hit a hard ground ball to Johnny Pesky. After Pesky had trouble getting the ball out of his glove, he was given an error. Dan Daniel of the *New York World Telegram* convinced official scorer John Drebinger that it shouldn't have been an error since the ball was stuck in Pesky's glove. Drebinger agreed and changed his ruling from an error to a hit. Three innings later, when Rizzuto's hit was the only one on the board, Drebinger started to second-guess himself. He called and talked to Pesky in the dugout and the shortstop told him it should be an error. Drebinger then reversed his ruling and changed the call again, thus preserving the no-hitter.

In a rematch of the 1949 World Series, the Yankees met the Brooklyn Dodgers in the Fall Classic. The result was the same as the Yankees captured their fourth consecutive World Championship title four games to three. It was their third World Series victory over the Dodgers in six years and their 15th overall.

The 35-year-old Rizzuto started to show signs of slowing down in 1953. He stole only four bases and played his fewest games in five years but still made the All-Star team and finished sixth in the MVP voting. Although his batting average increased, most of his other offensive numbers started to decline. Rizzuto and the veteran Yankees still had some fight left in them though, as was evident in a game on April 28. While playing against the Browns, Rizzuto was spiked by Clint "Scrap Iron" Courtney in the tenth inning. A fight ensued in which umpire John Stevens dislocated his collarbone. Courtney was retaliating for a play in the top of the tenth when Gil McDougald knocked him over to score the go-ahead run in the eventual 7-6 Yankee win. The scrappy Yankees went on to win their fifth straight pennant and were looking to win their fifth straight Series. For the third time in five years, the Yankees met the Dodgers in the World Series.

After jumping out to a two-games-to-none lead the Yankees eventually won their unprecedented fifth straight World Series title in six games. Rizzuto batted .316 and led all players with 19 assists in his eighth World Series. Phil was one of 12 players who played on all five championship teams and became legends. The other 11 are pitchers Allie Reynolds, Vic Raschi, and Eddie Lopat; catchers Yogi Berra and Charley Silvera; infielders Bobby Brown, Gerry Coleman, Johnny Mize, and Joe Collins; and outfielders Gene Woodling and Hank Bauer.

Rizzuto's role began to diminish in 1954 and 1955 as he played in 127 and 81 games, respectively. In 1954, Rizzuto and the Yankees struggled as they finished eight games behind the Indians to end the most dominant run in baseball history. In a game on July 22, Phil played second base for the first time in his major league career. In an effort to get more power in the Yankee lineup manager Casey Stengel put Rizzuto at second and Mantle at shortstop. The Yankees won the game in the tenth 3-2 on a Mantle home run.

It didn't take long for the Yankees to make another run as they captured the 1955 flag by three games. Although he played in only 81 games during the season, Phil appeared in all seven games of what was to be his last World Series. The 38-year-old veteran performed well as he batted .267 with five walks and his two stolen bases led both teams. Unfortunately, the Yankees failed to start another streak as they lost to the Brooklyn Dodgers in seven games. This was the sixth World Series meeting between the two teams but the first time the Yankees didn't walk away as the World Champs.

Rizzuto played a backup role in 1956 as he was used primarily for his defense. On August 25, the Yankees gave him his unconditional release in order to make room for Enos Slaughter.

Rizzuto finished his career having played in nine Fall Classics. In seven of those Octobers, Phil Rizzuto and the Yankees were left as the last team standing.

Phil Rizzuto wasn't gone for long, as he was signed as a TV-radio broadcaster for the Yankees on December 18, 1956. He would remain the team's broadcaster until his retirement on August 18, 1995, after a dispute with WPIX-TV: the station refused to allow him to miss a game to attend former teammate Mickey Mantle's funeral. Eventually Rizzuto returned for the 1996 season.

To this day, Phil Rizzuto's World Series rankings are remarkable: third best in stolen bases; sixth best in games played; seventh best in at-bats and hits; and tenth best in runs scored.

The Yankees honored Rizzuto by retiring his number 10 on August 4, 1985. A monument was placed in Yankee Stadium's Monument Park that reads:

PHILIP FRANCIS RIZZUTO
"A MAN'S SIZE IS MEASURED BY HIS HEART"
SCOOTER SPARKED YANKEES TO 10
PENNANTS AND 8 WORLD CHAMPIONSHIPS
1950 MAJOR LEAGUE PLAYER OF YEAR
MVP OF WORLD SERIES IN 1951
HAS ENJOYED TWO OUTSTANDING CAREERS
ALL-TIME YANKEE SHORTSTOP
ONE OF GREAT YANKEE BROADCASTERS
"HOLY COW!"
ERECTED BY NEW YORK YANKEES
AUGUST 4, 1985

In 1990, Rizzuto received one of his most prestigious awards from the New York Baseball Writers. They unanimously selected him for the Long and Meritorious Service to Baseball Trophy.

Four years later, on February 25, 1994, the Veterans Committee elected him to the Hall of Fame. On July 31, he was inducted along with Leo Durocher and Steve Carlton.

"HOLY COW!" Scooter was finally in.

REGINALD MARTINEZ JACKSON
"MR. OCTOBER"
KANSAS CITY, A.L., 1967
OAKLAND, A.L., 1968-1975, 1987
BALTIMORE, A.L., 1976
NEW YORK, A.L., 1977-1981
CALIFORNIA, A.L., 1982-1986

EXCITING PERFORMER WHO PLAYED FOR 11 DIVISION WINNERS AND FOUND SPECIAL SUCCESS IN WORLD SERIES SPOTLIGHT WITH 10 HOME RUNS, 24 RBI'S AND .357 BATTING AVERAGE IN 27 GAMES. IN 1977 SERIES, HIT RECORD 5 HOMERS, 4 OF THEM CONSECUTIVE, INCLUDING 3 IN ONE GAME ON 3 FIRST PITCHES OFF 3 DIFFERENT HURLERS. MAMMOTH CLOUT MARKED 1971 ALL STAR GAME. 563 HOMERS RANK 6TH ON ALL-TIME LIST. A.L. MVP, 1973.

Reggie Jackson

(Elected 1993)

During their careers, very few athletes are recognized by first name alone. Baseball fans recognize Mickey, Willie, and the Babe as Mantle, Mays, and Ruth. The name Reggie unmistakably refers to "Mr. October"—Reggie Jackson.

Born in Wyncote, Pennsylvania, in 1946, Jackson starred as a running back in football and a pitcher/first baseman in baseball for Wyncote High School. He received a scholarship to play football at Arizona State University and Reggie tried out for the baseball team on a $5 bet with his friends. Jackson went on to make All-American honors in baseball his sophomore year. As the team went 41-11 Reggie played center field, hit 15 home runs, and led the team in runs, total bases, hits, and RBIs.

The A's chose Jackson second in the first round of the 1966 amateur draft after the New York Mets selected catcher Steve Chilcott. After six years in the minors Chilcott retired and became the first number one pick to never play in the majors. Reggie signed with Kansas City for $85,000.

Reggie wasted little in the minors as he was called up to Kansas City in 1967. Although he struggled at the plate, he was installed as a starting out-fielder for the A's in 1968, the team's first year in Oakland. Jackson responded by hitting 29 home runs in 553 at-bats.

In 1969 Reggie was two weeks ahead of Roger Maris's pace with 40 home runs. He then slumped and finished with 47. His slump lasted throughout the 1970 season and up until the 1971 All-Star Game. Jackson finished the 1971 season with 32 home runs and wowed the baseball world as he hit a home run off of the light tower in the All-Star Game at Tiger Stadium.

In 1972 the A's captured the American League West pennant en route to the World Series. Due to a torn hamstring in the American League

Championship Series against Detroit, Jackson sat out the series as the A's beat the Reds in seven games.

Jackson won the MVP in 1973 as he led the A's to their second consecutive World Series title. Oakland beat the Mets in seven to rub salt in the wound left by passing over Reggie in the amateur draft some years earlier. The A's repeated as champs again in 1974 as they beat Los Angeles in five games.

After Catfish Hunter left via free agency in 1975, A's owner Charlie Finley took a page from the Connie Mack Owners Handbook and started selling or trading off his stars. Jackson was traded to the Baltimore Orioles in 1976 for pitcher Mike Torrez and outfielder Don Baylor. Reggie, the consummate professional, responded with another fine season.

On November 29, 1976, Reggie Jackson signed a then-record contract with the New York Yankees for $2.96 million.

The courtship with the Yankees began on November 4, 1976. Being one of the 13 teams in the hunt for Jackson, Steinbrenner and the Yankees pulled out all the stops trying to obtain him. After entertaining offers from many teams including San Diego, Montreal, and Baltimore, Reggie had decided to bring his traveling show to New York.

When Reggie arrived at the airport from Montreal, George Steinbrenner picked him up in a limo and they went to lunch at one of the "in" spots in New York City, the restaurant *21*. During that lunch, Steinbrenner told Jackson, "You can own the town Reggie . . . with your charisma and charm you'll be even bigger than you already are. And we can win with you. We can bring a World Championship back to the Yankees, where it belongs. You and I are going to make a great team."

After lunch Reggie and George walked the streets in what Jackson later described as a two-man St. Patrick's Day parade. The clever Steinbrenner then took Reggie to his house, a multifloor brownstone with an indoor pool, to talk money. Reggie said that he and his moneyman Gary Walker were looking for $3 million while George offered $2 million, claiming he didn't want to upset his salary structure.

Reggie left town without a deal and a few days later had set up camp in Chicago with friend and advisor Walker. Jackson was set up to take final bids and listen to any late offers. George agreed to pay $2.96 million and the deal was written on a napkin. The $60,000 tacked on the end was for a Rolls-Royce Corniche. Contrary to popular belief, Steinbrenner did not by the car for Jackson. Reggie wanted the car and bought it himself.

The big reason Reggie wanted to play in New York was the fans that he felt would appreciate him more. He also thought he could make the difference between losing the World Series, as the Yankees had done a couple of months earlier, and winning it. Reggie had said earlier in his career that if he played in New York they would name a candy bar after him, and the prophetic Jackson was right.

Reggie started earning his money on opening day 1977 en route to a fine season. As his past and current teammate Catfish Hunter shut out the Brewers 3-0, Reggie had two hits and two runs scored. He would finish with 32 home runs and 110 RBIs—respectable numbers for what was at best a tumultuous season for him. Fighting between Billy Martin and Jackson as well as the fall-out from a magazine article in *Sport Magazine*, which quoted Reggie as saying he was "The straw that stirs the drink," made Reggie feel like a man alone on an island.

The low point however, came on June 18 in Boston. During a game with the Red Sox, Martin got upset about a play that he felt Reggie didn't make and removed him in the middle of an inning during a pitching change. This led to a nationally televised donnybrook in the dugout between Martin and Jackson. A few days later, after Steinbrenner attempted to play peacemaker as Billy and Reggie rode in a taxi together to Tiger Stadium for a game with Detroit. Even though they lost that night the corner had been turned and they were focusing on the playoffs. The Yankees went on to win 40 of their last 53 games to win the division with Reggie contributing 13 home runs and 49 RBIs during the run.

New York beat Kansas City three games to two in the ALCS, then faced the Dodgers in the World Series. After splitting the first two games in New York the scene switched to Los Angeles for Games Three and Four. In Game Three Reggie walked in the fifth on four pitches and later scored the final run of an eventual 5-3 win. In Game Four, with the Yankees leading 3-2 in the sixth inning, Reggie gave them an insurance run with a homer to left-center field. The game would end 4-2 as New York took a three-to-one-game lead in the Series. Jackson homered off the foul pole the next day in Game Five as the Yankees fell 10-4 to Los Angeles.

The Yankees were back in New York for Game Six on October 18 as they tried to close out the Series. In the second inning Jackson walked and later scored on a home run by Chris Chambliss to tie the score at two. After L.A. went ahead on a run in the third Jackson came up in the fourth with Thurmon Munson on first. It would have been impossible for anyone to know what was about to transpire. Reggie stepped in and hit the first offering from L.A. pitcher Burt Hooten into the right field stands to give the Yankees a 4-3 lead. Jackson came up again in the next inning and remarkably

did it again. With Elias Sosa now on the mound he hit a homer to what looked like the identical spot, giving the Yankees a 7-3 lead. It was the third home run that Jackson had hit over two games, on the last three pitches he had seen. Three innings later Jackson came up again, and what happened next is the stuff from which legends are made. This time he was facing Charlie Hough, but it didn't seem to matter as the crowd cheered "Reg-gie, Reg-gie!" Everyone watched in amazement as Jackson again sent the first pitch he saw out of the park, forever becoming "Mr. October." Jackson had just hit four home runs over two games on four swings and became the first player since Babe Ruth, 50 years earlier, to hit three home runs in a Series game. Jackson also set a record with his five home runs as the Yankees won their first World Series in 15 years. For the second time in his career Reggie was deemed the Fall Classic's MVP.

As the 1978 season rolled around, things were back to normal as Jackson, Martin, and Steinbrenner began to square off again. As Jackson and the Yankees slumped the Red Sox built up a huge lead halfway through the season. After Martin was replaced by Bob Lemon as manager, Reggie and the Yankees somehow caught the Red Sox to force a one-game playoff for the pennant. After a slow start Reggie had rebounded to post 27 home runs and 97 RBIs. During the chase Reggie helped the Yankee cause by hitting a two-run homer in a 3-2 win over Boston on September 16. After winning the one-game play-off with Boston that decided the division, the Yankees went on to win the ALCS over the Royals in four games as Jackson hit .462 with two home runs and eight RBIs.

In a rematch from the year before, New York faced Los Angeles in the Fall Classic. After the performance of a year before anything Jackson did would pale in comparison. He finished the Series leading all players with eight RBIs and a .696 slugging average and two home runs. New York won their second consecutive World Series four games to two.

The Yankees slumped in 1979 and after Thurmon Munson died the team floundered and finished in third place. Reggie hit 29 home runs and batted .297, which was 35 points higher than his career mark.

Under new manager Dick Howser the team rebounded in 1980 as Jackson hit an even .300, marking the first time in his career he had reached that milestone. On August 11 Reggie hit home run number 400 off Chicago's Britt Burns in the third inning of a 3-1 New York win. He won his third home run crown as he belted 41 round-trippers, sharing the title with Milwaukee's Ben Oglive. The Yankees won the A.L. East title, their fourth in five years, but fell in the ALCS to Kansas City in three straight.

The year 1981 was unusual on two fronts—an actor entered the White House and the baseball playoffs were a tale of two seasons. Although Jackson slumped badly that year, hitting only .237 with 15 home runs, the team somehow made the playoffs. In the strike-interrupted season, the winners of each "half-season" would have a best-of-five playoff series to determine who would go on to play in the League Championship Series. The Yankees, who had won the first half, played the Brewers who had won the second half. New York prevailed in five games as Reggie hit two two-run homers in the series.

In the ALCS, New York swept Oakland in three games, and for the 11th time the Yankees and the Dodgers faced off in the World Series. After appearing in only two games with four at-bats in the ALCS, Jackson sat out the first three World Series games as he continued to nurse a calf injury. With the Yankees up two games to one, Reggie returned in Game Four and contributed to the cause with the last World Series home run of his career, but it wasn't enough as the Dodgers won 8-7 to even the Series. Los Angeles won Games Five and Six to take the Series as Jackson batted .333.

After Reggie filed for free agency Steinbrenner chose not to sign him and Jackson signed with the California Angels on January 22, 1982, for a reported four-year, $4 million contract. Jackson would go on to become the 13th player to hit over 500 home runs in his career and retired after playing the 1987 season with the Oakland A's.

On August 1, 1993, Reggie Jackson was inducted into baseball's Hall of Fame and would be remembered as "Mr. October" on baseball's all-time calendar.

On July 6, 2002, the Yankees honored Jackson by dedicating a plaque in Monument Park that reads:

REGGIE JACKSON
"MR. OCTOBER"
NEW YORK YANKEES
1977–1981
ONE OF THE MOST COLORFUL AND EXCITING
PLAYERS OF HIS ERA
A PROLIFIC POWER HITTER WHO
THRIVED IN PRESSURE SITUATIONS
IN FIVE YEARS IN PINSTRIPES,
HELPED LEAD THE YANKEES TO FOUR
DIVISION TITLES, THREE AMERICAN LEAGUE PENNANTS
AND TWO WORLD CHAMPIONSHIPS
AT HIS BEST IN OCTOBER,
BELTED FOUR HOME RUNS ON FOUR
CONSECUTIVE SWINGS IN THE 1977 WORLD SERIES
—INCLUDING THREE IN
GAME SIX AT YANKEE STADIUM
INDUCTED INTO THE BASEBALL HALL OF FAME IN 1993
DEDICATED BY
THE NEW YORK YANKEES
JULY 6, 2002

ANTHONY MICHAEL LAZZERI

"POOSH 'EM UP TONY"
NEW YORK, A.L., 1926 - 1937
CHICAGO, N.L., 1938
BROOKLYN, N.L., 1939
NEW YORK, N.L., 1939

FEARED CLUTCH HITTER WITH LONG BALL POWER.
PLAYED SECOND BASE WITH QUIET PROFICIENCY
ON FAMED 'MURDERER'S ROW' YANKEE TEAMS WITH
RUTH AND GEHRIG. A .300 HITTER FIVE TIMES WITH
CAREER .292 MARK. DROVE IN OVER 100 RUNS
SEVEN TIMES. SET A.L. SINGLE GAME RECORD WITH
2 GRAND SLAMS AND 11 RBIS, 5/24/36. BELTED 60
HOMERS FOR SALT LAKE CITY (PCL) IN 1925.

Tony Lazzeri
(Elected 1991)

With teammates such as Babe Ruth and Lou Gehrig, it may not have been easy to get attention, but Tony Lazzeri had little problem getting credit for all that he brought to the Yankees. *The Sporting News* editor J. G. Taylor Spink wrote that he was ". . . a greater ballplayer than anybody knows."

Known as "Poosh 'em up" for his clutch hitting with men on base, it's ironic that one of Lazzeri's most remembered moments in baseball came on a strikeout with the bases loaded in the 1926 World Series. Lazzeri acquired the nickname while playing for the Salt Lake City Bees of the Pacific Coast League in 1922. During a dry hitting spell, a local restaurateur provided him with free spaghetti dinners for three nights running in order to get him to "Poosh 'em up." Although the food didn't stick to the thin, 170-pound Lazzeri, the nickname did, and fans would cheer it whenever he came to the plate.

After shuttling between Peoria in 1923 and Lincoln in 1924, Lazzeri returned to Salt Lake City in 1925. After putting up some remarkable numbers, this would be his last stop before jumping to the majors. While playing in the extended Pacific Coast League schedule Tony put up a .355 batting average, drove in 222 runs, and hit 60 home runs in his 197 games. Lazzeri became the first professional baseball player at any level to hit 60 homers in a single season.

That was all the Yankees needed to see as they gave up $55,000 in cash and $20,000 worth of players to obtain him. Lazzeri's acquisition paid immediate dividends as he batted .275, hit 18 home runs, and had 114 RBIs in 1926. After finishing second in the league in RBIs and third in home runs, Lazzeri finished tied with Lou Gehrig for tenth in the MVP voting. Afterwards, Miller Huggins was quoted as saying, "Tony is a great natural player, make no mistake about it. This is his first year in the majors, but he's no flash in the pan. He should improve." Although there was no Rookie of the Year Award in 1926, *Total Baseball* speculated that if there had been, Tony Lazzeri would have won it.

Huggins proved prophetic as Lazzeri was seventh in home runs from 1926 to 1937 behind Ruth, Gehrig, Jimmie Foxx, Al Simmons, Earl Averill, and Goose Goslin, all future Hall of Famers. During that same period he was also sixth in RBIs behind Gehrig, Simmons, Foxx, Ruth, and Goslin.

The Yankees would go on to win the 1926 pennant by three games and it was not lost on the team that Lazzeri was a major part in that success. The previous year their starting second baseman finished the season with a .246 batting average, four home runs, and 38 RBIs. The upgrade to Lazzeri's numbers almost certainly resulted in that three-game margin.

The Yankees returned to the World Series after a two-year absence and split the first six games with the Cardinals. Playing the deciding Game Seven at home, the Yankees trailed 3-2 in the bottom of the seventh. With Gehrig, Earle Combs, and Bob Meusel on base, Lazzeri came to the plate. Trying to unnerve the rookie, St. Louis player/manager Rogers Hornsby came to the mound and replaced Jesse Haines with the great Grover Cleveland Alexander. Alexander had pitched a complete-game victory in Game Six as Lazzeri went 0 for 4 against him. Rumored to have been hungover from the previous nights festivities, Alexander strode to the mound showing no obvious signs of being worse for the wear. With the count 1-1 against Lazzeri, Alexander hung a pitch out over the plate and Tony turned and crushed the ball deep to left field. The ball landed a few feet foul and on the next pitch Lazzeri swung and missed to end the rally. Any hopes Lazzeri and the Yankees had ended there as Alexander finished the game for the save and the World Series Championship. Now linked forever in baseball history, ironically, both Lazzeri and Alexander were also linked in their medical history as both suffered from epilepsy.

After the game Alexander, referring to how lucky he was that Lazzeri's hit went foul, commented that "less than a foot made the difference between a hero and a bum." The incident damaged Lazzeri's reputation as a clutch hitter, prompting manager Miller Huggins to say, "anyone can strike out, but ballplayers like Lazzeri come along once in a generation."

The accolades wouldn't end there. Not long after coming into the league veteran umpire Tommy Connolly remarked, "When things get tough out there, the others don't look to Ruth or any of the veterans. They look to Lazzeri, and he never fails them."

Although he failed to capture immortality as a hero in the 1926 World Series, Lazzeri went on to perform as a member of the famed 1927 "Murderer's

Row" lineup. Playing second base for the greatest team of all time, Lazzeri batted .309 with 18 home runs and 102 RBIs. He finished third in the league in home runs behind teammates Ruth and Gehrig and fifth in stolen bases. That fall, sportswriters thought enough of the youngster to give him MVP consideration.

On May 31 the Yankees played a doubleheader against the A's. Lazzeri was witness as Ruth hit home runs in both to run his string to four straight games. In Game Two he also witnessed the first home run in the illustrious career of rookie strong-boy and future Hall of Famer Jimmie Foxx. On July 8 Lazzeri hit three home runs against Chicago. The first two were off of Red Faber and the third tied the game in the bottom of the ninth. The Yankees went on to win 12-11 in 11 innings.

In mid-July 1927 manager Huggins said, "There are several reasons why we are winning so many games. Lazzeri is one of them. He was a good player last year, but now he is one of the greatest in baseball."

In the 1927 Series against the Pirates the Yankees led three games to none and were tied 3-3 in the bottom of the ninth of Game Four. Experiencing what must have been déjà vu, Lazzeri came to the plate with the bases loaded. He wouldn't be the goat this time, as Pittsburgh pitcher Johnny Miljus uncorked a wild pitch that allowed Earle Combs to score both the game and Series-clinching run. Lazzeri led all players with 18 assists in the four games.

Lazzeri's power numbers slipped in 1928 (10 HR, 82 RBI) as his average rose to .332, good enough for fifth in the league. Despite the lack of power, Tony finished fourth in the MVP voting as the Yankees clinched their third pennant in Lazzeri's first three years with the club.

On May 24, 1928, Lazzeri was a participant in a most unusual game. In Game One of a doubleheader with the A's there were a record 17 future Hall of Famers on the field, with 13 playing in the game.

The Yankees swept the World Series again, this time avenging their 1926 World Series defeat as they dispatched the St. Louis Cardinals in four straight.

As the Yankees slipped to second in 1929, Lazzeri stepped up his game as he finished fourth in the league in on-base percentage and batting average. He had a career high .354 batting average, with 18 home runs and 106 RBIs.

The Yankees again failed to capture the pennant in 1930, as Lazzeri hit over .300 for the fourth consecutive year finishing at .303. On May 22, 1930, the Yankees played a doubleheader against the Philadelphia Athletics. In Game Two Tony went 4-4 with four RBIs and five runs scored as the two teams combined for 14 home runs in the twin bill, including a then-record 10 in Game Two.

In 1931 the Yankees' slide continued as they finished 13½ games out. Lazzeri, who finished fifth in the league in stolen bases, saw his offensive production tail off. In what was an otherwise forgettable season, Lazzeri had a couple of memorable games. On April 2 the Yankees played an exhibition game against the Chattanooga Lookouts of the Southern Association. Miss Jackie Mitchell, a 17-year-old gate attraction was pitching. Babe Ruth came up and after swinging and missing twice he watched a third strike go by. Lou Gehrig then gallantly timed his swings to miss the ball. Lazzeri was next and after trying to bunt he eventually drew a walk and Miss Mitchell left the game. The Yankees would go on to win the game 14-4. As for Miss Mitchell, she would go on to pitch for the House of David barnstorming team in 1933.

On September 13, 1931, the Yankees played the Tigers in a doubleheader. After reaching first, Lazzeri stole second, reached third, and then stole home in the twelfth inning to give the Yankees and Lefty Gomez a 2-1 win.

An interesting incident would occur between Lazzeri and the quirky Gomez some years later. Lazzeri had a quiet but well-respected presence. Throughout his career he had a reputation as one of the smartest players in baseball. In one game a ball was hit back to Lefty Gomez and he threw it to Tony who was in no position to make any kind of play. Lazzeri ran in to Gomez and asked why he threw the ball to him. Lefty replied, "I've been reading in the papers how smart you are and I just wanted to see what you'd do with that one."

Lazzeri and the Yankees were back in 1932 as they ran away with the pennant. Tony, who finished third in the league in triples with 16, rebounded with a .300 batting average, 15 home runs, and 113 RBIs. On May 21, before a crowd of 60,000 at the Stadium, the Yankees swept a doubleheader against Washington. Lazzeri went 6-7 with a home run, two doubles, and a triple.

On June 3, 1932, Lazzeri hit for the cycle as the Yankees beat the Athletics in a slugfest 20-13. In this game Gehrig hit four consecutive home runs and narrowly missed a fifth. The two teams set a record for extra bases on long hits in a single game.

The Yankees strolled through the World Series by sweeping the Chicago Cubs four games to none. In the clincher Lazzeri had what may have been his best offensive performance of his World Series career. He went three for five with two home runs, four RBIs, and two runs scored in leading the Yankees to their first World Championship in four years.

Although 1933 found Lazzeri, Ruth, and Gehrig finishing in the top five in home runs, the Yankees finished eight games back. Tony, who also came in the top five in stolen bases, was the starting second baseman for the American League in the first-ever All-Star Game.

In 1934 the Yankees' 94 wins were only good enough for second place. They finished seven games out of the running as they were runner-up to Detroit. Lazzeri, who finished the season with a .267 average and 14 home runs, would say goodbye to a longtime teammate as an aging Babe Ruth finished his stellar Yankee career.

The mild-mannered Lazzeri had played a practical joke on the Babe some years earlier. After arriving late for a game, Ruth was trying to pull a shoe out of his locker and found it wouldn't move—he didn't even have to ask who nailed it to the floor.

A new era for Lazzeri and the Yankees began in 1935. As Ruth's career was ending it seemed that the Yankees run of dominance was as well. For the third straight year they failed to capture the flag, finishing second once again to Detroit. Tony finished the season with a .273 batting average, 13 home runs, and 83 RBIs.

The return to excellence didn't take long as Lazzeri, the Yankees, and new rookie left fielder Joe DiMaggio won the pennant by 19½ games in 1936. Lazzeri, whose numbers rebounded as he hit .287 with 14 home runs and 109 RBIs, had a memorable series on May 23 and 24 at Philadelphia. Playing a doubleheader on May 23, Tony hit three home runs as the Yankees won 12-6 and 15-1. The crowd of 24,240, one of the largest in several seasons for the Athletics, pelted the field with debris including cushions and bottles. The next day Lazzeri set several slugging marks as he became the first player in major league history to hit two grand slams in one game. In addition to his two slams he hit a solo home run and a triple, for an astounding 15 total bases. His performance carried the Yankees to a 25-2 slaughter of the A's. Lazzeri had now hit six home runs in three games and seven home runs in four games. This feat would go unbroken until Ralph Kiner hit eight home runs in four games in 1947. Lazzeri's 11 RBIs in one game set a new American League record.

In their first World Series without Babe Ruth the Yankees beat the New York Giants four games to two. In the third inning of Game Two Lazzeri became only the second player in history to hit a grand slam in the World Series. Lazzeri had fully atoned for his strikeout with the bases loaded in the 1926 Series.

Lazzeri's swan song with the Yankees came in 1937 as he batted .244 and hit 14 home runs. Tony would go out the way he came in with the Yankees, as they captured the flag and once again played in October. In a rematch from the year before, the Yankees again dominated the Subway Series, this time by a four-games-to-one margin. In Game One Lazzeri hit his final World Series home run in the eighth inning as the Yankees rolled 8-1. In the clinching Game

Five, Lazzeri witnessed Joe DiMaggio hit his first of eight career World Series home runs. Lazzeri finished with his highest Series batting average ever, coming in at .400 to lead both teams. He also led all players with a .733 slugging average. On October 15, 1937, only five days after helping the team win another World Championship, the Yankees released Tony Lazzeri.

While with the Yankees, Lazzeri had seven 100-RBI seasons, hit over .300 five times, and had 18 home runs four times. He was a vital part of six World Series teams and a winning participant in five of them.

Although known as the quiet man of the Yankees, Lazzeri always seemed to be the one to take charge when his teammates needed him. One writer complained that "trying to interview him was like trying to mine coal with a nail file," but when Lazzeri spoke, people listened. On one occasion Gomez filled the bases and Lazzeri came in to reassure the pitcher. When asked after the game what words were exchanged Lefty claimed Lazzeri said, "You put those runners on there. Now get out of the jam yourself."

A man of few words, he possessed the leadership skills to know which words were appropriate for the situation. This was never more evident than it was one day in a St. Louis hotel lobby. Lazzeri, along with teammates Joe DiMaggio and Frank Crosetti, sat quietly for one hour and 20 minutes. When DiMaggio cleared his throat, veteran newsman Jack Mahon, who was sitting near the trio, inquired, "What did you say?" The usually mild Lazzeri snapped, "Shut up! He didn't say nothing."

Tony went on to play parts of two more major league seasons before retiring after the 1939 season. He would go on to manage a few years in the minors before dying prematurely due to a fall during an epileptic seizure at the age of 42.

Although he played with Ruth, Gehrig, Hoyt, Pennock, and DiMaggio among others, famed baseball writer Red Smith would write in his column on August 9, 1946, that Tony Lazzeri "was the man who made the crowds and who made them roar."

The Veterans Committee elected Lazzeri to the Hall of Fame on February 26, 1991, along with former major league team owner Bill Veeck.

GAYLORD JACKSON PERRY

SAN FRANCISCO, N.L., 1962-1971
CLEVELAND, A.L., 1972-1975
TEXAS, A.L., 1975-1977, 1980
SAN DIEGO, N.L., 1978-1979
NEW YORK, A.L., 1980
ATLANTA, N.L., 1981
SEATTLE, A.L., 1982-1983
KANSAS CITY, A.L., 1983

ACHIEVED PITCHERS' MAGIC NUMBERS WITH 314 WINS
AND 3,534 STRIKEOUTS. PLAYING MIND GAMES WITH
HITTERS THROUGH ARRAY OF RITUALS ON MOUND WAS
PART OF HIS ARSENAL. 20-GAME WINNER 5 TIMES WITH
LIFETIME ERA OF 3.10. NO-HIT CARDS FOR GIANTS
9/17/68. OUTSTANDING COMPETITOR. ONLY CY YOUNG WINNER
IN BOTH LEAGUES.

Gaylord Perry
(Elected 1991)

After three consecutive trips to the World Series resulting in wins in 1977 and 1978, the Yankees not only failed to make the playoffs in 1979, they didn't even come close. Finishing 13½ games out, the Yankees could do nothing but watch as Baltimore ran away with the division. Trying to avoid another miserable "failure" in 1980 the Yankees, who were leading the Orioles by 3½ games with 50 to play, were looking for more pitching.

"Will the real oldest guy please stand up?" was the greeting from Ron Guidry to the newly acquired Gaylord Perry, as he sat in front of his locker talking to Luis Tiant. Perry, who was just a month shy of his 42nd birthday, looked more like a coach than a player when he was traded from the Rangers for two minor leaguers. But few coaches or players could lay claim to the achievements that Perry had amassed up to that point.

Although his current season mark was only 6-9 with a 3.43 ERA, his career statistics were second to none. At the time he joined the Yankees he was the winningest active pitcher with 285 victories. The 19-year veteran was the only pitcher in history to win the Cy Young in both leagues, and is still only one of three to have done it, joined later by Pedro Martinez and Randy Johnson. He brought with him five 20-win seasons, 50 shutouts, and 3,248 strikeouts, as well as being one of only four pitchers to have won 100 games in each league. He had led the league in wins three times, innings pitched twice, complete games twice, and winning percentage and shutouts once each.

In 1974 Gaylord pitched with his brother Jim for the Indians. Winning 21 and 17 games, respectively, their 38 combined wins represented half of Cleveland's total victories that season. The Perry brothers combined for 529 career victories, which was the highest total by brothers until another former Yankee and future Hall of Famer Phil Niekro and his brother broke it in 1987.

His most memorable moment, however, may have come on September 17, 1968, as he no-hit the great Bob Gibson and the Cardinals.

Perry, an admitted proponent of the spitball, entitled his autobiography *Me and the Spitter.* He claimed to rarely throw it but the idea that he might was enough to put the hitter at a disadvantage. His odd herky-jerky delivery only heightened everyone's suspicion.

Perry's debut with the Yankees was a memorable one as he beat the Orioles 4-1. He put on his usual show before every pitch as he rubbed his hand across his eyebrows, his shirt, his hair, and his cap at least 15 times. On one occasion he touched those areas 27 times. Although they were in a pennant race with Baltimore at the time, the game took a back seat to a classic Earl Weaver tirade. Many Yankees said they would have paid to see it.

Another memorable moment came on August 30 as Perry started his second game for the Yankees and the 600th game of his career. Gaylord, seemingly not quirky enough, started the game with a red glove that brought Seattle manager Maury Wills onto the field in the second inning to protest. The umpires did nothing as the Mariners played the game under protest. Under the rules, the pitchers glove cannot be white, gray, or two-toned, and while odd, Perry's glove was legal. Perry would later say he wanted the hitters to think about the glove—another head game by the crafty veteran.

Although Perry was with the Yankees for only 10 games, he had a front row seat as the Yankees dedicated a plaque to the late Thurman Munson prior to his start on September 20, 1980. Munson, the MVP catcher, died tragically in a plane crash on August 2, 1979. The plaque was later placed in Monument Park, located beyond the center field fence of Yankee Stadium.

Perry's last win with the Yankees was on October 1 as he came in to relieve Tommy John who had slipped on the mound and hurt his back. Perry relieved John and recorded the team's 100th win of the season, giving them a 2½-game lead with four to play.

That same day Perry must have felt like a 42-year-old kid as the Chicago White Sox reported that they were going to activate 57-year-old Minnie Minoso for the final three games of the season. In what can only be described as a publicity stunt, Minoso would become the only player to appear in a major league game in five decades.

After the Yankees won the division the Royals swept them in the American League Championship Series three games to none. This was only the second time Perry technically qualified for postseason play in his 22-year career. It is no wonder the spitballer needed a little extra help to win 314 games. Although he was on the roster, he did not make an appearance in the postseason and became a free agent after the season ended.

Gaylord signed with Atlanta on January 12, 1981, and retired after the 1983 season. He returned to the American league and faced the Yankees in Seattle on May 6, 1982, as a member of the Mariners. Only 27,369 fans filled the 59,418 seat Kingdome to witness Perry capture career win number 300.

Perry was elected to the Hall of Fame in 1991 by the Baseball Writers Association of America, alongside Rod Carew and Fergie Jenkins.

JAMES AUGUSTUS HUNTER
"CATFISH"

KANSAS CITY, A.L., 1965 – 1967
OAKLAND, A.L., 1968 – 1974
NEW YORK, A.L., 1975 – 1979

THE BIGGER THE GAME, THE BETTER HE PITCHED.
ONE OF BASEBALL'S MOST DOMINANT PITCHERS FROM
1970-76, WINNING OVER 20 FIVE STRAIGHT TIMES. COMPILED
224-166 MARK WITH 3.26 ERA BEFORE ARM TROUBLE
ENDED CAREER AT AGE 33. HURLED PERFECT GAME
VS. TWINS IN 1968. 1974 A.L. CY YOUNG AWARD WINNER.
5-3 IN 12 WORLD SERIES GAMES.

Catfish Hunter

(Elected 1987)

James Augustus Hunter was signed by Charles Finley, owner of the then Kansas City A's, in 1965. Finley, wanting a nickname for his new find named him "Catfish" because he liked to fish. Thus a household name was born.

A hunting accident a year earlier resulted in Hunter losing one of his toes. After the accident many professional scouts passed on Hunter. This was not the case nine years later as 23 of the 24 teams in the league were bidding for his services.

Hunter was declared a free agent in 1974 after Finley breached his contract by failing to make a $100,000 annuity payment on time. Steinbrenner outbid all others as he paid $3.75 million to bring Hunter to the Yankees for five years. This was the richest deal in baseball history at the time and would be the beginning of a financial revolution in baseball. "I was probably the first player who broke it open for other players to be paid what they're worth," Hunter said in 1987, a few hours after he was elected to the Hall of Fame.

Not a power pitcher, Hunter's success came from his outstanding control and wide assortment of pitches. In his book *The Umpire Strikes Back,* former major league umpire Ron Luciano said, "Catfish Hunter had the finest control of any pitcher I've ever seen. He was so good he could pick the sprinkles off an ice cream cone from the pitcher's mound."

Although only 28 years old at the time, Catfish Hunter had accomplished everything a player dreams of by the time he signed with the Yankees. Having never played in the minors, Hunter was already a 10-year veteran with a full trophy case. The 1974 Cy Young Award winner had already won at least 20 games four times, played in six All-Star Games, and thrown a perfect game against the Twins in 1968 (the first one in the American League since 1922).

He also had led the league in wins, winning percentage, and ERA. But his crowning achievement had been his three consecutive World Series Championships from 1972 to 1974, as he won four Series games and lost none.

Hunter didn't miss a beat in 1975, his first year with the Yankees, as he went 23-14. Catfish led the league in wins (23), complete games (30), innings pitched (328), lowest hits allowed per nine innings (6.80), lowest opponent's batting average (.208) and lowest opponent's on-base percentage (.260). He was also second in shutouts (7) and ERA (2.58) and fifth in fewest walks allowed per nine innings (2.28). Hunter was runner-up for a second consecutive Cy Young Award to future Hall of Famer Jim Palmer, who had one of the best seasons of his illustrious career. Catfish was also elected to his seventh All-Star Game.

Hunter's acquisition started to pay off in 1976 as the Yankees won their first pennant since the days of Mantle and Maris 12 years earlier. Although they were winning again, the Yankees were swept in the World Series by the Cincinnati Reds four games to none. Catfish pitched a complete game in Game Two as the Yankees fell 3-2. This was the closest game of the Series.

Years of arm strain and the effects of diabetes started to take their toll on Hunter as he spent time on the disabled list for parts of the next two seasons. Clearly not at his best, Hunter still went a respectable 21-15 over this span. Hunter's competitiveness may have been the difference as the Yankees won the pennant by 2½ games in 1977 and by one game in 1978. The Yankees would claim World Series crowns both seasons, as Hunter won the clincher in 1978 in what was Thurmon Munson's last postseason appearance. Catfish started that Game Six and was removed with no outs in the eighth with a 7-2 lead. After six outs of scoreless relief from Goose Gossage, Hunter was a World Champion for the fifth and final time.

James "Catfish" Hunter retired after his contract expired following a lackluster 1979 season. Due to physical problems, Hunter could no longer compete at the level he had been accustomed. Only 33 years old, Hunter retired to his hometown of Hertford, North Carolina, and became a full-time farmer. "He exemplified class and dignity and taught us how to win," George Steinbrenner said of Catfish Hunter. Steinbrenner never questioned whether Hunter earned his money, calling him the cornerstone of the team's 1970s championships.

During his Hall of Fame acceptance speech Hunter thanked Mr. Steinbrenner for giving him enough money to retire in five years.

It is not often that the most memorable achievement for a Hall of Fame pitcher would come 20 years after his retirement. But such is the case with Catfish Hunter. Hunter was diagnosed with amyothropic lateral sclerosis (ALS), also known as Lou Gehrig's disease, in September 1998.

With only a year left to live Hunter achieved what will ultimately be his legacy. With the help of many friends from his hometown as well as others including Reggie Jackson, George Steinbrenner, and Jim Pagliaroni, the catcher who caught his perfect game, Jimmy, as he was known at home, founded the Catfish Hunter ALS Foundation on May 8, 1999, the 31st anniversary of his perfect game. The first meeting of the Board of Directors was held October 9, 1999, exactly one month after Hunter's death at the age of 53.

On the very day that the Yankee family could have been celebrating the 100th anniversary of the birth of their Hall of Fame pitcher Waite Hoyt, they instead were mourning the loss of Catfish Hunter.

Hunter was elected to the Hall of Fame in 1987.

ENOS BRADSHER SLAUGHTER
"COUNTRY"
ST. LOUIS N.L. 1938-1953
NEW YORK A.L. 1954-1955, 1956-1959
KANSAS CITY A.L. 1955-1956 MILWAUKEE N.L. 1959
HARD-NOSED, HUSTLING PERFORMER WHO PLAYED
THE GAME WITH INTENSITY AND DETERMINATION.
FLAT, LEVEL SWING MADE HIM A LIFETIME .300
HITTER WHO INVARIABLY CAME THROUGH IN
CLUTCH SITUATIONS. EXCELLENT OUTFIELDER WITH
STRONG ARM. DARING BASERUNNER FAMOUS FOR
HIS MAD DASH HOME TO WIN 1946 WORLD SERIES
FOR CARDINALS. BATTED .291 IN 5 WORLD SERIES.

Enos Slaughter
(Elected 1985)

Prior to ever coming to the "Big City" and the Yankees, the boy known as "Country" was immortalized with a 10-second dash to glory to win the 1946 World Series.

Enos got his start after *Durham Morning Herald* writer Fred Haney urged St. Louis to give the Roxboro, North Carolina, native a look. The tryout was successful and the Cardinals assigned Slaughter to Class B Columbus of the South Atlantic League for the 1934 season.

Early in his career Enos, who made his reputation by running, was not very quick. In 1935 Cardinal Billy Southworth pointed out to him that he ran flat-footed and told him to run on the balls of his feet. After a few days of practice, Slaughter had cut four steps off of his run from homeplate to first.

During a game in 1936, Columbus manager Eddie Dyer saw Enos moping around the dugout in response to his poor performance and said, "Son, if you're tired, we'll try to get you some help." The words hit Slaughter like a ton of bricks and he later recalled, "I suddenly realized people don't care how sorry I felt for myself. That's when I started running." Some say the original Charlie Hustle never stopped.

After hitting .382 to pace the American Association in 1937, Slaughter was brought up to the big club in 1938. Enos learned that the Chicago Cubs had offered $100,000 for him and he demanded a raise. At the time he was making $400 per month and the Cardinals obliged by giving him a 50 percent raise to $600.

Over the next 16 years Slaughter played 13 seasons with the Cardinals and batted over .300 eight times. Just hitting his stride, Slaughter had one of his best seasons in 1942 as he led his team to the World Series. Enos led the league in hits (188), triples (17), and total bases (292). He also finished second in the league in batting average (.318) and runs scored (100) and third in slugging average (.494) and RBI (98).

Facing the defending World Champion Yankees in the Series, St. Louis certainly had an uphill climb. In Game Two Slaughter threw out Tuck Stainback at third in the ninth inning to help the Cardinals beat them 4-3. St. Louis went on to win the Series in five games and handed manager Joe McCarthy his only World Series loss with the Yankees.

Enos spent 1943 to 1945 in the service but returned in time for the 1946 season. While in the service, Slaughter played service ball to entertain the troops, including a game on recently captured Iwo Jima.

Upon his return Enos promptly picked up where he left off as he led the Cardinals to another pennant. He hit .300 for the fifth straight season and led the league in RBIs with 130. Slaughter also had career highs with 18 home runs, 100 runs scored, 609 at-bats, and 156 games played.

Playing against the Red Sox in the World Series, Slaughter immortalized himself in the eighth inning of Game Seven. With the score tied 3-3, Slaughter led off the eighth with a single. After the next two batters made outs, Enos remained at first base. Feeling like he had to do something, Slaughter broke for second and later said, "I feel I caught the infield by surprise . . . I was just stealing second." When left fielder Harry Walker saw Slaughter running he slapped the ball to center. With two outs Slaughter kept on running as the ball dropped in for a hit. Center fielder Leon Culberson, who replaced an injured Dom DiMaggio, scooped up the ball and fired it to the cutoff man, Johnny Pesky. Pesky immediately turned to stop Walker from running to second. Meanwhile, Slaughter ran through third base coach Mike Gonzalez's stop sign and was headed for home. By the time Pesky realized what was going on it was too late, as the hustling Slaughter scored the eventual winning run.

Although Slaughter hit .300 or better three times over the next seven years with a high of .336 in 1949, the Cardinals couldn't win the pennant. In 1952, when Enos hit less than 15 home runs while driving in more than 100, he became the first player in major league history to accomplish the feat twice. He had done it previously in 1950.

On April 11, 1954, as they were trying to regroup, the Cardinals traded Slaughter to the Yankees to make room for promising rookie outfielder Wally Moon. In exchange for Slaughter the Yankees sent center fielder Bill Virdon, pitcher Mel Wright, and outfielder Emil Tellinger to the Cardinals. Yankee co-owner Del Webb said, "We gave up no one and got a ball player we can use very much."

When Slaughter found out about the trade he wept openly at his locker. He would later say, "I never felt as bad when my father died as when I was released by the Cardinals." St. Louis owner August A. Busch called Enos "one of the greatest players in Cardinal history."

After 15 hard-nosed years in St. Louis the country boy was in for a culture shock in the Big Apple. Former New York teammate Bobby Richardson recalled the following story: "I'll never forget it. They teamed Whitey Ford with Slaughter (as roommates) and they couldn't be more different. Every morning Enos was out of bed early, showered and shaved by 5:30 a.m. and ready to head out the door. Of course, at that time, Whitey was just coming home from a night of carousing."

Knowing there was no crying in baseball, Slaughter helped the Yankees win 103 games. Unfortunately it wasn't enough, as the Indians won 111 games to capture the pennant. Playing in only 69 games due to a broken arm, Slaughter's highlight came on September 9 as he had the only hit against Baltimore's Joe Coleman. This marked the third time in his career that Slaughter had broken up a no-hitter.

Enos led the American League in pinch hits in 1955 as he split time between the Yankees and the A's. Slaughter was traded to Kansas City along with Johnny Sain on May 11, 1955, but a little more than a year later he was waived back to the Yankees. In August 1956 the Yankees had injury troubles and Stengel went to general manager George Weiss and said "Buy Slaughter back." Weiss said, "Heck, he's 40 years old," and Casey replied, "I don't care, buy him back." In order to make room for Slaughter the Yankees waived longtime shortstop Phil Rizzuto on August 25.

Enos was a key factor in manager Casey Stengel's platoon system. In 1956 Slaughter hit .350 with a home run in the World Series as the Yankees won their first World Championship in three years. With the home run he hit in Game Three, he became the oldest player (40 years, 162 days) to homer in World Series history. In Game Five Slaughter recorded a putout and witnessed what many consider to be the greatest game ever pitched, Don Larsen's perfect World Series game. After the Series the team voted Slaughter a partial share of World Series money, which prompted Enos to say, "Where else could I make $4,200 for four weeks work?"

Slaughter was used primarily as a pinch hitter in 1957 and 1958. He had 48 pinch hit at-bats each season and led the league in 1958 as the Yankees returned to the World Series both years. New York split the two championships with the Milwaukee Braves, as they lost in 1957 and won in 1958.

In September the Yankees sent Slaughter to the National League contending Braves. Slaughter retired at the end of the season with an even .300 career batting average and 2,383 hits in 19 seasons.

The Veterans Committee elected Enos "Country" Slaughter to the Baseball Hall of Fame on March 6, 1985. Later that summer, on July 28, Slaughter was inducted in Cooperstown alongside Arky Vaughn, Hoyt Wilhelm, and Lou Brock.

Sadly, Slaughter passed away on August 12, 2002, at the Duke University Medical Center. He was 86 years old. At his funeral the president of the Hall of Fame announced that for the first time the institution would have a black canopy hanging over its doorway and its flag would fly at half-staff.

Quite an honor for a country boy from North Carolina.

JOHN ROBERT MIZE
"THE BIG CAT"
ST. LOUIS N.L., NEW YORK N.L.,
NEW YORK A.L., 1936-1953

KEEN-EYED SLUGGER SMASHED 359 HOME RUNS
AND BATTED .312 IN 15-YEAR CAREER WHILE
TOPPING .300 MARK NINE SEASONS IN A ROW.
SET MAJOR LOOP RECORDS BY HITTING THREE
HOMERS IN A GAME SIX TIMES AND TRIO IN
SUCCESSION ON FOUR OCCASIONS. WON N.L.
BATTING TITLE ONCE, LED OR SHARED LEAD
IN HOMERS AND SLUGGING PCT. FOUR TIMES,
RUNS BATTED IN AND TOTAL BASES THRICE.

Johnny Mize
(Elected 1981)

In August 1949, New York Giants manager Leo Durocher, who had just jumped from the rival Dodgers in the middle of the previous season, determined that a running team would stand a much better chance of competing in the National League.

Durocher felt that somewhat slow-footed slugger Johnny Mize did not fit into his plans, and on August 22, 1949, the 6-foot 2-inch, 220-pound first baseman was sold to the neighboring Yankees for the sum of $40,000 cash. Weeks prior, the Giants had faced the Yankees in an exhibition game, where Mize and old National League friend Casey Stengel had a conversation. Mize mentioned that he hadn't been playing much, and Stengel told him that if he were with the Yankees he would see more action. When Big John became available, Stengel encouraged the acquisition.

The 35-year-old Mize had never appeared in a World Series in his 10 major league seasons, but donning the Yankee pinstripes would change his career dramatically in that regard. Virtually no other player has ended the final several seasons of his career with a similar volume of team success.

Coming to Yankee Stadium, Mize, the first cousin of Babe Ruth's second wife, Claire, brought with him several impressive offensive accomplishments, most recently having been only the ninth player to reach the 300 home run plateau. John had led the league in homers on four occasions, and spending three prime years in the military during World War II may well have deprived him of more than 100 off his career total. Mize also led the N.L. in slugging percentage four times, but evidence of the notion that he was so much more than just a power hitter lies in his batting title in 1939, and the fact that his career batting average when he joined the Yankees was a lofty .320. Mize remains the only man in history to hit at least 50 home runs in a season (51 in

1947) while striking out less than 50 times (42). Not to be overlooked was Mize's defensive prowess; his agility around the first base bag earned him the nickname "The Big Cat."

Joining the Yankees in August 1949, Johnny played a minor role in the heated pennant race with Boston, which New York clinched in the final game. Mize then would see his first Fall Classic action, as the Yankees were set to face local rival Brooklyn. His first appearance came in Game Two at the Stadium as he pinch-hit for catcher Charlie Silvera, singling in the eighth inning. Mize's only other at-bat came in Game Three at Ebbets Field, helping to secure a victory for the Yankees. Again in a pinch-hitting role, this time for Cliff Mapes, Johnny delivered a single off Ralph Branca with the bases loaded that scored two runs to make it a 3-1 game. New York held on to win 4-3 and took the Series in five games to give Mize his first Championship ring.

In 1950 Mize spent his first full season in pinstripes, and as he would do for the remainder of his career, he split time at first base with Joe Collins. He would also be used by Casey Stengel increasingly as a pinch-hitter. Johnny went on to have his most productive season as a Yankee in 1950, clouting 25 home runs with 72 RBIs in just 274 at-bats. His season's biggest highlight came on September 15 when he slugged three home runs in a game versus Detroit. This marked the sixth time in his career that he hit three in one game, which still stands as a major league record.

With New York back in the World Series that fall against Philadelphia's "Whiz Kids," Mize appeared in all four games at first base. His offensive contributions were minimal, but the Yankees prevailed in a four-game sweep.

With 113 games, Mize saw action in more Yankee games in 1951 than he would in any other year with the team. The husky 38 year old managed to leg out a triple that season, his first in a few seasons and the final of his career, to go along with his last stolen base. It was the first of three consecutive seasons that he would lead the A.L. in pinch hits, and he also registered the 350th home run of his career. In that season's World Series, Mize was able to gain a measure of revenge against the Giants and Leo Durocher as the Yanks bested their neighbors in six games. Johnny's most prominent hit was a double in Game Five that scored Berra in a 13-1 Yankee blowout.

In 1952, his playing time started to decline significantly, with pinch hitter becoming his most prominent role. Facing the crosstown rival Dodgers in that October's World Series turned out to be one of Mize's finest performances in the Yankee uniform. In his first at-bat in the Series in Game Three he batted for pitcher Tom Gorman in the ninth inning and tagged a solo home run. In Game Four at the Stadium he started at first base and homered

to open the fourth inning. In his next at-bat Mize led off the sixth with a ground rule double, and Allie Reynolds subsequently completed the 2-0 shutout. The next game, also at home, saw Johnny hit a three-run homer into the right field stands.

Brooklyn however, squeaked out a 6-5 win. Finally, it all came down to Game Seven in Brooklyn as Mize continued his hot hitting. He singled in the fourth, scoring Rizzuto to make it 1-0, and singled again in the sixth as New York went on to wrap up the Series with a 4-2 win. His .400 average for the Series, along with three home runs and six RBIs earned Mize, three months shy of his 40th birthday, the 1952 World Series MVP Award.

His final campaign in the big leagues came in 1953, and he only saw action in the field in 15 games. Mize was called upon quite often to pinch-hit however, and was very effective in that role, going 19 for 61 for a .311 average. Stengel rewarded him for his excellence as a pinch hitter with a spot on the 1953 A.L. All-Star squad. In the Mid-Summer Classic on July 14 at Cincinnati's Crosley Field he was called upon to bat in the ninth for Hank Bauer, and his single led to the A.L.'s only run of the game. One of Mize's big highlights in that final season was hitting a pinch hit grand slam against Washington when the Yankees were trailing 1-0.

New York once again squared off against Brooklyn for the championship of baseball, and the Yankees made history with their fifth consecutive title. Mize made only three appearances in the six-game Series, unsuccessful in three stints as pinch-hitter. His last major league at-bat came in the eighth inning of the clincher, grounding out for Joe Collins. This closed the book on a marvelous career, one for which he is ranked by many historians as being among the five best first baseman to have ever played the game. Though having missed three prime years to military service, Mize still registered 359 home runs, 1,337 RBIs, and a .312 batting average. As for his time with the Yankees, he would say years later that he knew when he joined them in August of 1949 he was going to make the most of it. It is doubtful, however, that he could have imagined five World Championship rings in his final five years.

Mize watched comparable contemporary sluggers such as Hank Greenberg and Ralph Kiner gain enshrinement to the Hall of Fame via the baseball writer's ballots, but he himself was still on the outside looking in. In his 15 years on the BBWAA ballot he never received the required 75 percent for election, topping out at 58 percent in 1971. Finally, the long overdue call to Cooperstown came after the Hall's Veterans Committee cast their ballots in early 1981.

Mize returned to his native Georgia, where in 1993 at the age of 80 he passed away in the house in which he was born in Demorest.

LELAND STANFORD MacPHAIL
"LARRY"

DYNAMIC, INNOVATIVE EXECUTIVE MADE HIS
MARK AS PROGRESSIVE HEAD OF THREE CLUBS-
CINCINNATI REDS, BROOKLYN DODGERS AND
NEW YORK YANKEES-FROM 1933 TO 1947. WON
CHAMPIONSHIPS IN BOTH LEAGUES-WITH
DODGERS IN 1941 AND YANKEES IN 1947.
PIONEERED NIGHT BALL AT CINCINNATI IN
1935. ALSO INSTALLED LIGHTS AT EBBETS FIELD
AND YANKEE STADIUM. ORIGINATED PLANE
TRAVEL BY PLAYING PERSONNEL AND IDEA
OF STADIUM CLUB. HELPED SET UP EMPLOYEE
AND PLAYER PENSION PLANS.

Larry MacPhail
(Elected 1978)

S till mourning the death of Casey Stengel two days prior, the Yankee organization experienced another loss from their glorious past with the passing of former top executive Larry MacPhail on October 1, 1975. Gabe Paul, then president of the Yankees, said upon hearing the news, "Larry MacPhail was dynamic, bombastic, and smart. He made many outstanding contributions to baseball, and I have a special place in my heart and memories for him."

MacPhail's association with the team may have been brief at just less than three years, but his impact was felt in many significant ways. He brought a vision and a pioneering spirit with him that the major leagues had seen in his days as president and general manager of the Cincinnati Reds and later the Brooklyn Dodgers.

MacPhail was a high achiever from early on, getting a law degree from George Washington University at age 20. By 24 he had risen to the position of president of a large department store in Nashville. He entered the world of pro baseball in 1930 when he bought a badly in debt Columbus team of the American Association.

Along with helping to make the franchise solvent, he was hailed for innovating a playoff system in the league and was subsequently recommended to the owner of the Reds by Branch Rickey.

It was with Cincinnati that MacPhail pioneered night baseball for the major leagues in 1935, and became the first to have his team regularly travel by air. He laid the groundwork with his personnel moves that led to back to back pennants for the Reds in 1939 and 1940, though he had moved on to Brooklyn by that point.

In 1937, the Dodgers were $500,000 in debt, and the Brooklyn Trust Company was able to lure MacPhail to the organization to weave his magic

and help turn the struggling franchise around. He renovated Ebbets Field and began acquiring players that helped Brooklyn capture the National League pennant in 1941, their first in 21 years. Unfortunately, they ran up against a Yankee team in that year's World Series, and were topped by a slim margin in seven games.

MacPhail left the Dodgers in 1942 and entered the Army at 52 years of age to serve during World War II. He had also seen action in World War I 25 years prior, but by 1944 he would attain the rank of Lieutenant Colonel.

It was January of 1945 that MacPhail had formed a partnership with Dan Topping and Del Webb and purchased the Yankees from the estate of Jacob Ruppert for $2.8 million. The sale not only included the team, but the stadium, four minor league teams, and the rights to 400 players. Larry entered into a contract with his co-owners that called for him to act as general manager and also have final say on all team matters for 10 years. He would be assuming a position held by executive giant Ed Barrow for 24 seasons. MacPhail went right to work, spending nearly $1 million to upgrade and modernize the park. He added new seats, lights for night games, and created the posh "Yankee Stadium Club." There were rumors that Larry was considering hiring Babe Ruth as a coach when he took over, though it never materialized. It was he who had brought Babe to the Dodgers as a coach back in 1938.

When the Yankees won the World Championship by defeating Brooklyn in the 1947 Series, MacPhail was credited with rebuilding a Yankee mystique that had begun to wane by the end of World War II. He shocked many by tearfully announcing his resignation during the Series victory celebration. He said, "I'm finished. I promised my wife I'd retire after a team of mine won the World Series." With that, he retreated to his horse farm in Maryland and sold his share of the team to partners Topping and Webb.

Leland Stanford MacPhail had a relatively short but brilliant career as a baseball executive, leaving an indelible mark at each stop. A little over two years after his death he was elected to the Baseball Hall of Fame by the Veterans Committee as one of the more noteworthy front office men in the history of the game. Twenty years later, his son Lee would join him in the Cooperstown shrine.

JOSEPH WHEELER SEWELL
CLEVELAND A.L., NEW YORK A.L.,
1920 - 1933
POSTED LIFETIME .312 BATTING AVERAGE,
TOPPING .300 IN TEN OF 14 YEARS. MOST
DIFFICULT MAN TO STRIKE OUT IN GAME'S
HISTORY. CREATED RECORDS WITH: FEWEST
CAREER STRIKEOUTS (114), FOUR SEASONS
OF FOUR WHIFFS OR LESS IN 500 AT-BATS
AND 115 GAMES IN ROW WITHOUT FANNING.
LED A.L. SHORTSTOPS IN FIELDING TWICE
AND IN PUTOUTS AND ASSISTS FOUR TIMES.

Joe Sewell
(Elected 1977)

When the Yankees had a bit of uncertainty at third base going into their 1931 training camp, they couldn't have done better than they did in obtaining excellent all-around infielder Joe Sewell from Cleveland. Several teams were interested in acquiring the veteran, but GM Ed Barrow had beaten them all to it. In a strictly cash deal without sacrificing players in return, they had received a player who was likely the finest A.L. shortstop of the 1920s before his switch to third base in 1929.

To that point, Sewell had distinguished himself in a variety of ways. He had batted .315 or better nine times; he had showed his durability with a 1,103 consecutive game streak; and most noteworthy of all, he had established himself as the hardest batter to strike out in baseball history, whiffing a total of only 30 times in his last five full seasons. Illness had prevented Sewell from having his typical good year in 1930, but he felt that having had his tonsils removed in the off-season would return him to form.

He reported to Yankees camp and new manager Joe McCarthy in St. Petersburg in March 1931, and the 32 year old immediately began to impress observers. In a Yankees column dated March 8, 1931, in *The Sporting News*, it stated:

> Joe Sewell, who looks like a schoolboy, is full of pep, ready to play wherever McCarthy places him. He has tried his hand at second, short, and third, and is as spry as a college boy.

McCarthy was using Tony Lazzeri more at third base early in camp, but when he switched him back to second, Sewell began to see more action at third. Ultimately, however, Lazzeri was named as the third baseman to start the season, while Sewell was temporarily relegated to backup status. He made his Yankee debut in the sixth game of the 1931 season on April 20 when he pinch-hit for pitcher Lefty Gomez at the Stadium.

But by late May, Lazzeri was struggling badly at bat, and Sewell, who hadn't seen much action, was anxious to get in the lineup. The Alabama native and graduate of the University of Alabama was finally installed in the starting lineup on May 25 and went on to spend 121 games there for the season. Batting sixth in the order, he responded with several hits in his first few games, and by early July he was moved up to second in front of Babe Ruth. By mid-July, distinguished New York writer Joe Vila wrote that Sewell was "covering third base brilliantly."

He went on to be an effective cog in the Yankee offense in 1931, hitting for a .302 average and scoring 102 runs. Sewell also lived up to his reputation for being near impossible to strike out, with only eight in 484 at-bats. He was an excellent choice as a number-two hitter behind Earle Combs, setting the table for the big guns Ruth, Gehrig, and Lazzeri. The Yankees finished second to Philadelphia in 1931, the closest Sewell had come to a pennant in many a year.

Joe was again the Yanks primary third sacker for 1932, giving way on occasion to rookie Frank Crosetti. Sewell found the confines of Yankee Stadium to be friendly this season as he showed a bit more power in his bat and struck a career-high 11 home runs. Remarkably, he did so while striking out only three times in 503 at-bats. One of his most memorable games that season was a 5 for 5 day with a home run against Lefty Grove and the World Champion Athletics.

Sewell was fortunate to be a member of the powerful Yankees, and they also benefited from having a veteran of his caliber in their lineup, as his contributions helped win 107 games, earning a trip to the World Series for the first time in four years. For Sewell, it was his first time back to the Fall Classic since his rookie season of 1920. The Indians had called him up to the majors in August of that year to replace shortstop Ray Chapman, who had tragically died as the result of a pitched ball. Less than two months later, young Joe was celebrating a World Series victory over Brooklyn.

The 1932 World Series got underway in New York on September 28. Sewell's main highlights included walking in the sixth inning and scoring on a Bill Dickey single, and driving in Combs with a single in the eighth. New York prevailed easily by a 12-6 margin. They came out on top again in the second contest 5-2 as Sewell scored a run, again on a Dickey single. The Series then moved on to Chicago for what would be a very eventful Game Three.

Though Sewell didn't hit safely in the game, he did reach base three times, twice via a walk and getting hit by a pitch once. After his walk in the first he scored when Ruth slugged a three-run home run for what would be his first of two for the game. Later on in the fifth inning, Sewell would watch from the Yankee dugout as the famous "called shot" incident occurred with Babe belting his second home run of the game. With a 7-5 win, New York was now one win away from a Series sweep.

Sewell then had his best individual performance in Game Four by slashing three singles in six trips to the plate, driving in two and scoring one as New York topped the Cubs by the widest margin yet, 13-6. Sewell had ascended to the top of the baseball world as a member of the 1932 World Champion New York Yankees.

Again Sewell was the team's full-time third baseman as they attempted to defend their title in 1933. His 131 games at third would be his most in his time spent with New York. The Washington Senators edged out the second-place Yankees for the pennant, and though Sewell had a respectable year, batting .273, he decided at 35 years old it was time to walk away. His ability to avoid strikeouts remained with him to the end, going down on strikes only four times in 524 at-bats in 1933. For his entire career, he whiffed a total of 114 times in 7,132 at-bats, history's best ratio. Making this all the more remarkable is the fact that the 5-foot 6-inch, 155-pound Sewell used a substantial piece of lumber—a 35-inch, 40-ounce Louisville Slugger Ty Cobb model. More remarkable still is that he used only this one same bat throughout his entire career, continually seasoning it with tobacco juice and rubbing it with a coke bottle.

Sewell was retained as a coach by the Yankees through the 1934 and 1935 seasons, and even came back into the organization as a scout in 1963.

By the mid-1970s, many of Sewell's contemporaries had been elected to the Hall of Fame, and he seemed rather conspicuous in his absence from the shrine. His baseball achievements seemed to warrant his inclusion: .312 lifetime batting average; all-time best at-bat-per-strikeout ratio; and excellent defense at shortstop, which included leading the league in various categories numerous times.

Finally, in 1977, 44 years after the conclusion of his playing days, the Veterans Committee corrected the oversight. Joe Sewell enjoyed his status as a Baseball Hall of Famer for 13 years before passing away in Mobile, Alabama, on March 6, 1990.

STANLEY RAYMOND HARRIS
"BUCKY"

SERVED 40 YEARS IN MAJORS AS PLAYER,
MANAGER AND EXECUTIVE, INCLUDING 29 AS
PILOT. SLICK SECOND SACKER EARNED TAG
OF "BOY WONDER" BY GUIDING WASHINGTON
TO 1924 WORLD TITLE AS 27-YEAR-OLD IN
DEBUT AS PLAYER-PILOT. WON A.L. FLAG
AGAIN IN 1925. LED 1947 YANKEES TO
WORLD TITLE. MANAGED DETROIT, BOSTON
RED SOX AND PHILADELPHIA PHILLIES.

Bucky Harris

(Elected 1975)

Following the split with legendary manager Joe McCarthy and three consecutive years without winning a pennant, the downward spiral of the Yankees seemed hopelessly out of control in 1946. With his low-key approach and extensive knowledge of the game, Stanley "Bucky" Harris not only stopped the free fall but also returned the team to postseason glory.

Harris, the son of a coal miner, was raised in Pittston, Pennsylvania. Bucky left school at the age of 13 to work at a local coal plant and play baseball for several minor league teams in the area. His father, Thomas, had played semipro baseball and was a teammate of Hall of Famer Hughie Jennings, a fellow Pittston resident. It was Jennings who secured Harris a tryout with the Tigers in 1915.

After several seasons in the minors, former Yankee manager and current Washington Senators owner Clark Griffith signed Harris in 1919. While playing second base for the Senators, Harris was only 27 years old when Griffith tabbed him to be the team's manager for the 1924 season. After initial hesitation by some veterans who thought they were more deserving, including Walter Johnson, the club rallied around "the boy manager." The Senators then landed a one-two punch on New York, as Washington beat the Yankees for the pennant and the Giants for their first and only World Series Championship.

Harris led the team to the pennant again in 1925 but dropped the World Series in seven games to the Pittsburgh Pirates. Bucky's first stint as Senators manager lasted until 1928 when he was traded to the Detroit Tigers for outfielder Jack Warner. He was then immediately installed as the Tigers' new skipper. While in Washington, Harris married a U.S. Senator's daughter and President Coolidge attended his wedding.

Although he failed to duplicate his initial managerial success, Harris's reputation preceded him as a knowledgeable manager who got the most out of his player's talent. Hall of Famer Goose Goslin said Harris was "the best manager I ever played for." Unfortunately for Harris, he rarely had the players to compete in the first division and it wasn't until he joined the Yankees in 1947 that he again finished higher than fourth. From 1929 through 1943 Harris never went without major league work as he managed the Tigers (1929–1933), Red Sox (1934), Senators (1935–1942), and Phillies (1943). Known as a player's manager, Harris was so well liked and respected that the Philadelphia players threatened to strike in protest after he was dismissed 92 games into the 1943 season. Prior to coming to the Yankees, Bucky managed in the International and Pacific Coast Leagues.

After manager Joe McCarthy left the Yankees in mid-1946, Bill Dickey and then Johnny Neun finished the managerial duties for the year. For the third straight year the Yankees failed to capture the pennant. This equaled the team's longest dry spell since they captured their first World Series title in 1923.

Bucky Harris joined the Yankees on September 9, 1946, in an executive capacity. After the completion of the 1946 season, team executive Larry MacPhail appointed Harris manager in November and Bucky tied a record by leading his fifth team. MacPhail had said for weeks that Harris was not going to be the team's next manager but had a change of heart. Harris said, "It was a big surprise to me when Larry MacPhail phoned last September and asked me to come with the Yankees. I didn't even know what my job would be, other than to report on how the team looked. 'I want your advice on the team,' MacPhail said, 'and the only way for me to get that is to have you look them over out west.'" Harris signed a two-year deal reported to be worth $35,000 a season.

When Harris took over the team the only active manager with more experience was the A's Connie Mack. For only the second time in his 21-year managerial career, Harris was at the helm of a good team as he took over for the 1947 season and delivered with splendid results. As he had done with his only other good team, the 1924 Senators, Bucky promptly led the Yankees to the pennant, their first in four years. Harris's influence was evident as the team won 10 more games than it had the previous year, finishing with 97 wins. One of the highlights of the season was a 19-game winning streak, which remains the longest in team history. They also led the league in runs, hits, triples, home runs, batting average, and slugging average. *The Sporting News* named him the Manager of the Year.

One key ingredient to the team's success came when Harris converted struggling starting pitcher Joe Page into a reliever. Page, who had good stuff

but lousy control, responded with one of the first great seasons by a closer. While earning the nickname "Fireman," Page appeared in 56 games and posted a 14-8 record with 116 strikeouts, a 2.49 ERA, and 17 saves. He finished fourth in the Cy Young Award voting and led all pitchers in the MVP voting.

Also making a mark was pitcher Allie Reynolds, who was acquired from Cleveland for Joe Gordon and Ed Bockman. Reynolds would not only pay dividends in 1947 but would be an integral part of many more Yankee championships. Reynolds finished the season with a team-leading 19 wins and league-leading .704 winning percentage.

Veteran Joe DiMaggio had another stellar year en route to the MVP and rookie catcher Yogi Berra split duties with Aaron Robinson as he started what can only be described as a storybook career.

The Yankees met the Brooklyn Dodgers, who featured Rookie of the Year Jackie Robinson, in the World Series. Playing before a Yankee Stadium record crowd of 73,365 in Game One, the Yankees got off to their typical World Series start with a 5-3 win. All five runs came off Ralph Branca in the fifth inning. The Yankees took Game Two 10-3 behind Reynolds for a two-to-none Series lead. Berra hit the first World Series pinch homer ever in Game Three but it wasn't enough as the Yankees lost 9-8. Game Four featured an 8⅔ innings no-hitter by Yankee starter Bill Bevens that was eventually won by the Dodgers 3-2. With the Series tied at two the teams split the next two to force a seventh game. Harris rehab project Joe Page got the call in the fifth inning with the Yankees leading 3-2. Page held the lead as the Yankees won the game and secured their 11th World Championship.

After the 1947 World Series, Larry MacPhail retired and sold out to his partners. George Weiss took over as the senior-ranking baseball man in the Yankee organization. In January of 1948 the New York baseball writers presented Harris with the 25th annual William J. Slocum Memorial Award for outstanding service to the game over a long period of years. This accolade carried little or no weight for Harris, as his future with the team seemed unsure at best. It was common knowledge that Harris wasn't Weiss's guy and the two bickered quite often in 1948. Although the fights were usually about bringing up farm prospects for help, they also included Bucky's refusal to act on Joe Page's chronic curfew violations. Harris said, "I don't kid myself, Page's great relief work last season put me back in business after I had been forgotten. I'd be an ungrateful so-and-so to turn on him now. This job isn't that important to me."

The Yankees finished third in 1948 in a three-way pennant race with Boston and Cleveland. Despite Harris's popularity with players and fans, Weiss felt he had all the reasons he needed to dismiss him and hire Casey Stengel. Casey even took over Harris's uniform number 37 while with the team.

After sitting out the 1949 season Harris landed back in Washington for his third stint with the Senators, this time a five-year hitch. He finished his managerial career with a second go-round in Detroit in 1955 and 1956. After serving as assistant general manager with the Red Sox and a scout with the White Sox and Senators, Harris retired in 1971, completing 57 years in baseball.

Stanley "Bucky" Harris, the fourth-winningest manager of all time with 2,159 wins, was elected to the Hall of Fame in 1975. Harris died on November 8, 1977—his 81st birthday.

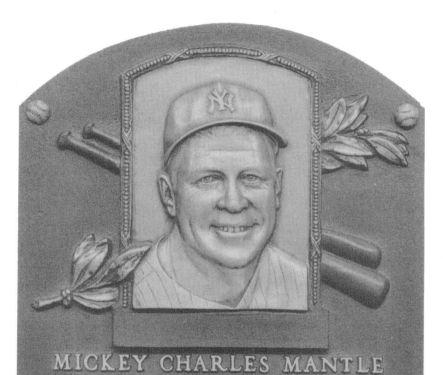

MICKEY CHARLES MANTLE
NEW YORK A.L. 1951-1968
HIT 536 HOME RUNS. WON LEAGUE HOMER TITLE
AND SLUGGING CROWN FOUR TIMES. MADE
2415 HITS. BATTED .300 OR OVER IN EACH
OF TEN YEARS WITH TOP OF .365 IN 1957.
TOPPED A.L. IN WALKS FIVE YEARS AND
IN RUNS SCORED SIX SEASONS. VOTED
MOST VALUABLE PLAYER 1956-57-62. NAMED
ON 20 A.L. ALL-STAR TEAMS. SET WORLD
SERIES RECORDS FOR HOMERS, 18; RUNS, 42;
RUNS BATTED IN, 40; TOTAL BASES, 123;
AND BASES ON BALLS, 43.

Mickey Mantle
(Elected 1974)

There are few images that better symbolize the golden age of the 1950s than a photo of a young, smiling Mickey Mantle in his pinstriped Yankee uniform.

His is a great American story that evokes memories of a simpler time. A blond-haired country boy from rural Oklahoma taking his remarkable baseball skills—an unusual blend of raw power and blinding speed—all the way to Yankee Stadium at the tender age of 19. In the following years he would achieve success on the field beyond his wildest dreams and become a hero to countless fans in the process.

If not for his abundant natural abilities, young Mantle was destined for a life working in the copper and lead mines like his father and many other men in northeastern Oklahoma. His discovery by Yankee scout Tom Greenwade when Mantle was 17 was the first step in his journey to the Bronx. A shortstop at the time, Mickey spent 1949 with Independence of the K.O.M. League, 1950 with Joplin of the Western Association, and was expected to be promoted to Binghamton of the Eastern League for 1951. But something happened on the way to Binghamton. Mantle so impressed Yankee management in Spring Training of 1951 that they decided to keep him with the major league team as the season opened. It had been decided early in training camp, however, that Mantle was better suited to the outfield. He was thought to be a good potential replacement for Joe DiMaggio in center field when the great man finally decided to retire.

It was April 17, 1951, with the Yankees opening their season against Boston that Mickey found himself starting in right field in front of the Stadium crowd. Sporting the number 6 on his uniform rather than what would later become his familiar number 7, he roamed the outfield beside the

36-year-old DiMaggio and batted third in the order. In the 5-0 Yankee win, he drove in a run with a single and also scored a run.

Stengel tried Mantle in the leadoff spot several times early on, and even gave him a start in left field. On May 1 in Chicago he slugged his first career home run, then three days later added a prodigious clout in St. Louis. But there was a growing concern that the youngster was trying to hit mammoth home runs every time he came to the plate, and he was being given special attention and instruction from Stengel, coaches Bill Dickey and Tommy Henrich, and even instructions on bunting from shortstop Phil Rizzuto.

Mantle slumped badly in June and early July, and management made the decision to send him down to Kansas City. He would be managed there by former Yankee outfielder George Selkirk, who was Babe Ruth's replacement when he left the team after the 1934 season. The first week with Kansas City saw Mickey continue to struggle, but then his performance began to take a turn for the better. After 40 games, his .364 batting average helped to earn him a recall to the Yankees, rejoining them on August 24. Now wearing number 7, he was primarily the team's leadoff hitter for the duration of the 1951 season and began to be a component in the team's offensive attack. A few of his home runs hit down the stretch in September were big factors in Yankee victories. Though Cleveland was threatening to overtake New York late in the season, they dropped out, leaving the Yanks five games ahead at the end. Like Joe DiMaggio 15 years before, Mantle would be heading on to the World Series in his rookie year. In the 341 official at-bats over 96 games with the Yanks, Mantle contributed 13 home runs and 65 RBIs.

On October 4, the day after Bobby Thomson's "shot heard 'round the world" clinched the N.L. pennant for the New York Giants, Mantle made his World Series debut. A little over two weeks away from his 20th birthday, Mantle could not have possibly imagined that this would be the first of 12 Fall Classics in which he was to appear.

The Yankees hosted the Giants in the opener, and Mantle, leading off in the bottom of the first, flied out to right. In all, he was hitless in three at-bats but also walked twice as the Giants prevailed 5-1. Game Two started off well enough for Mantle as he led off the home half of the first by laying down a well-placed bunt for a single. He was later driven in by a Gil McDougald single for the first run of the game. Later on in the top of the fifth inning, an incident occurred that would be significant in young Mickey's career. Stengel had instructed Mantle to catch every ball hit to right-center field due to a bad heel that had been troubling DiMaggio. When Willie Mays led off the inning with a fly ball in that direction, Mantle gave chase, but pulled up when he realized that Joe had made it there to make the catch. At that moment, Mickey caught his right spike on a rubber drain cover and went down in a heap with a knee injury. He was carried off on a stretcher, the Series ending for him with a trip to the hospital, where he would watch his team clinch the championship in six games. This was the first of numerous leg injuries during his major league career that would eventually rob him of his exceptional speed. Mantle wore a knee brace throughout the winter and was declared fit to play come Spring Training 1952.

With DiMaggio having announced his retirement in December 1951, Mantle was generally considered the heir apparent. Because of his knee, they brought him along slowly in camp, alternating him with Jackie Jensen in center field. But by the start of the 1952 season, it was Mick in Joe D.'s old spot. Aside from an occasional start in right field and one ill-advised game at third base, center field was his main position.

It was this season that Mickey really began to engage in high jinks with Billy Martin, exploring all the night life New York City had to offer. When Whitey Ford returned to the team from the military the following year, they formed an inseparable trio whose nocturnal escapades were legendary until Martin's trade to the Kansas City Athletics in June 1957.

Mickey was also struck with a personal loss in 1952 when his father, Elvin, succumbed to Hodgkin's disease during the season. It was his father who had encouraged him to become a switch-hitter at five years old, and worked tirelessly with him to improve his skills.

The 1952 Yankees beat out Cleveland again for the pennant, this time by a mere two games. Mantle continued to make progress in proving that he belonged, batting .311, third best in the A.L., with 23 homers and 87 RBIs. He also ranked second in doubles, slugging percentage, and total bases, and was named to his first A.L. All-Star team that summer.

Batting third in the New York lineup now, he would get his first taste of the Yankee–Dodger rivalry as the teams were set to begin the Series on October 1 in Brooklyn.

Mantle saved his most lasting performances for the final two games. Down three games to two in Game Six at Ebbets Field, he homered for the final Yankee run in a game that they would squeak out 3-2. The next day he homered in the sixth to give the Yankees a 3-2 lead, and in the seventh he singled home McDougald, which finalized the 4-2 clinching win. A World Champion for the second time, it was the first time he actually got to celebrate a Series win with his teammates. Days later, he was the guest of honor at a parade back in Commerce, Oklahoma.

In April 1953, Mantle created a considerable amount of attention on his potential for power. While playing the Senators in Washington, he hit a towering home run off Chuck Stobbs that was estimated at a whopping 565 feet. Mantle went on to hit many a tape-measure shot over the years, but this was likely his most titanic.

Mickey reinjured his right knee in August while making a throw, tearing ligaments. He didn't miss much playing time, but was forced to wear a brace for the rest of the season. In all, he hit 21 home runs and led the team in runs scored with 105. With 99 victories, the Yankees earned their fifth straight trip to the World Series, a rematch with the crosstown Dodgers.

Mantle emerged as the hero in Game Two at Yankee Stadium on October 1. With the score tied at two with two outs in the home half of the eighth, he slugged a two-run home run off lefty Preacher Roe as New York won 4-2 to go up two games to none. Three days later in Game Five with the Series now tied, Mickey hit a grand slam in the third inning of a game that ended in the Yankees favor 11-7. He would later call this one of his biggest thrills. Moving back to the Stadium, New York won the next game for their fifth straight title. Mantle's Series batting average of .208 does not begin to tell of his contributions as his timely slugging played a big part in two of the four wins.

Mantle added to his injury troubles as he hurt his knee playing basketball shortly after the 1953 season. He had surgery to remove cartilage from the knee at that time. Shortly before training camp of 1954 he had to have a large cyst removed from behind his knee. It took a while to play at full speed in camp, but he was ready for the opening of the 1954 season. Mickey had a relatively injury-free season, participating in 146 of the 154 games. He batted an even .300, hit a career-high 27 home runs, and led the A.L. with 129 runs scored. He also showed off his strong right arm by leading all major league outfield assists with 20, which would be the highest figure of his career. In July he got his first two hits in All-Star Game competition as the A.L. topped the senior circuit in Cleveland 11-9.

But despite New York winning 103 games, the Indians had a year for the ages with 111 victories in 1954. For the first time in his four-year big-league career, Mantle was heading back to Oklahoma at the end of the regular season.

The Yankees bounced back in 1955 and relegated Cleveland to second place, as they had in 1951, 1952, and 1953. Mantle emerged as a major home run threat, leading the league for the first time with 37—seven more than the player in second place. He also topped the A.L. in walks and slugging percentage, and was still able to display his speed with the lead in triples with 11. With increasing problems with his legs in the following years, he would never come close to that figure again.

Across town, Mickey's center field rival Duke Snider was leading Brooklyn to another October matchup with the Yankees. The teams kicked off the Fall Classic on September 28 at Yankee Stadium, but a leg injury to Mantle caused him to miss the first two games. New York was able to win the first two games without him, putting Brooklyn in a hole as the Series moved to Ebbets Field. Back in the lineup Mantle hit a solo homer to lead off the second inning, but it was wasted as the Yankees were beaten by young Johnny Podres 8-3. The following game was the only other game in the Series Mantle was able to start, and the Dodgers won it 8-5 to even it at two games apiece.

As it came to Game Seven on October 4, the teams were tied up at three games apiece and Brooklyn held a 2-0 lead going into the bottom of the seventh inning at Yankee Stadium. Mantle was sent up to pinch-hit for pitcher Bob Grim in the home half of the seventh representing the tying run. He got under it, however, and popped out to short to end the inning. New York could get nothing going as Brooklyn won 2-0 to clinch their only Series.

In 1956, Mantle finally lived up to the enormous potential that everyone knew he had. He set the pace by homering twice on Opening Day, and by season's end he had slugged a whopping 52-20, more than the man in second place. Right to the end of the season he battled the great Ted Williams for the batting title, and with a big final weekend against the Red Sox he finished at .353 to Ted's .345. Mick was extremely pleased to surpass Williams, whom he thought was the greatest hitter he ever saw. Also leading in RBIs with 130, Mantle had captured the elusive triple crown. He led the circuit in runs with 132, and his slugging percentage of .707 had not been exceeded by anyone in either league since Williams's .735 in his legendary 1941 season.

Mantle hit several amazingly long home runs in 1956, but likely none more impressive than one against Washington on May 30 that came a little over a foot away from traveling completely out of Yankee Stadium. He also happened to homer for the second straight year in the 1956 All-Star Game held in Washington, D.C. With his astonishing performance in 1956 he was an easy choice for the Most Valuable Player Award and was also *The Sporting News* Player of the Year.

Mantle continued his home run exploits right into the World Series, with the Yankees facing Brooklyn once again. In the opener he wasted no time, connecting for one over Ebbets Field's right field screen with Enos Slaughter on base to start the scoring. Unfortunately, Brooklyn went on to win the contest 6-3. Moving ahead to Game Four, the Yanks were looking to even the Series up and Mantle's solo home run in the sixth inning helped to achieve that in the 6-2 win.

Game Five on October 8 at Yankee Stadium would stand as a game that Mantle, or anyone else who witnessed it, would never forget. With two out in the fourth inning, Mickey got the first hit of the game, a solo home run down the right field line. New York had added one more run in the sixth, and by the time Yankee starter Don Larsen threw his final pitch, he had recorded the only perfect game in World Series history.

Despite the history-in-the-making game, the outcome would still come down to Game Seven at Ebbets Field, which also happened to be the last game Jackie Robinson would ever play.

Mantle scored on Bill Skowron's grand slam in the seventh inning as the Yankees embarrassed Brooklyn 9-0 on their own turf to reclaim the world title.

By early 1957, Mantle, with his triple crown season and boyish good looks, had become hot property in the world of product endorsements. He could be seen hawking breakfast cereal, pancake syrup, and orange juice. He was working with a business manager and exploring numerous outside interests, earning nearly as much off the field as he was from the Yankees.

Mickey followed up his award-winning 1956 season with another terrific year. Although his home runs dropped to 34, his average rose to .365, which was second only to Ted Williams. His stellar on-base percentage of .512 was behind only Ted as well, and he managed to lead the A.L. in runs scored and walks. With Mantle's name found at or near the top of virtually all of the major offensive categories, he was voted as the league's MVP for the second year in a row.

One occurrence brought sadness to Mantle during the 1957 season, as he saw the Yankees trade his great friend Billy Martin to Kansas City in mid-June. Martin had been Mick's roommate on the road for much of his career with New York.

New York found itself at the top of the league once again at the close of the 1957 schedule, finishing eight games better than the second-place White Sox. The Milwaukee Braves, having risen from the ashes after their move from Boston in 1953, were now at the top of the N.L. and were set to challenge the Yankees for the title. Mantle and young Henry Aaron would pose for photos before Game One at the Stadium on October 2.

Relying more on speed than power, Mantle beat out two infield grounders for singles in his four trips to the plate as Whitey Ford beat Warren Spahn 3-1. The Braves evened the Series the next day and it was off to Milwaukee, hosting its first ever World Series game. But the Yankees spoiled the party as they punished the Braves in front of their fans 12-3. Mantle walked and scored on a sacrifice fly in the first, singled in the third, and slugged a two-run homer in the fourth in the winning effort.

Mantle was unable to start Game Five with a bad shoulder he had hurt
sliding in Game Three and was used only as a pinch-hitter. Lew Burdette's 1-0
shutout gave the Braves a 3-2 advantage heading back to New York. Mickey
was again unable to play in Game Six as the Yanks squeaked out a 3-2 win. He
was in the lineup the next day for the finale, but managed only one single as
Burdette was just too tough. He recorded his third win of the Series as the
Braves were able to wrestle the trophy away from the Bronx.

With the Dodgers and Giants now departed for the west coast in 1958, the
Yankees had New York all to themselves. With Willie Mays in San Francisco
and Duke Snider in Los Angeles, no longer was there the question of who was
the greatest center fielder in New York. Mickey could now lay claim to the title
unequivocally.

Mantle had shoulder surgery in the off-season, and was not quite 100 percent in the spring of 1958. He got off to a bit of a slow start, but still ended
with the league lead in home runs with 42, runs scored with 127, and walks
with 129. The Yankees once again made bridesmaids of Chicago, this year by
10 games, and earned a rematch with the Braves in the Fall Classic.

Mantle's best individual performance in Game Two at Milwaukee was
wasted as New York lost by a wide margin 13-5. He had led off the fourth with
a solo home run off Burdette, and came back with a two-run shot off him in
the ninth. Days later in Game Six, Mantle singled and scored the tying run on
a sacrifice fly in a game that the Yankees won 4-3 in the tenth inning. Faced
with a Game Seven against Milwaukee for the second consecutive year, the
Yankees would not fail, regaining the World Championship for New York.

The 1959 season turned out to be one that both Mantle and the Yankees
would just as soon forget. Nagging injuries throughout the season to Mickey
as well as many of his teammates helped prevent them from winning more
than 79 games, finishing a distant third. Though many players would have
been extremely pleased with such production, Mantle was disappointed to hit
only .285 with 31 home runs and 75 RBIs. Despite his drop-off he still found
himself second in the A.L. in runs scored and third in slugging percentage. The
Yankees would be missing the World Series for only the second time in Mickey's
nine years with the Yankees.

There was not a lot of optimism heading into the 1960 season, either. The
Yankees had performed very poorly in the spring training season, finishing
with an 11-21 record, and Mantle was letting a $10,000 pay cut affect his play.
But with the addition of Roger Maris in right field, New York showed it was
back in contention. Mickey put his contract issues behind him and appeared
in a career-high 153 games, missing only one, and slugged 40 home runs. He

also led the league once again in runs scored as well as total bases as the Yankees held off the surprising young Orioles to return to the Series. Though Maris was voted the A.L. MVP, Stengel indicated to reporters that he thought Mantle should have won.

The Pittsburgh Pirates beat out the Braves to earn their first World Series invitation in 33 years. Most of the experts didn't give the Pirates much of a chance against the Yankees' Series experience.

The Yanks dropped the opener in Pittsburgh, but came back the next day and pummeled the Bucs 16-3. Mantle hit a two-run home run in the fifth, then pounded an estimated 475-foot, three-run shot in the seventh. Two days later with the Series moved on to Yankee Stadium, New York dished out another shellacking, embarrassing Pittsburgh 10-0 with Whitey Ford getting the shutout. Mantle's four-for-five day included a two-run home run, a double, and two singles.

It all came down to Game Seven at Forbes Field with the scored tied 9-9 going into the bottom of the ninth inning. Like millions who watched, Mantle was positively stunned to witness Bill Mazeroski's long fly sail over Yogi Berra's head in left field and over the ivy-covered wall. It was one of his most disappointing moments on a baseball field, and his .400 average, three home runs, and 11 RBIs for the Series became just a footnote.

Stengel, the only big-league manager Mantle had known, was let go after the Series and replaced by Ralph Houk. A former teammate of Mickey's, the new manager approached him at the beginning of spring training and asked him to assume a leadership role on the team, mainly leading by example. On the verge of turning 30, Mantle responded by having one of the greatest years of his career. The home run race between Mantle and Maris created national attention in the second half of the season. An abscess on his hip forced Mantle to drop out of the race by mid-September, finishing with 54 home runs to Maris's record 61. The two players shared an apartment during the season and became great friends, despite reports in the press that they were bitter rivals.

The team, with 109 wins, had what was likely the greatest season any Yankee team had since the "Murderer's Row" 1927 edition. They were considered almost a shoo-in to dominate the underdog Cincinnati Reds in the Series.

Mantle was still unavailable for the first two games of the Series due to his hip. He was able to play all of Game Three, which the Yankees won 3-2, but after singling in his second at-bat of Game Four his hip began bleeding and he was removed for a pinch runner. New York was able to handle the Reds with relative ease in five games, for all intents and purposes without Mantle.

Injuries cut into Mickey's 1962 season also, though he still posted a very high quality performance. He suffered injuries to both legs in mid-May, missing about a month's worth of action. But in the end, in his 123 games played he produced 30 home runs and led the league in slugging percentage and walks. In September he hit his 400th career home run, and this year he would win the only Gold Glove of his career. For the third time, he would be deemed the American League's Most Valuable Player.

The Yankees held off the upstart Minnesota Twins, and at the conclusion of a three-game playoff in the National League between the Dodgers and Giants, they were set to match up against Willie Mays and company. Mays and Mantle had met in the World Series for the first time 11 years before, back in their rookie year of 1951.

In Game Three at the Stadium with the Series tied at one, Mantle singled and scored in the seventh inning of a game they would win by the slim margin of 3-2.

The Series boiled down to Game Seven at Candlestick Park with New York's Ralph Terry holding a 1-0 lead in the bottom of the ninth. Terry had been the goat two years prior on the Mazeroski home run, and now had runners on second and third with powerful young Willie McCovey up, one out away from another Yankee title.

Mantle witnessed incredible drama right in front of him as McCovey lined out to second baseman Bobby Richardson to make New York World Champions for the second year in a row. Mickey would be taking his last sips of Series-winning champagne.

Coming off of his third MVP season, Mick signed a contract for $100,000 for 1963, the first time he had reached the figure. He got off to a good start that season, but broke his foot in June scaling an outfield wall to make a catch. He was able to play only 65 games, and for the first time since 1954 he failed to hit at least 30 home runs, ending with 15.

The Yankees finished their 1963 schedule 10½ games ahead of second place Chicago, and like the year before they would be taking on one of their former New York rivals in the World Series. The Los Angeles Dodgers were coming back to the city to begin the 1963 Fall Classic on October 2.

But the Yankees soon found out that the Dodger pitching staff was going to be a major obstacle, between Sandy Koufax, Don Drysdale, and Johnny Podres. Mantle's one noteworthy highlight was homering off Koufax in Game Four to tie Babe Ruth with 15 career World Series home runs. But in the end the Dodgers came away with what would be the first time the Yankees were swept in four games in a World Series.

Shortly after, Houk was promoted to general manager and Mantle's old pal Yogi was taking over as field boss for 1964. Berra was able to lead the team to 99 wins and the pennant by just one game over the White Sox. Mantle bounced back from his injury-plagued season and though he still was in constant pain, he was able to appear in 142 games. Teammates admired his courage immensely, as he endured the process of having his legs taped up before limping through every game. Oftentimes when he swung, he grimaced in obvious pain. Posting what would be his last truly All-Star caliber season, Mickey slugged 35 home runs, drove in 111, and recorded his last average above .300 at .303.

In the National League, the St. Louis Cardinals capitalized on the Phillies late season collapse to steal the pennant by one game. The Yankees would be meeting the Cardinals in the Fall Classic for the first time since 1943. For Mantle it would be his 12th Series in his 14 years with the club.

In Game Three at Yankee Stadium, Mantle was set to lead off the bottom of the ninth with the teams locked in a 1-1 duel. Just before he approached the batter's box he told on-deck hitter Elston Howard that he was going to hit the first pitch out, which is exactly what he did for a 2-1 win. The home run had broken Ruth's World Series record of 15.

Back in St. Louis in the Sixth Game, Mantle followed a Maris home run with a homer of his own. Later in the eighth inning he walked and scored on Joe Pepitone's grand slam as the Yankees forced a Game Seven with an 8-3 win.

The Yankees had to face tough young Bob Gibson in enemy territory in the final game and found themselves down 6-0 going into the top of the sixth. Mantle came up with two runners on and deposited a Gibson pitch into the left-center field bleachers for his record 18th and final World Series home run. New York made a late surge with two solo homers in the ninth, but could get no closer as St. Louis prevailed 7-5 to clinch the Series. Mickey Mantle had made his last appearance on the grand stage of World Series play.

The Yankees had decided to replace Berra as manager with Johnny Keane, who had just resigned from the Cardinals after their victory over New York in the Series. In Spring Training of 1965, Keane decided to play Mantle mainly in left field, where it would be easier on his legs. Now 33, his seemingly countless injuries had diminished his ability severely. His average dropped to .255 with 19 home runs and 46 RBIs. In the event that Mickey decided to retire after the season, the team held "Mickey Mantle Day" to honor him in September.

The Yankee dynasty appeared to be over with the team dropping to sixth place with a record of 77-85. Mickey had a shoulder operation in the off-season and by training camp of 1966 he had regained enough mobility to give it a go.

While Mantle's legs were giving him serious trouble, he managed to rebound slightly in 1966 with 23 homers and a .288 batting average. Among his home runs was his 494th against the White Sox in September, which moved him past Lou Gehrig and into sixth place on the all-time list.

After winning just 4 of the first 20 games in 1966, Keane was fired, with Houk stepping down as GM and getting back into uniform as Yankee manager. In Spring Training 1967, Houk moved Mantle to first base where he would play exclusively his final two seasons.

One month into the season, on May 14, Mickey reached a major milestone by hitting his 500th career home run. But with the Yankee lineup a shadow of its former self and virtually no protection in the batting order, Mantle was being walked at a very high rate. Opponents still showed great respect for his power.

Despite his aching legs, Mantle remarkably managed to get into 144 games in 1968. He was very disappointed to learn that his .237 batting average for the season had dropped his lifetime average below .300, down to .298. He hit his final home run on September 20, which gave him his 536 career total, good for third on the all-time list temporarily behind only Ruth and Mays.

Mantle reported to Spring Training in 1969 just to find out for himself if he felt he could do it for one more year. He quickly concluded, however, that his body wasn't able. On March 1, he announced to the world that he was officially done. Three months later on June 8, the Yankees held another day in his honor at the Stadium that featured an outpouring of love and affection by more than 60,000 of Mantle's closest friends. It was on that day that a plaque was erected for Mickey in center field, and his number seven was officially retired. The plaque reads:

MICKEY MANTLE
A MAGNIFICENT YANKEE
536 HOME RUNS
THE MOST POPULAR PLAYER OF HIS ERA
IN RECOGNITION OF HIS TRUE GREATNESS
IN THE YANKEE TRADITION AND
FOR HIS UNEQUALED COURAGE
THIS PLAQUE PRESENTED TO MICKEY MANTLE
BY JOE DiMAGGIO IN A CEREMONY AT
YANKEE STADIUM ON JUNE 8, 1969

EDWARD CHARLES FORD
"WHITEY"

NEW YORK A.L. 1950-1967
POSTED BEST WINNING PERCENTAGE (690)
AMONG TWENTIETH CENTURY PITCHERS
WITH 200 OR MORE DECISIONS. HAD 236
VICTORIES AND 106 LOSSES. LIFETIME EARNED
RUN AVERAGE 2.74. PACED A.L. IN VICTORIES
AND WINNING PCT. THREE TIMES AND IN
EARNED-RUN AVERAGE AND SHUTOUTS
TWICE. WON CY YOUNG AWARD IN 1961. SET
WORLD SERIES STANDARDS FOR GAMES
PITCHED, 22; INNINGS, 146; WINS, 10, AND
STRIKEOUTS, 94, AND WITH 33⅔ CONSECUTIVE
SCORELESS INNINGS.

Whitey Ford

(Elected 1974)

I t is an all-New York story—from the sandlots of Astoria, Queens, to the pitcher's mound in Yankee Stadium, to the Hall of Fame in Cooperstown—such is the baseball life of "The Chairman of the Board," Edward "Whitey" Ford.

Born in New York City on October 21, 1928, Ford became a Yankee fan by the mid-1930s. A couple of months after he graduated from Manhattan High School of Aviation, where he had been primarily a first baseman on the baseball team, the blond-haired, blue-eyed youngster attended a Yankee tryout with about 40 other hopefuls. Shortly after, famed Yankee scout Paul Krichell went to Ford's house in the summer of 1946 with a contract in hand, offering a $6,000 bonus. At that same time, a New York Giants scout called the Ford home with a contract offer of his own. Krichell then said to Ford, "I'll give you $7,000 if you sign right now," which Whitey did. Krichell suggested to young Ford at that time that he switch to pitching, which he had never really done before, but was willing to give it a try.

He began the long climb up the ladder of the Yankee organization in 1947 in Pennsylvania with Butler of the Mid-Atlantic League. Pitching for Binghamton of the Eastern League in 1949, he led the league with an impressive 1.61 ERA. By 1950 Ford had worked his way up to New York's top farm club in Kansas City. Not long into the season, the supremely confident left-hander felt he was ready for the call up to the big club.

The call finally came in late June. Stengel gave him his first assignment against Boston out of the bullpen in Fenway on July 1, wearing the number 19 on his road jersey. In five innings he was manhandled by the hard-hitting Red Sox, giving up seven hits, six walks, and five runs. Ford was not tagged with a loss, however, and he was undaunted, confident he would prove himself. He proceeded to win the next six games he pitched. His first victory came on July 17 at Yankee Stadium as Yogi Berra's two-run double helped him beat Chicago 4-3. The brash, young New York native was quickly developing a reputation of having nerves of steel, which would stick with him throughout his career.

Ford, mainly known to his teammates as "Ed" early on, elevated his won-loss record to 9-0 before being tagged with his first defeat. Stengel showed his confidence in Ford by starting him very late in the season against Detroit, who had a half-game lead over the Yankees. Whitey dominated the Tigers in an 8-1 win which catapulted New York into first place, and the A.L. flag was captured shortly after.

By season's end Ford had pitched in 20 games for New York, 12 of which were starts. He had compiled a 9-1 record, which included two shutouts, and a fine 2.81 ERA. Ford would say later that breaking into the pitching rotation of Raschi, Reynolds, and Lopat was like passing the bar exam. Come October, he had the chance to participate in what would be his first of many World Series as the Yankees were set to be challenged by the Philadelphia Phillies.

With New York winning the first three games, albeit each by one slim run, Stengel felt he was in a position to take a chance in starting rookie Ford instead of going back to Game One starter Ed Lopat. Whitey justified Casey's confidence and pitched better than anyone had a right to expect a young man not quite 22 years old to pitch in his first Fall Classic appearance. He scattered seven hits and took a shutout into the ninth inning. He allowed two base runners in that final frame, and with two outs, left fielder Gene Woodling dropped a fly ball that would have ended the game. The two runs were allowed to score, and Stengel decided to bring in Allie Reynolds, who promptly struck out the final batter to end the Series. But Ford had his first World Series win, and demonstrated to the baseball world his ability to pitch in the spotlight.

After three-and-a-half years of paying his dues at the minor league level, young Ed Ford had proved that he belonged in the major leagues. But his career that had just gotten underway would now be put on hold for two years. After the 1950 season, he was drafted into the Army and would spend much of his time stationed not far away at Fort Monmouth, New Jersey. On Opening Day of 1951 at Yankee Stadium, Whitey threw out the first pitch in his Army uniform. He had a chance to keep his baseball skills in use by playing for the Fort Monmouth baseball team, but would not make his return to the Yankees until after the end of his two-year hitch in the spring of 1953.

He wasted little time in establishing himself as one of the very top pitchers on the Yankee staff. His 18-6 record included leading the team in wins, innings pitched, strikeouts, and complete games, and he was second in the entire league in winning percentage, fourth in ERA. The Yankees got hold of first place by early May and would not let go, aided by an 18-game winning streak that began later in the month. They cruised to their record-setting fifth straight pennant, and were to be opposed in the Series by the rival Brooklyn Dodgers.

With a two-games-to-one lead, the Yankees sent Ford to the Ebbets Field mound to start Game Four. Things got off on a bad note in the first when right fielder Hank Bauer misjudged a fly ball off the bat of Jim Gilliam that went for a ground rule double. After a rough first inning Brooklyn had a 3-0 lead and Stengel decided to bring in Tom Gorman to start the second inning. New York wasn't able to catch up in a game that ended 7-3, and Ford was hung with the loss based on his one inning pitched.

He got a chance to redeem himself in Game Six with New York only needing one win to capture the Series. Whitey worked seven strong innings, giving up only one run, walking one, and striking out seven. He even singled in his first at-bat and advanced Phil Rizzuto, who eventually scored what would be an important run. Though Ford was not involved in the decision, the Yankees won 4-3 for their record-setting fifth straight World Championship.

New York came back for their seemingly annual defense of their crown, and though their 103 wins was more than in any of the previous five years, it was eight less than pennant winner Cleveland. Ford chipped in with a 16-8 won-loss record and set the pace on his own staff with a 2.82 ERA, also leading Yankee hurlers in games started, innings pitched, and strikeouts. It was also 1954 that he was named to his first All-Star team, starting and pitching three innings for the A.L.

Whitey's name was for the first time scattered all throughout the A.L. pitching leader lists in 1955. He started the season beating Washington 14-1 with a two-hitter, getting three hits himself. Other highlights that season included two consecutive one-hitters in early September. He finished the year in the top three in the league in numerous categories, including being the runner-up in wins, ERA, and winning percentage. Most important, however, was that Ford's fine pitching helped return the Yankees to the World Series to face the Dodgers as they had in 1953.

Former staff stalwarts Raschi, Lopat, and Reynolds were all gone now, and Ford was the logical choice to start Game One against Brooklyn. He squared off against Dodger ace Don Newcombe, and as the team's battled back and forth, it was Ford who had a 6-5 lead at the end of the eighth. Bob Grim came in to pitch the ninth and got the save for Whitey as the Yanks were victorious in the opener.

Ford made his next appearance with everything on the line as Brooklyn had jumped out to a three-games-to-two advantage. The lefty rose to the occasion in front of the Yankee Stadium crowd and allowed only four hits in the 8-1 complete-game win. It was performances such as this that earned him the reputation as a terrific big-game pitcher. Unfortunately, he had done all he could and was unable to prevent a Dodger victory the next day for what would be Brooklyn's only World Championship.

Ford further added to his status as ace of the Yankee staff in 1956 by virtue of his 19-6 record and A.L. best 2.47 ERA. The Cy Young Award was created in 1956 but only one trophy was given out rather than one in each league. It has been speculated that if one had been awarded to both an A.L. and N.L. pitcher, Ford would have likely won in his circuit.

Outdistancing Cleveland again in the pennant chase by a good margin, the Yankees qualified for a return engagement with their nemesis from previous Octobers, the Dodgers. In the opener, the blue-eyed, blond-haired Whitey would be contrasted by the dark, mean, unshaven right-hander Sal Maglie.

Ford was helped out right away by a two-run home run by Mantle in the first, but then ran into trouble by giving up two in the second and three in the third. Stengel made a pitching change going into the fourth, and with the score ending up 6-3, Ford was the losing pitcher. The Yanks got pounded the next day 13-6, and switching to the Stadium for Game Three, Ford was handed the crucial assignment. He pitched as well as he needed to, going the distance and allowing three runs, while Enos Slaughter's three-run homer aided him in the 5-3 win. Whitey stated years later that because of the importance of this game, it was his biggest Series thrill.

Whitey saw no further action in the Series, but New York ultimately prevailed in seven games.

Ford experienced shoulder problems in 1957, causing him to miss several weeks of action. When he did pitch, he pitched well, ending with an 11-5 record with a 2.57 ERA. When the bell rang to end the season, New York had an eight-game bulge on second-place Chicago, and had a different team, the Milwaukee Braves, on their October schedule.

With his injury woes behind him, Ford got the ball to open up Game One against fellow lefty Warren Spahn. The 69,476 fans at Yankee Stadium were treated to a fine outing in which Ford gave up only five Braves hits and one run in nine innings as New York won 3-1.

Five days later with the Series now tied at two, Whitey was slated to oppose righty Lew Burdette, who was very tough in the Braves win in Game Two. Ford pitched seven strong innings, giving up only one run on six hits, but

Burdette dominated New York batters and recorded a complete-game shutout. Three days later in the seventh game Burdette tossed yet another shutout, his third win of the Series. Despite Ford's 1.13 ERA in his two appearances, the Yankees had lost their second World Series in three years.

Though his 14-7 record in 1958 sounds a bit modest, Ford did manage to lead the A.L. in ERA by a considerable margin at 2.01, and shutouts with seven. Three of his shutouts came in consecutive starts in July. Come the season's end, they had again made bridesmaids of the White Sox, this time by 10 games. With the Braves also dominating their league, a rematch of the 1957 Series was in place. Ford got the starting nod in the first game, just as in the previous year, against Spahn. Whitey pitched into the eighth inning and left with a 3-2 lead, but a runner he had left on third was allowed to score by Ryne Duren, who had relieved him. Duren later gave up the winning run in the bottom of the tenth, and the Braves were up 1-0. By Game Four, New York was seeking to even the Series up, and Ford again opposed fellow lefty Spahn. He again worked into the eighth inning, and left having given up only two earned runs, but Spahn's shutout left them in a 3-1 hole.

After Bob Turley shut out the Braves 7-0 in Game Five to keep the Yanks alive, Ford faced Spahn yet again in Game Six in Milwaukee. Stengel pulled Ford early, with one out in the second, as he got into trouble by loading the bases. The Yanks came back to win the game, and miraculously overcame the 3-1 deficit to gain revenge on Milwaukee just as they had on Brooklyn two years prior.

The Yankees came back with a vastly sub-par season in 1959, floundering in last place as late as May 20. They ultimately rose as high as third, but finished 15 games behind first-place Chicago. Ford recorded a 16-10 won-loss mark, and had the league's sixth-best ERA at 3.01. Seemingly well on his way to a Hall of Fame career, Ford had a combined 121-50 record in the decade of the 1950s.

After a poor 1959 season and a terrible exhibition season in 1960, there were many harsh critics of the Yankees coming out of the gate just before Opening Day. They were, however, able to pull it all together and stave off a late run by the upstart Orioles, cruising to the pennant by winning their last 15 games. Ford's 12-9 record does not accurately reflect his effectiveness, as he possessed the fifth-best ERA at 3.08 and was tied for the league lead in shutouts with four.

New York was to face the underdog Pittsburgh Pirates in the World Series, and for Ford, the incredibly unusual results provided a strange mix of emotions. Among his many fine Fall Classic performances, individually, 1960 may well have been his finest.

Ford was given his first start in Game Three as the teams moved to New York tied at one game apiece. Whitey was nearly unhittable on that early October day, with just four Pirates reaching base safely. New York put on an offensive display and Ford came away with a 10-0 complete game. Four days later back in Pittsburgh, Ford had the assignment of trying to even the Series as the Yankees had fallen behind three games to two.

He was masterful again, allowing just seven singles throughout the entire nine innings. When Ford himself drove in Yogi Berra with an infield single in the second inning, there was no way he could imagine that it was all the scoring he would need. Still, Yankee batters piled it on again, and Whitey had recorded his second shutout of the Series. The next day however, he could only watch as Bill Mazeroski slugged his way into history, creating one of Yankees fans darkest days.

After their disappointment in October 1960, the Yankees came back with a vengeance in 1961 with their most powerful lineup since Ford joined the team. Among New York's impressive 109 victories were Whitey's career-high 25. New manager Ralph Houk used him very wisely, allowing him to complete only 11 of the league-leading 39 games he started. He was living up to the "Chairman of the Board" nickname Elston Howard had given him, as overall he was the number one pitcher in the game at this time. The writers who voted on postseason awards confirmed this by voting him the winner of the only Cy Young Award that was given in 1961.

The surprising Cincinnati Reds were the opponents in the 1961 Series, and Ford seemed to pick up where he left off from the previous October. In the first contest with New York hosting, Whitey spun a marvelous two-hitter, allowing just one hit in the first inning and one in the fifth. Solo home runs by Howard and "Moose" Skowron provided all the support Ford needed in the 2-0 whitewash.

Whitey's next trip to the mound came in Game Four at Crosley Field with the Yanks looking to take a three-to-one advantage. On this October 8, Ford was set to write his name in the record book. When he had reached the end of the third inning with the Reds still scoreless, he had now pitched 30 consecutive scoreless innings in World Series play to break a mark set by Babe Ruth 43 years prior in 1918. Ford added two more innings to his new record before coming out of the game with no outs in the sixth inning with an injured ankle. Reliever Jim Coates came in and preserved the shutout over the final four innings in the 7-0 New York win. With Roger Maris having just broken Ruth's home run record and Ford surpassing his Series scoreless innings mark, Whitey would note after that "Babe had a bad year."

The Yankees put Cincinnati away in Game Five by the score of 13-5 to return to their place atop the baseball world. Somewhat ironically, in light of the record Ford broke, he was given the 1961 Babe Ruth Award as the Outstanding World Series Performer.

The Cleveland Indians had a hold on the top spot in the A.L. in 1962 until the All-Star break when they fell hard and allowed New York to take over. Ford's 17-8 season helped them top the second-place Minnesota Twins by five games. His annual appearance among league leaders saw him rank second in winning percentage and third in ERA. On May 22 he missed a chance at a no-hitter when he had to leave with back spasms after holding the Angels hitless for seven innings.

The Yankees were to face an old rival, the Giants, in the 1962 Series, but this time in their new home in San Francisco. Despite the fact that Ralph Terry had led the Yanks staff with a 23-12 record that year, it was old pro Ford whom Houk went to for Game One. He got a two-run lead on three Yankee base hits right away in the first, but when he allowed a run in the second, it brought an end to his Series scoreless streak at 33⅔ innings. The Giants managed to put across one more run the next inning, but the Yanks added four more for a 6-2 win that would be Ford's 10th win in World Series play.

Up two to one heading into the fourth game in New York, Whitey was set to face young Juan Marichal. Ford's only real mistake was a two-run home run by Tom Haller in the second inning. Though he would induce Willie Mays, Felipe Alou, and Orlando Cepeda to ground out in the sixth without any Giant reaching base, Houk opted to bring in Jim Coates to start the seventh. Leaving with the score tied at two, Ford was not involved in the decision when San Francisco ultimately won 7-3.

Three days of rain allowed Houk to send Ford back out to the mound for Game Six against lefty Billy Pierce. Ford was going along fairly well until his errant pick-off throw in the fourth paved the way for three Giant runs. In the fifth, he allowed four singles and two more runs and Houk decided to go to the bullpen. In the end, Pierce hurled a three-hitter and Ford was tagged with the loss in the 5-2 game.

The next day, October 16, the seventh game went right down to the wire, but New York held on to their championship banner with a 1-0 win. It would be the last world title that Ford would enjoy.

Whitey came back in 1963 with what would be his last 20-win season, finishing with a spectacular 24-7 record. Again, as in 1956, had a Cy Young Award been given in both leagues, Ford almost surely would have been the A.L. recipient.

That fall, the Yankees were to face the other former New York team, the Dodgers, in their new west coast home. Ford had the misfortune of being matched up against the dominating Sandy Koufax in both of his starts. In the opener in New York, Ford ran into trouble in the second, giving up four runs, and he was pulled after six trailing 5-0. Koufax went the distance and won 5-2. Ford was much more effective in Game Four in L.A., allowing only two hits in seven innings. But Koufax again was sharp, and his 2-1 win caused the Yankees to be swept four straight for the first time in Ford's career.

With old friend Yogi Berra taking over as manager in 1964, the Yankees barely squeaked out the pennant by just one game over Chicago. Whitey was experiencing shoulder problems, but still managed a 17-6 record and the A.L.'s third-best ERA at 2.13. His eight shutouts were more than he had in any previous season.

Facing yet another different N.L. team in the Series for the fifth year in a row, the Yankees only had the St. Louis Cardinals in the way of another world crown. For the fourth straight year Ford was called on to start Game One of the Fall Classic. It turned out to be Whitey's final appearance in a Series, and it was a game better soon forgotten. In his 5⅓ innings of work, he allowed five earned runs and suffered the loss in the 9-5 game. His shoulder problems would not allow him to be used in the remaining games.

The teams went back and forth, and eventually found themselves matched up in Game Seven, where the Yankees had the tough task of facing Bob Gibson. Trailing Gibson and the Cardinals 7-3 going into the ninth, the Yankees rallied with two home runs, but fell short 7-5 to lose the Series. Weeks after, Ford had his aching shoulder surgically repaired.

As the spring of 1965 rolled around, his shoulder was sufficiently recovered to allow him to resume his spot in the rotation. He was able to work 244 innings and compiled a 16-13 record for what was a very disappointing Yankee team that finished way down in sixth place. The end of the 1965 season signaled the end of Ford's time as a regular in the Yankee rotation.

In 1966, nearing 38 years old, his arm problem returned as he was only able to pitch 73 innings over 22 games. His season ended early with a 2-5 record as he underwent another operation in August. He tried to come back in the spring of 1967, pitching in seven games and even firing one final shutout before calling it a career. Troubled by a bone spur in his left elbow and experiencing circulatory problems in the arm, he could no longer go on. The following season, 1968, Whitey served as the Yankees pitching coach, overseeing fine young pitchers such as Mel Stottlemyre and Stan Bahnsen.

Ford retired from the game with many noteworthy distinctions. His 236-106 career won-loss record gave him a .690 winning percentage, third on the all-time list. He remains the all-time leader in numerous World Series categories, including games pitched, innings pitched, wins, and strikeouts, and ranks third in shutouts. His 236 regular season wins are the most in a Yankee uniform.

Ford became eligible for the Hall of Fame in 1973, but fell 30 votes shy. This paved the way for Whitey to be elected the next year with his old pal Mickey Mantle, who was eligible for the first time in 1974. The two buddies who had been through so much together on and off the field were able to take their places in Cooperstown together on August 11 of that year.

On August 2, 1987, Ford was honored with a plaque in Monument Park that read:

EDWARD "WHITEY" FORD
"CHAIRMAN OF THE BOARD"
NEW YORK YANKEES 1950, 1953–67
LED YANKEES TO 11 PENNANTS
AND SIX WORLD CHAMPIONSHIPS
LEADS ALL YANKEE PITCHERS IN GAMES,
INNINGS, WINS, STRIKEOUTS, AND SHUTOUTS
CY YOUNG AWARD WINNER IN 1961
HOLDS MANY WORLD SERIES RECORDS
INCLUDING 33 1/3 CONSECUTIVE SCORELESS INNINGS
ERECTED BY THE NEW YORK YANKEES
AUGUST 2, 1987

LAWRENCE PETER BERRA
"YOGI"
NEW YORK, A.L. 1946-1963
NEW YORK, N.L. 1965
PLAYED ON MORE PENNANT-WINNERS (14) AND
WORLD CHAMPIONS (10) THAN ANY PLAYER IN
HISTORY. HAD 358 HOME RUNS AND LIFETIME
.285 BATTING AVERAGE. SET MANY RECORDS
FOR CATCHERS, INCLUDING 148 CONSECUTIVE
GAMES WITHOUT AN ERROR. VOTED A.L. MOST
VALUABLE PLAYER 1951-54-55. MANAGED
YANKEES TO PENNANT IN 1964.

Yogi Berra
(Elected 1972)

While it is easy to dwell on Yogi Berra's well-documented penchant for making humorous statements, it should never be forgotten that he was one of the greatest, most accomplished catchers to ever pull on a mask. Yogi's contributions to the post–World War II Yankee dynasty both behind the plate and at bat are worthy of a most special place in the team's history.

Berra single-handedly bridged the gap from the championship teams of the late 1940s to those of the early-to-mid 1960s.

Born in the Little Italy section of St. Louis in 1925 to Italian immigrant parents, he was a childhood friend of future major league catcher Joe Garagiola. When the Cardinals signed Garagiola in 1942, they were also interested in Berra, but would only give a $250 bonus. Shortly after, the Yankees offered a $500 bonus, to which young Lawrence Berra agreed.

Berra would not acquire the nickname "Yogi" for a few more years, when a teammate saw him sitting cross-legged and thought he resembled a Hindu spiritual leader. Though many have assumed that the name came from the cartoon character "Yogi Bear," the opposite is actually true.

Berra began in pro ball with Norfolk in the Piedmont League in 1943, but missed the next two years serving time in the military. He was involved in the D-Day battle in Normandy in June of 1944. Upon his return, he was moved up to Newark of the International League in 1946, where he played well enough to earn a call up to the Yankees near the end of the season. Because of his squat, 5-foot 8-inch, 195-pound frame and rather unathletic, odd appearance, some of his new teammates called him "Ape" and did unflattering imitations. Even Casey Stengel would say years later that Berra was a man who "looked funny in uniform." In time however, he would become a respected and beloved member of the Yankee family.

Wearing number 35 on his Yankee jersey, Berra appeared as a catcher in a big-league game for the first time on September 22, 1946. He hit a home run in his first game, and the next day as well. In his 22 at-bats in that first brief stint for the duration of the 1946 season, he hit safely eight times.

Berra went to training camp in 1947 competing with Ralph Houk for the job as backup catcher behind Aaron Robinson. Both would split time in the role but Berra also played many games in right field. Fifty-five years later, Houk would joke that he wished Yogi had been a better right fielder, as he went on to be Berra's backup catcher with very limited playing time over the next seven seasons.

Under new manager Bucky Harris in 1947, the Yankees pulled together to capture the A.L. pennant for the first time since 1943, leaving second-place Detroit 12 games behind. Yankee fans got their first good look at Berra's distinct batting habits as a notorious pull hitter who would swing at almost anything. He walked very little yet made good contact, striking out very little as well. In 293 at-bats in 1947 he batted .280 with 11 home runs and 54 RBIs, walking only 13 times but striking out a miniscule 12 times. On April 18 he had his first four-hit day, coming against Washington.

When the World Series began against the nearby rival Brooklyn Dodgers, Harris had enough confidence in the 22-year-old Berra to give him the start behind the plate in Game One and bat him third in the order. This would mark the first of a record-setting number of World Series games in which Yogi would appear. The Yankee Stadium crowd was phenomenal, setting a Series attendance record at 73,365, and while Berra went hitless in this particular game, New York came out on top 5-3.

Yogi was the starting catcher again in Game Two, and while he didn't record a hit, he was intentionally walked in the seventh and eventually scored on a single. The Yankees went up two games to none with a big 10-3 victory. Game Three moved over to Ebbets Field, and though Berra didn't start, Harris sent him in to pinch-hit for catcher Sherm Lollar in the seventh inning. Facing Brooklyn pitcher Ralph Branca with the bases empty, Yogi slugged the first pinch hit home run in the history of World Series play. He brought the Yankees to within one run with the score now 9-8, but that's the way the game would end. Berra was very nearly a big part of an historic happening in Game Four as he caught the entire game in which pitcher Bill Bevens gave up his first hit with two outs in the ninth, losing the no-hitter and the game in the process.

Berra came into Game Six as a replacement in right field early in the game and got two hits in three trips to the plate. His single in the fourth gave New

York a 5-4 lead, but Brooklyn prevailed 8-6 to force a seventh game. Berra started in right field in that final game for what would be his last appearance in over a decade in a World Series game anywhere other than at catcher. Harris had a pinch hitter bat for Yogi in the sixth inning, and he joyously emerged from the dugout with his teammates when a ninth inning double play made him officially a World Champion for the first of more times than he could possibly imagine.

Berra split time again between catcher and right field in 1948. He was selected as a sub on the A.L. All-Star team, though he didn't get into the game. He compiled a .305 batting average and 98 RBIs for the season, and narrowly missed another Series as Boston eliminated the Yankees on the next-to-last day of the season.

In Spring Training 1949, the Yankees had brought their former catching great Bill Dickey in to give one-on-one instruction to Berra. One aspect that Yogi needed extra work on was handling foul pop-ups. New manager Casey Stengel would tab him as his starting catcher, but a broken thumb early in the season limited him to only 109 games behind the plate. This year it was New York's turn to eliminate the Red Sox from the race, which they did on the final day of the season. They were matched up against Brooklyn as they had been in the Series two years prior, though they had an easier time of it in October of 1949. Berra caught four of the five games, missing the only game the Yanks lost. Gil Hodges struck out to end Game Five, and when the ball pounded into Berra's mitt, New York was embarking on an unprecedented streak of success.

The 1950 season would bring about Yogi's breakout season, as he emerged as clearly the best all-around catcher in the American League. Appearing in all but three of the Yankees' games, he hit .322 with a potent slugging percentage of .533, socked 28 home runs, scored 116, and drove in 124. In addition, he led all A.L. catchers in numerous defensive categories. A great comeback season for Joe DiMaggio and help from rookie lefty Whitey Ford put New York back in the Series against a new opponent, the Philadelphia Phillies.

Berra caught Vic Raschi's outstanding two-hit 1-0 shutout in the opener at Philadelphia. Although New York went on to a three-games-to-none lead, it failed to indicate the closeness of the games, with each contest decided by only one run. But on October 7 at the Stadium, the Yankee fans were hoping for the clincher and they were not disappointed. Berra guided the rookie Ford through 8⅔ innings of fine pitching, and added help with his bat also. Yogi stroked an RBI single in the first inning, and a solo home run in the sixth to contribute to the championship-winning game. Only 25 years old, Berra had been a World Champion three times.

Yogi was garnering increasing attention from the national baseball press as he was now regarded among the top catchers in all of baseball. Writers were also picking up on his interesting personality quirks, particularly his fondness for comic books. Rooming on the road with Yankee infielder Bobby Brown proved to be an interesting contrast. Brown attended medical school and had a career as a surgeon ahead of him. Often in their hotel room at night, Brown could be found studying medical journals, while Yogi was engrossed in his funny books.

Aside from being named to the A.L. All-Star team yet again in 1951, which was becoming a perennial occurrence, Berra earned his first major postseason award. Having led the Yankees in home runs, RBIs, and runs scored; having served as an outstanding handler of pitchers; and leading New York to its third straight pennant, Berra was voted the Most Valuable Player in the American League. He also experienced the thrill of catching two no-hitters thrown by Allie Reynolds in 1951, the first two of his career in which he was on the receiving end. Berra's extremely memorable season was capped off by a four-games-to-two win in the World Series over the nearby New York Giants.

Yogi continued to lead the team with his bat in 1952. He topped the club in home runs, RBIs, and runs scored again, and reached 30 home runs for the first time in his career. The Yanks out-distanced the favored Indians by two games. As they had in Berra's first two World Series, they would be squaring off against the Dodgers for the title once again. This edition would be a hard-fought battle that went the full seven games.

In Game Three with the Series tied at one, Berra singled, doubled, and hit a solo homer, but his passed ball in the ninth allowed two runs to score in the 5-3 loss. But in Game Six with New York facing elimination, Yogi hit a solo home run that helped make the difference in the 3-2 win. The Yankees then dashed Brooklyn's hopes by stealing Game Seven at Ebbets Field 4-2 for their fourth straight championship.

The next quest was to surpass the Joe McCarthy-led 1936 to 1939 Yankees and their four consecutive World Series titles. Yogi, aside from his usual stellar work behind the plate, also provided with his bat by leading the team in home runs and RBIs, as was becoming his habit. The Yankees again topped second place Cleveland to earn their fifth straight World Series invitation and a chance to make history. Fittingly, the opponents would once again be the mighty Brooklyn Dodgers.

New York got off to a strong start in Game One on September 30 at Yankee Stadium, winning 9-5 with Berra contributing a solo home run. The next day he hit a sacrifice fly to start the scoring, and with a 4-2 win, the Yankees headed to Ebbets Field with a 2-0 lead. Game Three turned out to be the only game

Brooklyn would win, and Berra had two hits in each of the final two New York wins. He batted a lofty .429 for the Series and the Yankees accomplished what no team had done before or since—five straight World Series Championships.

Yogi drove in what would be a career-high 125 runs in 1954, falling one shy of league leader Larry Doby of the Indians. But despite a terrific year from Berra plus a well-balanced all-around lineup, the Yanks 103 wins was second to Cleveland's 111. There would be no chance to defend the crown once again in October, and Yogi's only consolation was to enjoy personal rewards. Again the voting members of the Baseball Writers Association of America deemed him the MVP of his league.

The Yankees returned to the top of the league in 1955, knocking Cleveland back into second place. And while Mickey Mantle was beginning to show his home run power, leading the A.L. with 37, Berra still had more RBIs, 108 to 99. New York batters combined for a league-high 175 home runs, but were set to face a powerful Brooklyn team in the Series that slugged 201. This, as the Yankees would find out, was a Dodger team to be reckoned with.

The Yankees took the first two games at home with Yogi going a combined three for six with two runs. No team had ever come back from losing the first two, but this year would be different. Brooklyn won Games Three, Four, and Five at Ebbets Field. Back at the Stadium for Game Six, Berra drove in the first run with a single in the first inning of a game Whitey Ford would win 5-1, setting the stage for the winner-take-all seventh game.

Young Dodger pitcher Johnny Podres was cruising along and had a 2-0 lead going into the bottom of the sixth when he let the first two batters reach base. Berra came up, representing the go-ahead run, and dramatically hit a fly deep into the left field corner that looked certain to be trouble. Left fielder Sandy Amoros, who had just taken over at the position at the start of the inning, ran it down for a terrific catch, then doubled Gil McDougald off first. The Yanks were unable to get anything further going, and Brooklyn had finally beaten the Yankees to celebrate what would be their only World Championship. Berra would take little solace in the fact that he led all participants in hits with 10, or that he batted .417.

His fine World Series performance had followed up a very productive season, and yet again, for the third time in five seasons, Yogi was voted the Most Valuable Player in his league. He was quietly taking his place among the elite catchers in the history of the game.

As they had in 1955, the Yankees made a runner-up out of Cleveland again in 1956. And for the sixth time in 10 seasons, they would face the Brooklyn Dodgers in the Fall Classic, this time with payback on their minds.

Brooklyn had edged out the up-and-coming Milwaukee Braves by one mere game. Yogi had matched his career high in home runs with 30, and for the sixth and final time of his career he achieved the impressive feat of having more home runs than strikeouts. For the Yankees, only Mantle, having his triple crown year, topped Berra in home runs and RBIs.

Yogi had what was his most productive and likely most memorable World Series of all in which he participated. Amid all of the heavy hitters and offensive firepower, it was Berra who led all in hits, home runs, RBIs, batting average, and slugging percentage over the seven-game Series. He hit a grand slam off Don Newcombe in Game Two; he doubled in the winning run in Game Three; and he ripped two home runs and drove in four in Game Seven as the Yanks clinched the championship.

But the moment that will live forever is Yogi, catching strike three to end Don Larsen's famed perfect game in Game Five and jumping into Larsen's arms. Berra's catcher's mitt from that game, like he himself, would become a treasured part of the Hall of Fame.

Berra began to see a very slight reduction in playing time in 1957, also playing a handful of games back in the outfield. Though some of his offensive numbers were below his usual standard, he still managed 24 homers and 82 RBIs. New York finished eight games better than the second-place White Sox in the A.L., and Hank Aaron, Eddie Mathews, and the Milwaukee Braves were on tap in October. Hitting .320 for the Series, Berra hit a two-run home run to help win Game Six 3-2, and scored more runs (5) in the seven games than any other Yankee. But tough Braves right-hander Lew Burdette won three games for Milwaukee, including a complete-game shutout in the clincher.

Berra was nearing his mid-30s by 1958, but was still sure-handed behind the plate. In one 148-game span stretching from 1957 into 1958, he did not commit a single error. Once again, he was good for second on the team behind only Mantle with 22 homers and 90 RBIs. The Yankees easily earned their 10th trip to the World Series in the previous 12 seasons, getting another crack at the Milwaukee Braves.

Things looked very bleak after the Yankees lost Game Four to go down three games to one. Berra added an RBI double in Game Five, helping Bob Turley shut the Braves out 7-0. Yogi singled in a two-run tenth inning rally in Game Six that New York won barely by a 4-3 score, and it came down to the finale in Milwaukee on October 9.

Tied at two going into the eighth, Berra started off a rally with a double, and eventually scored the go-ahead run in a four-run inning. The score would stand at 6-2 as Berra was part of a Series-winning team for the eighth time.

New York had a very sub-par season in 1959, winning only 79 games and finishing in third place. Berra caught only 116 games, but still led A.L. catchers in putouts and also had the top fielding percentage. He was still capable of hitting home runs, and his 19 was again second to only Mantle on the team. The Yankees bounced back in 1960 to return to the Series, this time facing Pittsburgh. Berra caught only 63 games, increasingly giving way to Elston Howard, with John Blanchard also in the mix. He was seeing more time in the outfield, as he had early in his career. In the Series against the Pirates, Yogi saw action behind the plate, in left field, right field, and even as a pinch hitter. His bat was quiet early on, but came alive in Game Six and Seven. In the sixth game he had two RBI singles and scored three runs in the Yankees' 12-0 blowout.

In the fateful Game Seven, Berra started in left field for the second straight day. He hit a three-run home run in the sixth inning that gave New York a 5-4 lead, walking and scoring in the eighth to increase it to 6-4. The Pirates rallied with five in the bottom of the eighth to take a 9-7 lead. New York came back with two in the top of the ninth, with Berra's ground out scoring Gil McDougald to make it 9-9. One of the most shocking home runs in baseball history lay just ahead.

Berra was camped in left field and watched helplessly as the first batter in the bottom of the ninth, young Bill Mazeroski, hit the ball over his head and over the wall to end the Series in an instant. The Yankees had outscored Pittsburgh 55-27 over the seven games, but went home empty-handed.

New York rebounded from its devastating Series loss by having a phenomenal 109-win season under Berra's former backup Ralph Houk, who had taken over for Stengel. Playing primarily left field, Berra contributed to the home run display with 22, his highest total since he had hit that same number in 1958. The Yankees were heavily favored over the upstart Cincinnati Reds in the World Series.

Berra's biggest highlight was a two-run home run in Game Two, but they were the only runs New York scored in the 6-2 loss. This was Yogi's 12th and final World Series home run. Few were surprised when the Yankees captured the Series in five games, but as for the clincher, it would be the first one that Berra did not appear in since he joined the team.

In 1962 Yogi appeared in less than 100 games for the first time since 1947. His 86 games were split between catcher, the outfield, and appearances as a pinch hitter. With no A.L. teams capable of knocking the Yankees off their throne, they were heading back to the Fall Classic. The N.L., sending its fifth different team in five years, would be represented by the San Francisco Giants.

With Elston Howard now the regular starting catcher and Tom Tresh the left fielder, Berra saw very limited action. He started behind the plate in Game

Two, his last World Series action there, and pinch-hit in Game Four. In all, he was 0 for 2 with two walks in a series that the Yankees narrowly squeaked out in seven games.

Berra was suiting up as an active player in 1963 for the 18th season, more than anyone had in Yankee history, but it would be his last. He manned his old position behind the plate in 35 games, and was used as a pinch hitter 29 times. His final hit as a Yankee was a home run on September 21 of 1963 off Moe Drabowsky of Kansas City, and his last regular-season at-bat came one week later when he pinch-hit for pitcher Al Downing. Just a few days later, Berra was set to compete in his record 14th World Series, this time against the Los Angeles Dodgers.

His only appearance came in Game Three as he pinch-hit for Jim Bouton in the eighth inning and lined out. The Dodger pitching, with Sandy Koufax, Don Drysdale, and Johnny Podres was just too strong and New York could not manage a win. It was the first time in their history that they had been swept in the Series in four straight games.

For Berra, it had closed the book on his World Series playing ledger, leaving totals in a few categories that may never be equaled. Decades later, he was still ranked first all time in Series games played, at-bats, hits, and doubles, and was in the top five in numerous other categories including home runs and RBIs. Berra was long thought to be a clutch performer and that reputation was further enhanced by his many key hits in the glare of the October spotlight.

Shortly after the Yankees' Series loss to Los Angeles, they promoted manager Ralph Houk to the general manager position and named Yogi the team's new skipper for 1964. He would now be in the unusual position of being the boss to a group of men to whom he had just been a teammate for so long, including Mantle, Ford, and Howard.

Berra was easygoing as the Yank's manager, but exerted discipline when it was needed. He was able to pilot the team to the pennant, actually bringing them from behind in his first year, beating out Al Lopez's Chicago White Sox by one game. His first October challenge came against the St. Louis Cardinals, managed by Johnny Keane, who were making their first Series appearance since 1946. Going in, Berra had lost Tony Kubek to a wrist injury and ace Ford hurt his arm in Game One. It came down to Game Seven, but Bob Gibson was a bit better than Yankee pitchers, as the Cardinals came away with the trophy.

The next day, Berra was dismissed as manager, and replaced later by Keane, who resigned from the Cardinals. Yogi's 19 seasons in a Yankee uniform had come to an end, at least for the time being.

After spending a decade as coach, then manager of the Mets, Yogi returned to coach the Yankees from 1976 through 1983. Once again he was immediately

part of Bronx glory as the team made four trips to the World Series between 1976 and 1981. Then, 20 years after his first stint as Yankee manager, he was elevated to the position again in 1984. The team finished third in the A.L. East with an 87-75 record, and though he returned in 1985, he was replaced 16 games into the season in favor of old teammate Billy Martin.

Berra had become eligible for the Hall of Fame in 1971, and while he was the leading vote-getter that year, he surprisingly fell 28 votes shy. It is difficult to understand why he wasn't a first-time inductee. He was universally regarded as an outstanding defensive catcher and terrific handler of the pitching staff; among his 358 career home runs, 306 came as a catcher, which remained a record until late in Johnny Bench's career; and Yogi meant so much to so many Yankee championships.

The following year, the voters got it right as he got elected with 42 votes to spare.

In later years, Yogi Berra has remained one of baseball's truly beloved figures and great ambassadors.

VERNON LOUIS GOMEZ
"LEFTY"

NEW YORK A. L. 1930-1942
WASHINGTON A. L. 1943
WON 20 OR MORE GAMES FOUR TIMES IN
HELPING YANKEES TO WIN SEVEN
PENNANTS. LED A. L. WITH 26-5 RECORD,
2.33 EARNED RUN AVERAGE IN 1934 AND
WITH 21 VICTORIES AND 2.33 ERA IN
1937. PACED A. L. IN WINNING PCT. TWICE,
STRIKEOUTS THREE TIMES. SET WORLD
SERIES MARK BY WINNING 6 GAMES
WITHOUT A LOSS.

Lefty Gomez

(Elected 1972)

I t was a horseback riding mishap at 13 years old, badly injuring the youngster's right arm that helped to give the baseball world a character know as
"Lefty" Gomez. It was at this time that the Southern California teen, naturally right-handed, began to rely almost exclusively on his left arm, and history
would show the conversion to be a considerable success.

Frail-looking 20-year-old Vernon Gomez, who hailed from the Spanish
community of Rodeo, California, was pitching for the San Francisco Seals of
the Pacific Coast League in 1929. He was discovered by the Yankees at that
time, and purchased by them in mid-August for the reported sum of $30,000.
When Gomez arrived at the Yankees training camp in 1930, he was tipping the
scales at a mere 146 pounds on his 6-foot 2-inch frame. He did, however, have
a good fastball and effective curve, and management felt that if he added
weight they could have another Lefty Grove on their hands. New manager Bob
Shawkey was impressed enough to bring Gomez north with the team to start
the season. After six starts and nine relief appearances, a 2-5 record and a 5.35
ERA showed that the 20 year old might benefit from more experience at the
minor league level. Gomez was sent to St. Paul of the American Association
where he went 8-4 with a 4.08 ERA.

In an attempt to add a bit of bulk and build up his strength, Gomez
spent much of the winter of 1930–1931 at a health resort back home in
California. In January 1931, he wrote to friends he had made in New York
that he had gained 20 pounds and that he expected to stick with the big-
league squad in the upcoming year. When he reported to the Yankees' training camp, the improvement was noticeable. New manager Joe McCarthy
informed Lefty he had indeed made the team, but wanted him to gain 15 more
pounds. At that time, players were allowed $4 per day meal money on the

road, and Gomez told him it would take a lot more than $4 for him to gain weight. As a result, management waived the limit for Gomez, telling him he could eat as much as he wanted.

Lefty's additional weight seemed to help make a difference, and he really got the attention of the league with a terrific season. The southpaw with the distinct high leg kick led the Yankee staff with an outstanding 21-9 record, as well as a 2.63 ERA, while the rest of his staff combined had an ERA of over 4.00. For the third straight year, the Yankees watched the Philadelphia Athletics top the circuit, as New York could do no better than second place.

Gomez had quickly developed a reputation as a comic and a practical joker, as well as being the prototype flaky left hander. It was not uncharacteristic of him to simply stop what he was doing on the mound during a game to watch a plane fly overhead. There was an incident early in his career when slugger Jimmie Foxx stepped up to the plate, and Lefty continued to shake off the signs from catcher Bill Dickey. When a frustrated Dickey finally went out to the mound and asked him exactly what it was he wanted to throw to Foxx, Gomez responded, "I don't like the way he's looking at me. If it's all the same to you, I'll just hold on to the ball."

Full of nervous energy, he earned the nickname "El Goofy," which stuck with him for the duration of his career and beyond.

Both Gomez and the Yankees came back in 1932 with better won-loss records than in 1931. Lefty compiled a 24-7 mark, while the team turned the tables on Philadelphia by copping the A.L. flag by 13 games over the second-place Athletics. Among his A.L. pitching contemporaries, the 24-year-old Gomez ranked second in winning percentage, and third in both wins and strikeouts. He would be seeing his first World Series action also, against the Chicago Cubs.

The day after the Yankees roughed up the Cubs 12-6 in Game One at the Stadium, Gomez was given the start in front of 50,000-plus fans. The Cubs put across one unearned run in the first inning and another run in the third, but Lefty would give up no more. The usually powerful Yankee bats struck no extra base hits, but their singles proved timely enough and Gomez came away with a 5-2 win in his Series debut. New York rallied on to sweep, and Lefty had his first taste of championship champagne.

Off to another fine start in 1933, Gomez was given the opportunity to take part in a very historic baseball event. When the first All-Star Game was held at Comiskey Park on July 6, A.L. manager Connie Mack not only brought Gomez, he allowed him to start the game. Young Lefty then had the distinction of throwing the first pitch in All-Star Game history, and went on to give up only three hits and no runs in his three innings of work. But Gomez, a notoriously weak hitter, may have experienced his biggest thrill and distinction with his bat. In the bottom of the second inning, he shocked many by lining a single to center field, scoring Jimmie Dykes of the White Sox for the first run in the Mid-Summer Classic's history. Ruth later homered, and Gomez came away with the victory in the 4-3 game.

The Yankees played second fiddle to the Washington Senators in 1933, finishing seven games back. Though Gomez's 16-10 record doesn't sound overly impressive, he did lead all A.L. pitchers in strikeouts, while ranking second in shutouts and fourth in ERA. But if there was even the slightest doubt as to the quality of his performance in 1933, he made his greatness very apparent in 1934.

Gomez himself promised before the start of the season that he'd win 25 games, and even that turned out to be slightly conservative. He got off to a phenomenal start, and in late June *The Sporting News* speculated that Lefty's wife, actress June O'Dea, might be partially responsible. Apparently, she had been feeding him steak for breakfast on days that he pitched, which she claimed made him stronger, especially in the later innings. A review of his record would make it difficult to refute the claim. When all was said and done, he had achieved a 26-5 record, and won what is considered the pitcher's equivalent of the triple crown by leading the league in wins, ERA, and strikeouts. Added to this relatively rare achievement, he also finished first in shutouts, complete games, innings pitched, winning percentage, and fewest hits per nine innings. Gomez clearly would have won the Cy Young Award had such an honor existed. As it was, when fellow A.L. players were polled at the end of the season as to the best in the league at the various positions, Gomez was the runaway winner as best left-handed pitcher. Lefty even earned a little extra money on the side with his normally weak bat in 1934. It was said that when he got a hit it was cause for a Spanish festival back in his California hometown. With this in mind, Babe Ruth made a bet with him that if Gomez got more than 10 hits during the season he would pay him $500. If he got less than 10, Gomez would have to pay Ruth $50. Gomez, amazingly, got four on Opening Day, and ended up with 13 at season's end.

After the 1934 season, Gomez was selected to join an All-Star team of players who went on an extended tour of Japan to engage in exhibition games versus Japanese players.

He came back with a rather unspectacular 1935 season, compiling a 12-15 record. It would be the only sub-.500 full season of his entire major league career. A victim of mediocre support, he still managed the league's third-best total in strikeouts, and its fourth-lowest ERA. Lefty's winning percentage increased significantly in 1936 with a 13-7 mark, in what was the beginning of another special period in the Bronx. Yankee manager Joe McCarthy had young rookie Joe DiMaggio room with Gomez on the road to help relax the phenom. Joe D. played like he was very relaxed as he, Lefty, and their mates earned a World Series date with the New York Giants 15 years after the two teams had met in October the first time.

The Giants took the first game 6-1 at the Polo Grounds, and Gomez got the start in Game Two. The Yanks offense exploded, and Lefty pitched every bit as well as he needed to. Going the distance, he gave up only six hits and four runs as the Giants were embarrassed on their own turf by their neighbors from across the river.

The Giants didn't win another game until Game Five, and Lefty got the ball to start the sixth game in hopes of clinching the Series. He pitched well, but after getting into a bit of a jam with one out in the seventh inning, Lefty came out with a 5-4 lead. Johnny Murphy hung on to save the game for Gomez as the Yanks put many more runs on the board and clinched the championship with a 13-5 win. Lefty and company not only returned to the top of the baseball world, they were on the threshold of a very memorable period of Yankee dominance.

In 1937 Gomez returned to the level he had attained in 1934 when he was the A.L.'s top hurler. He once again captured the pitcher's triple crown, one of the very few to do so twice. In addition, he also occupied the top spot in strike-outs and shutouts while leading New York to the pennant by 13 games over Detroit. Again, as in 1934, he had what would have likely been a Cy Young Award-winning season. And once again, the Yankees would be pitted against the Giants in October for bragging rights.

Gomez was to face the Giants' Carl Hubbell in the opener, and what looked like a potential pitcher's duel turned out to be a blowout in favor of the Yankees. Hubbell was chased from the mound in the sixth inning, and Gomez went the distance, giving up only six hits in the 8-1 win. Hubbell came back to win Game Four, the Giants only win, but there was Lefty the next day, poised to wrap up the Series for the second year in a row.

Gomez yielded two Giant runs in the bottom of the third, but when the bell sounded after nine, Lefty was standing on the Polo Grounds mound with a 4-2 win and another World Championship. He had done his part with a 2-0 record and a microscopic 1.50 ERA.

Gomez and Red Ruffing once again formed a very effective one-two punch on the mound in 1938 as New York cruised to the pennant over sur-prising second-place Boston. The two pitchers tied for the league lead in shutouts with four, and Gomez was third in wins, ERA, and complete games.

Facing the Cubs in the Series, Ruffing dispatched them in the first game, and Gomez was opposed by former Cardinal great Dizzy Dean in Game Two on a cold October day at Wrigley Field. The game remained close until the Yankees broke it open late and chased Dean from the mound. With a save from Johnny Murphy, Gomez was credited with his sixth World Series victory without a defeat. His Yankees went on to take the next two Series games, out scoring Chicago in the four-game sweep by a combined score of 22-9.

New York continued its amazing run in 1939 by capturing their fourth straight pennant, this time by an impressive 17 games. It was an up and down year over all, as the team endured the death of owner Jacob Ruppert, as well as the loss of Lou Gehrig from the lineup due to his tragic condition. Gomez, experiencing a sore arm, started the fewest amount of games he had started since 1931 and compiled a comparatively modest 12-6 record. The Yankees would be facing a new World Series opponent in the upstart Cincinnati Reds, who came in as heavy underdogs.

Manager McCarthy gave Lefty a chance to start Game Three in Cincinnati with the Yanks up two games to none. The Reds got three hits and one run in the opening frame, and though Gomez struck out Harry Craft to end the inning, he was replaced by Bump Hadley to start the second. Lefty had made his final appearance in a World Series. New York went on to win the game and the Series with relative ease for the unprecedented fourth straight world title.

More serious arm woes in 1940 limited Gomez to just nine games. After the season, he decided to learn to throw a knuckleball in an attempt to take the strain off of his arm, and extend his career in the process. The pitch seemed to temporarily revive his performance as his 15-5 record topped the A.L. in winning percentage, and he also tossed his final two shutouts. The Yankees returned to the World Series in 1941 after a one-year absence, this time to face the nearby Brooklyn Dodgers. Though Gomez was on the Series roster, he saw no action in the five-game Yankee win.

Nearing the end of the line, Gomez pitched in only 13 games in 1942. One of the highlights of the season came on May 28 against the Senators. He gave up only four hits, and miraculously got four hits himself in the 16-1 win. He finished the season with a 6-4 record and again watched the World Series, this time as the Yankees lost to the Cardinals. Lefty then took off his familiar number 11 jersey for the final time. Three months later in January 1943, the Yankees sold Gomez to the Boston Braves. Though he attended Spring Training with Boston, he never appeared in an official game with the team. He was picked up by the Senators, for whom he pitched one game before he retired.

Gomez had left behind many achievements and distinctions in his 13 years in Yankee pinstripes: 189 victories and only 102 losses for a brilliant .649 career winning percentage; two seasons, 1934 and 1937, that were Cy Young Award-quality years; more strikeouts in the decade of the 1930s than any other major league pitcher (1,337); three All-Star Game wins, and the record for most innings pitched in one Mid-Summer Classic (6); and the most World Series victories (6) without a defeat, aided by his 2.86 Series ERA in 50⅓ innings pitched.

Thirty years after his final Yankee season, the Veterans Committee elected Gomez to the Hall of Fame. During his speech at the Hall on Induction Day on August 6, 1972, he said, "I want to thank the New York Yankees for giving me the chance and my teammates who scored so many runs and helped me. And Joe DiMaggio, who ran down all my mistakes."

Fifteen years after his induction into Cooperstown, the Yankees erected a plaque in Monument Park to Gomez on the same day that they similarly honored Whitey Ford. The plaque reads:

VERNON "LEFTY" GOMEZ
NEW YORK YANKEES 1930–42
KNOWN FOR HIS EXCELLENT WIT AS HE
WAS FAST WITH A QUIP AND A PITCH
SET WORLD SERIES RECORD WITH SIX
VICTORIES AND NO DEFEATS.
LEADING YANKEES TO SEVEN PENNANTS
AND SIX WORLD CHAMPIONSHIPS.
ERECTED BY NEW YORK YANKEES
AUGUST 2, 1987

The old left-hander passed away on February 17, 1989.

GEORGE MARTIN WEISS
MASTER BUILDER OF CHAMPIONSHIP TEAMS.
WAS CLUB EXECUTIVE IN MINORS AND
MAJORS FROM 1919 TO 1966.
DEVELOPED BEST MINOR LEAGUE CHAIN
IN GAME AS NEW YORK YANKEE FARM
MANAGER, 1932-1947 GENERAL MANAGER
OF THE YANKEES FROM 1947-1960 WHICH
WON 10 PENNANTS AND 7 WORLD SERIES
DURING THIS PERIOD.
PRESIDENT OF THE NEW YORK METS
1961-1966.

George Weiss

(Elected 1971)

When Yankees general manager George Weiss stepped down shortly after the 1960 World Series, he had amassed a resume virtually unmatched for efficiency among front office executives. His record would show 10 American League pennants, which led to seven World Series titles in his 13-season reign.

Much the same way Ed Barrow had done in the previous few decades, Weiss became the architect of the Yankees phenomenal success between 1948 and 1960. In the process, he managed to win the Major League Executive of the Year Award on four occasions. But Weiss's personality was such that he preferred to work behind the scenes, remaining in the shadows while the uniformed personnel received the bulk of the credit for the team's success.

Weiss's ascent to the most coveted front office position in baseball began at the grassroots level back in his hometown of New Haven, Connecticut, where at 18 years old he coached the local high school varsity team. Three years later he was managing the semipro New Haven Colonials, who on occasion would play exhibition games against major league teams. In 1919 at age 24 and having graduated from Yale University, he took a big step by purchasing the Eastern League's New Haven team.

It was there throughout the 1920s that he honed his skills as a savvy front office executive, acting virtually as a one-man staff. *The Sporting News* of April 12, 1928, stated that Weiss was basically the team's manager, coach, secretary, and salesman, referring to him as "champion salesman of the minors" for his ability to sell players to the majors for top prices.

Late in 1928, Jack Dunn, who ran the Baltimore Orioles of the International League and had first signed a young Babe Ruth back in 1914, passed away, and Weiss was asked to take over. He operated the franchise efficiently and effectively for three full seasons, and got the attention of Yankee owner Jacob Ruppert, who admired the manner in which Weiss conducted business. When Ruppert needed someone to run the organization's newly formed minor league system, they tabbed Weiss for the post. In a move that was the turning point of his baseball life, New York officially hired George on December 31, 1931.

One of Weiss's bigger contributions fairly early on was convincing Barrow to sign 20-year-old Joe DiMaggio despite a knee injury that made several teams shy away. After passing a physical exam that the Yankees had arranged, Joe was purchased for what turned out to be a phenomenal bargain at $25,000. Weiss could also claim a share of the credit for the team's remarkable eight-season period from 1936 through 1943, in which they only failed to reach the World Series once. His shrewd farm system maneuverings had provided the major league squad with several keys to their success, including George Selkirk, Tommy Henrich, Spud Chandler, Joe Gordon, Charlie Keller, Phil Rizzuto, and later, Yogi Berra, to name the more prominent.

When Yankees co-owner Larry MacPhail sold out to his partners Dan Topping and Del Webb late in 1947, they subsequently promoted Weiss to the general manager position. He would also carry the title of team vice-president. After 15 years of loyal service as the team's minor league guru, George now had front office control of the major league's most storied and powerful franchise.

One of Weiss's first major moves came after the 1948 season when manager Bucky Harris was let go and replaced by Casey Stengel. Many questioned the move, but in time, Weiss was vindicated as Stengel embarked on the unprecedented and unequaled string of five straight World Championships.

The productive Yankee system under Weiss continued to yield key components, including Whitey Ford, Mickey Mantle, Vic Raschi, Bobby Brown, Gil McDougald, Billy Martin, Hank Bauer, Bill Skowron, Bobby Richardson, Elston Howard, Tony Kubek, and more. Weiss was also adept at reaching outside the organization to augment the roster with shrewd acquisitions that included in part, Johnny Mize, Johnny Sain, Don Larsen, Enos Slaughter, and Roger Maris. When making trades, the highly detail-oriented Weiss seemed to possess a knack for asking for a throw-in with value that might serve as an effective backup down the line.

Weiss's Yankees experienced unparalleled success in the decade of the 1950s, failing to reach the World Series only twice, 1954 and 1959. In October 1960, they had reached the Series yet again and were the favorites to prevail over the Pittsburgh Pirates.

Though the teams were tied at three games apiece going into Game Seven, the Yankees had outscored Pittsburgh 46-17. In a game that contained a num-

ber of rather freaky and unusual occurrences, Bill Mazeroski broke the hearts of Yankee fans with his famous home run that gave the Pirates the victory and the Series. Days later, Yankee ownership decided to make a change and opted not to bring Stengel back. A couple of weeks later, Weiss decided that it was time to step down as well, leaving the organization he had been a part of for 28 years. The team that Weiss had built however, continued its winning ways, appearing in the next four World Series.

The 66-year-old Weiss had retired to his country estate in Greenwich, Connecticut, but the following year, both Weiss and Stengel were hired as part of the management team heading the newly created New York Metropolitans. Five years later, on November 14, 1966, Weiss retired from his position as Mets general manager. However, when the team shocked the baseball world with their World Championship of 1969, he was given a bit of credit for having assembled a good part of the squad.

When the Hall of Fame's Veterans Committee met on January 31, 1971, they cast the required amount of votes to enshrine George Weiss among the most distinguished and noteworthy figures in the history of the game. He would be joining a fellow Yankee executive, the great Ed Barrow, having done for the Yankees what Barrow had done for them a few decades prior. Unfortunately, when induction ceremonies were held in Cooperstown in the summer of 1971, Weiss was unable to attend, having suffered a stroke in May. Confined to a nursing home in Greenwich thereafter, he passed away on August 13, 1972. That day, a sellout Yankee Stadium crowd observed a moment of silence in his honor. Yankee president Mike Burke said at the time, "We have been striving to regain the level of excellence he set." The team then went out and swept a doubleheader from the Milwaukee Brewers. The week before, Yogi Berra had been inducted to the Hall of Fame, and in his speech he remembered to thank Weiss for bringing him to the majors. The day after his passing, Red Smith wrote of Weiss in his *New York Times* column:

> No other man, not even Babe Ruth or Ty Cobb, had a more profound and lasting influence on the game. No one ever built as George Weiss built, defying time to obliterate his work.

The Hall of Fame not only benefited by the mere inclusion of a front office guru like Weiss to the plaque gallery; many of the souvenirs he had accumulated over the decades are now part of their unequaled museum collection as well.

EARLE BRYAN COMBS
NEW YORK YANKEES 1924-1935

LEAD-OFF HITTER AND CENTER FIELDER OF
YANKEE CHAMPIONS OF 1926-27-28-32.
LIFETIME BATTING AVERAGE, 325, 200 OR
MORE HITS THREE SEASONS. LED LEAGUE
WITH 231 HITS IN 1927 WHILE BATTING .356.
PACED A.L. IN TRIPLES THREE TIMES AND
TWICE LED OUTFIELDERS IN PUTOUTS.
BATTED .350 IN FOUR WORLD SERIES

Earle Combs
(Elected 1970)

While the bulk of attention on the Yankees famed "Murderer's Row" team of the mid-to-late 1920s may naturally be focused on the likes of Babe Ruth and Lou Gehrig, outstanding center fielder and lead-off hitter Earle Combs was an integral part of their success. As Babe and Lou were busy driving in runs during those glory years, it was Combs, the consummate table-setter, whom they were most often driving in. Combs would become the first modern player to score over 100 runs in his first eight full seasons (minimum 450 at-bats per season).

Long before he achieved glory in baseball in the big city of New York, Earle roamed the mountains of Kentucky, where he was born in 1899. He went on to become a schoolteacher, but later began to distinguish himself on the ballfield with a semipro team in Lexington. Combs caught the eye of a scout for the Louisville team of the American Association, and was subsequently signed, making his debut with the team in the spring of 1922. He would be playing under manager Joe McCarthy, who was to play a part in the Yankee years down the line. Earle starred for the Colonels for two seasons, and compiled a .380 batting average while leading the American Association in hits with 241 in 1923.

With little left to prove at the minor league level, his contract was purchased by the new World Champion Yankees after the 1923 season for a figure reported to be between $30,000 and $50,000. In Earle's first training camp with New York in 1924, he performed well enough to displace incumbent center fielder Whitey Whitt from the starting lineup. He came to the major leagues with a reputation as a speedster on the base paths, but was instructed immediately by manager Miller Huggins to simply reach base, stay put, and wait to be driven in by the heavy hitters that would follow him. This goes a long way toward explaining Combs's rather modest career stolen base total of 96.

He got off to an impressive start in his inaugural season of 1924, stroking 14 hits in his first 35 at-bats for an even .400 average. Misfortune intervened however, as he suffered a fracture in his ankle, ending his season by early May. In hindsight, one can only wonder if Earle's presence all season might have helped the second-place Yankees win the four more games they would have needed to pass the eventual A.L. champion Senators.

Combs recovered fully and was poised to have his breakout season in 1925. He appeared in the outfield in 150 of the 154 games New York played that season, and with his unusual crouched batting stance he rapped 203 base hits for a .342 average, scoring an impressive 117 runs. The 26-year-old Kentuckian had arrived as a force in the major leagues. He would be described as a "superfast fielder and leadoff man supreme."

While many of his offensive numbers slipped a bit in 1926, Combs still managed to score 113 runs, and would be seeing his first World Series action. That year's Fall Classic got underway on October 2 at Yankee Stadium with New York hosting St. Louis. The Cardinals had put a run on the board in the opening frame, but Combs led off the bottom of the inning with a walk and later scored on a fielder's choice to make it a 1-1 game. Earle connected for his first World Series hit with a single in the sixth, and also made a nice running catch to end the eighth. Pitcher Herb Pennock had come through with a three-hit masterpiece to help make Combs's World Series debut a success as the Yankees prevailed 2-1. St. Louis ultimately captured the Series in seven games, but Combs fared very well with a 10 for 28 (.357) performance at the plate. It would be far from his last chance to experience the ultimate victory.

The 1927 season would turn out to be not only special for Earle Combs; it went down as likely the most legendary season in the history of the Yankee franchise. The team's 110 wins; Ruth's 60 home runs, and Gehrig's fabulous MVP season would slightly overshadow Combs's greatest year. While the sluggers were garnering the lion's share of the attention from the baseball public, it was Combs who led the league in hits with 231 and triples with 23, setting a Yankee record in that category that still stands. On September 22, 1927, he tied a major league record with three triples in one game, a mark later equaled by Joe DiMaggio. Earle's .356 batting average in 1927 would be his career high.

The Yankees dominated the overmatched Pittsburgh Pirates in that year's World Series with a four-game sweep. Combs got New York's first hit and scored its first run in Games Two, Three, and Four, and had the thrill of scoring the winning run in the clincher. The teams were tied at three runs apiece at the Stadium going into the bottom of the ninth. Combs led off the inning with a walk, and a couple of batters later he had advanced to third with the bases loaded. Pirate pitcher Johnny Miljus then threw a wild pitch and Combs scampered home to give the Yankees the 4-3 win and the Series sweep.

Combs followed up his brilliant 1927 season with another fine year in 1928, scoring 118 runs and leading the A.L. in triples with 21 as the Yankees again captured the flag. Unfortunately, after crashing into the outfield wall in Detroit and breaking a finger late in the season, Earle was limited to just one appearance as pinch hitter in another four-game Series sweep, this time over St. Louis.

As the 1929 season opened and the Yankees became the first team to feature numbers on the back of their uniform jerseys, Combs sported the number 1 to signify his leadoff spot in the batting order. Though several noteworthy Yankees have worn the number, including Billy Martin for whom it was retired in 1986, Combs was the original and would carry it with him for the rest of his playing career.

The "Kentucky Colonel," as he was called on occasion, still had a few achievements of note remaining as he entered his 30s. For the third time, he led the American League in triples in 1930 with 22, and the following season he put together a 29-game hitting streak. In 1932, having scored a career high 143 runs, Combs made his final World Series appearance as the Yankees returned to the Fall Classic for the first time in four years. In retrospect, he seems to have saved his finest Series performance for last in the event-filled four-game sweep of the Cubs. His totals for the Series include 6 for 16 for a .375 average, an impressive eight runs scored, and his only World Series home run. In the historic Game Three on October 1, 1932, at Wrigley Field, Combs was a witness to the legendary "called shot" home run by Babe Ruth in the fifth inning. He had also scored on Ruth's three-run homer in the first.

In the Series finale the next day, Earle had a particularly fine game, going three for four with four runs scored. He led off the ninth inning with a home run in what would be his final postseason at-bat as the Yankees won 13-6 and were once again World Champs. In all, in World Series play he had appeared in 16 games, had 21 hits (.350), and 17 runs.

In the middle of the 1934 season, Combs had another encounter with an outfield wall that produced near tragic results. On July 24 at Sportsman's Park in St. Louis, he fractured his skull and broke his collarbone chasing a long fly. It would be weeks before he could leave the hospital, and his teammates felt that his loss was a huge blow to their pennant hopes for 1934.

An incident that occurred a couple of days later while he was recovering in a St. Louis hospital gives a glimpse into the character of Earle Combs. Teammate Joe Sewell went to visit him, and though he could barely speak, Combs whispered to him, "Joe, that clubhouse boy at Sportsman's Park, I owe him 30 cents for a Coke. Pay him. Give him a buck and I'll make good with you." A frequent

reader of the Bible who neither drank nor smoked, Earle was thought to be the classiest of all the Yankees of the 1920s and 1930s. Bill Dickey once said, "The only one I could guarantee as a full-fledged gentleman was Earle Combs."

In the wake of Combs's absence from the Yankee lineup, renowned baseball writer Dan Daniel wrote in his *Sporting News* column in the August 2, 1934, issue:

> You cannot appreciate what the loss of Combs means to the Yankees, to their morale, their happiness, and their baseball abilities unless you have been with the club on its tours, and have been with it in its victories and in its defeats. Combs is almost in a class by himself. He has all the gameness in the world, and every fan knows how great an outfielder he has been.

Regarding his abundant defensive ability, some were of the opinion that playing next to Ruth in the outfield, he actually made Babe look even better than he was. When a young Joe DiMaggio was breaking in with New York, it was Combs who helped to train him as his replacement in the Yankee Stadium center field. DiMaggio, in turn, gave pointers to a young Mickey Mantle.

Not really fully recovering from the effects of his injuries, Combs acted as a player/coach in 1935, retiring as an active player after that season. He then served as a coach for the Yankees until 1944.

Though his playing career was somewhat abbreviated due to serious injuries, Combs built up an impressive resume that included a .325 career average, 154 triples, 1,186 runs scored, and having contributed greatly to three World Championship teams. When it came to receiving votes in Hall of Fame elections, Combs suffered the same fate as when he was playing, being overshadowed by heavier hitters. Finally in 1970, the Veterans Committee recognized the oversight and he had his day in the sun at the podium in Cooperstown that summer. Combs humbly told the crowd that he considered himself the luckiest player that ever lived. He reminded them that in his 20 years with the team as player and coach he had the good fortune to be part of 11 pennant and 9 World Series winners. He added that he also felt he was lucky to play with Babe Ruth and Lou Gehrig, two players he thought were the greatest.

As the years went on, Combs continued to maintain his 400-acre farm in Richmond, Kentucky, where his main crops were tobacco and corn. He died there on July 21, 1976, at the age of 77.

WAITE CHARLES HOYT
"SCHOOLBOY"

NEW YORK YANKEE PITCHER 1921-1930.
LIFETIME RECORD: 237 GAMES WON, 182
GAMES LOST, .566 AVERAGE, EARNED RUN
AVERAGE 3.59. PITCHED 3 GAMES IN 1921
WORLD SERIES AND GAVE NO EARNED RUNS.
ALSO PITCHED FOR BOSTON, DETROIT AND
PHILADELPHIA A.L. AND BROOKLYN,
NEW YORK AND PITTSBURGH N.L.

Waite Hoyt

(Elected 1969)

A week and a half before Christmas of 1920, Brooklyn native Waite Hoyt's father came in to wake him after reading the morning newspaper and exclaimed, "You've received a wonderful Christmas present! You've been traded to the Yankees!"

The 21-year-old Hoyt, who had seen limited pitching duty with the Red Sox over the past two seasons, would now be joining ex-teammate Babe Ruth and others in what could only be described as a positive career move. For the next decade, Hoyt would experience numerous highlights as one of the truly integral components of the Yankee pitching staff.

Born in 1899 in Brooklyn, Hoyt lived on Hawthorne St. and went to Erasmus Hall High School where he was discovered and signed by the New York Giants at age 15. Given the nickname "Schoolboy," the right-hander made one relief appearance with the Giants in 1918, and was shuffled off to the Red Sox the following season. He never really was given the opportunity to start on a regular basis with the Red Sox, and after two seasons he had a combined record of 10 wins and 12 losses.

Hoyt immediately paid dividends for the Yankees by becoming one of the stalwarts of the pitching staff, compiling a 19-13 record, and a 3.09 ERA that was fourth best in the A.L. More importantly, his efforts contributed to the Yankees first trip to the World Series to face Hoyt's original team, the Giants. It was during that Series that he showed his old manager John McGraw that he made a mistake in letting him slip away after the 1918 season.

It was slated to be a best-of-nine affair, and the Yankees captured the opener by shutting out the Giants 3-0 in the Polo Grounds, the ballpark the two teams shared. Yankees manager Miller Huggins sent Hoyt to the mound in Game Two, and the youngster, just one month past his 22nd birthday, completely dominated Giant hitters. Allowing only two hits, harmless singles in the third and ninth innings, Hoyt recorded an impressive 3-0 complete-game shutout. In decades to come, he regarded this as his finest performance on the mound.

Four days later Hoyt was given the ball to start Game Five with the Series now tied at two. While he wasn't quite as sharp as he was in Game Two, he managed to scatter 10 hits, only allowing one unearned run over nine innings. The Yankees, with better use of only six hits, outscored the Giants 3-1 to give Waite his second win and a three-games-to-two lead. Unfortunately, Babe Ruth would be lost from the starting lineup for the duration of the Series due to an infection on his arm, which left a significant hole in the Yanks offensive attack. The Giants came back with 8-5 and 3-1 victories, and Hoyt was given the assignment in Game Eight of keeping the Yankees alive.

Hoyt was exceptional, allowing just one unearned run in the first inning and only six hits over the entire nine innings. The Yankee offense could get nothing going, however, managing only four hits of their own and failing to put across even one run of support as the Giants closed out the Series with a 1-0 win. It was a heartbreaking loss for Hoyt, but he had shown the baseball world that the spotlight did not intimidate him and he just might be a force to be reckoned with for some time.

Hoyt followed up his fine breakthrough year with the Yankees with another fine performance on the mound in 1922. He again won 19, while losing only 12 for the circuit's fourth-best winning percentage, tossing three shutouts in the process. The Yankees narrowly edged the surprising St. Louis Browns by one mere game, and would again be facing McGraw's Giants in a rematch of the previous year's World Series. The Yankees started Bullet Joe Bush in the opener and carried a 2-0 lead into the bottom of the eighth. The Giants came up and got four straight singles off Bush to tie the score, and with runners on first and third with no outs, Huggins brought in Hoyt to stop the bleeding. The first batter he faced, Ross Youngs, flied out to center, and Frankie Frisch on third was able to make it home as the Giants now led 3-2. Hoyt then struck out George Kelly and Casey Stengel to end the inning, but the Yankees were unable to get anything going in the top of the ninth as the 3-2 margin stood.

A very unusual situation transpired in Game Two. With a 3-3 tie in the ninth inning, the umpires called the game on account of darkness and declared it a tie. The Giants retained their 1-0 advantage going into Game Three, which Hoyt was set to start. He hurled the first seven innings that game, and though the Giants scored three runs, only one was earned. Again the Yankees offense let him down, scoring no runs as they went down to a 3-0 defeat. Giants victories in the next two games allowed them to prevail over the Yankees in the Series for the second straight year. And though Hoyt compiled a microscopic 1.13 ERA for the 1922 Series, he had no wins to show for it.

Yankee Stadium opened in 1923 and Hoyt further established himself as a premier pitcher in the league. His 17-9 record gave him the second-highest winning percentage in the A.L., and he was also the league's runner-up in ERA and hits allowed per nine innings pitched. More importantly, the Yankees once again dominated the A.L. by a wide margin and earned the right to gain revenge on their rivals from across the Harlem River in the Fall Classic.

Getting the starting assignment in the Series opener at Yankee Stadium gave Hoyt the distinction of being the first pitcher to throw a World Series pitch in the ballpark that would go on to witness such a vast amount of Series history. He only ended up working 2⅓ innings and was not involved in the decision as the Giants came out on top 5-4. He saw no more action in the Series, but the Yankees went on to capture four of the remaining five games for their first title. Hoyt could now add "World Champion" to his growing list of baseball achievements.

The Yankees three-year run of postseason play took a two-year hiatus as the Washington Senators ruled the A.L. in 1924 and 1925. Hoyt went 18-13 in 1924 as New York finished in second place, three games back. He experienced his first taste of adversity as a Yankee in 1925, an aberration of a season in which the team finished seventh and not one regular starting pitcher had a record above .500. Being next to last in the league in runs scored as a team contributed to Hoyt's 11-14 record. Ironically, though New York collectively experienced offensive woes, Hoyt had the best season of his career as a hitter, going 24 for 79 at bat for a .304 average.

New York returned to the top of the A.L. roost in 1926, as Hoyt pitched in with 16 victories next to 12 defeats. Their opponents for the 1926 Series were Rogers Hornsby's St. Louis Cardinals, making their first ever postseason appearance. Hoyt got his first start in St. Louis in Game Four with the Cardinals holding a two-games-to-one advantage. He lasted the distance, and though St. Louis scored five runs, only two were earned. Luckily, the Yankee attack was bolstered by three Babe Ruth home runs and 13 hits in the 10-5 New York win.

It all came down to Game Seven, with Hoyt taking the hill in New York with the teams now tied at three games. He was cruising along fine until two errors in the fourth inning allowed the Cards to score three unearned runs. That would be the extent of their scoring, and going into the seventh inning down 3-2, Huggins put lefty Herb Pennock in to pitch. Unfortunately, the damage was done as the game and Series ended in the Cardinals favor. Hoyt had pitched 15 innings in this Series and had struck out 10, walked only one, and had an ERA of 1.20, yet there would be no championship this year. But the best of times lay just ahead.

While Hoyt could likely call 1927 the pinnacle of his pitching career, he would modestly declare that year that "The secret to success as a pitcher is getting a job with the Yankees." Backed by the so-called "Murderer's Row" offense, the team was about to embark on a two-year span that was nothing short of legendary. Hoyt reigned as the ace of the Yankees staff in 1927, leading the league with 22 wins and a .759 winning percentage, placing second in ERA (2.63), and third in fewest walks per nine innings pitched. But while some credited the team he was playing for as the main reason for his success, it was also pointed out that the Yankee bats did not help him throw multiple low-hit games, including three shutouts.

Come late September when the Yankees were set to face Pittsburgh in the upcoming World Series, Hoyt confidently predicted to radio listeners that a title for New York was a sure thing. He then had the chance to get the Yankees off on the right foot as the starter in Game One in Pittsburgh. New York had a 4-1 lead by the top of the third inning, and it was a lead they would not relinquish. They were ahead 5-3 in the top of the eighth inning when Huggins removed Hoyt with one out in favor of Wilcy Moore, who was able to preserve the 5-4 win. That would be Hoyt's only appearance as the Yankees sailed to a 4-0 sweep.

Hoyt embraced the charmed life of being young, living in New York, being a Yankee, and being a champion. He reveled in the night life, and was a member of the so-called "Playboy Trio," along with Ruth and third baseman "Jumpin'" Joe Dugan. But Waite was also considered very intelligent, articulate, and well-rounded. He dabbled in singing on stage, painting, and writing, and even took the New York State undertakers exam in hopes of someday running a funeral home.

Another very effective season lay ahead for Hoyt in 1928 as he complied a 23-7 record, missing a tie for the league lead in wins by one. Aside from his 31 starts he was also helpful to the staff coming out of the bullpen, and his eight saves topped the league. His performance was such that when *The Sporting News* named its All-Star team for 1928, Hoyt was the only right-handed pitcher to be selected. He also received a bonus of $2,500 from general manager Ed Barrow for winning 23 games. New York would be returning to the Series yet again, this time a rematch of the 1926 edition, with drastically different results.

Like the previous year, Hoyt had the ball to open the Series, which began October 4 in New York. He started out sharp and didn't allow a hit until one out in the fifth inning. His only real mistake came with one out in the seventh as Jim Bottomley hit a solo home run, but New York still had a 3-1 lead. In all, Hoyt only gave up three hits in the 4-1 Yankee win. None of the games were terribly close as Hoyt had the assignment of putting the Cardinals away for good in Game Four at St. Louis.

In what was to be Hoyt's final World Series game with the Yankees, he gave up only two earned runs while going the distance, and Ruth's three home runs along with one by Gehrig helped finish off the Cardinals 7-3. Hoyt was now a World Champion for the third time, and his Series performances in pinstripes showed a remarkable ERA of 1.62 in 77⅔ innings pitched with six wins and three losses. As good as Hoyt had pitched in the regular season, he elevated his game in the postseason.

A 10-9 record for Hoyt in 1929 was rather disappointing, as was the Yankees distant third-place finish. As the decade of the 1920s came to a close, Hoyt had been the one constant on the pitching staff, the only one left who had been there virtually the entire decade. His 157 victories in the 1920s was far more than any other Yankee pitcher.

Early in the 1930 season, Ed Barrow made the decision to ship Hoyt, along with infielder Mark Koenig, off to the Tigers in return for three players. Hoyt would bounce around to several teams as the years went on, concluding his career with Brooklyn in 1938. By that time, he had built up a 237-182 won-loss record. Hoyt stayed in the game by going to work as a broadcaster for the Cincinnati Reds, a position he remained at for 25 years.

When the Hall of Fame's Veterans Committee gathered for their annual meeting in February 1969, they voted to enshrine Hoyt, largely for his standing as one of the Yankee greats of the 1920s.

Hoyt passed away on August 25, 1984, and coincidentally was buried at Spring Grove Cemetery in Cincinnati just a few yards away from his former Yankee manager Miller Huggins.

STANLEY ANTHONY COVELESKI

PHILADELPHIA A.L.   1912
CLEVELAND A.L. 1916-1924
WASHINGTON A.L. 1925-1927
NEW YORK A.L.   1928
STAR PITCHER WITH A RECORD OF 214 WINS,
141 LOSSES, AVERAGE .603, E.R.A. 2.88.
WON 20 OR MORE GAMES IN 5 SEASONS. WON
13 STRAIGHT GAMES IN 1925. PITCHED AND
WON 3 GAMES FOR CLEVELAND IN 1920
WORLD SERIES WITH E.R.A. 0.67.

Stan Coveleski

(Elected 1969)

A fter dominating the league in 1927, the Yankees, not ones to rest on their laurels, did what champions always do, they made changes to get better. One change was adding a shoo-in future Hall of Famer, five-time 20-game winning pitcher Stan Coveleski.

Born Stanislaus Kowaleski, he started pitching as a child with a few stones and a tin can. As he recalled some 80 years later, "The plate's a lot bigger than a tin can to throw at. When it came to throwing a baseball, it was easy to pitch." Easy as it was, Coveleski didn't become a star until he mastered the spitball after seeing it used in the Pacific Coast League in 1915. Although the spitball was outlawed at the end of the 1920 season, "Covey" and 16 others were grandfathered as legal until they retired.

Coveleski debuted in the majors on September 10, 1912, with Philadelphia, coincidentally, five years to the day after his older brother Harry debuted with Philadelphia of the National League. Harry went on to have three 20-win seasons for Detroit.

Although by 1928 the 38-year-old Stan's better days were behind him, his resume was impressive. Twice he had led teams to the World Series (winning with Cleveland in 1920 and losing with Washington in 1925). At the time of his retirement Coveleski held six World Series records for one seven-game series, including starts, innings pitched, complete games, wins, and shutouts. He also had the second-lowest ERA between 1920 and 1941 with a 2.89 mark. Prior to coming to the Yankees, he had 210 wins and 141 losses. After winning 19 games during his sophomore season of 1917, he went on to four consecutive 20-win seasons as he won 22, 24, 24, and 23 games, respectively. He also won 20 games in 1925.

In 1920 with the Indians, Coveleski was no less than spectacular as he started, finished, and won three Series games as Cleveland clinched the championship five games to two. After winning Game One 3-1 behind Coveleski, Cleveland lost the next two to the Brooklyn Robins. Trailing two games to one, he again carried his team to victory as the Indians won 5-1. The Series was closed out in Game Seven as Coveleski threw his third complete game and first shutout for a 3-0 win. His ERA for the Series was a paltry .067 as he allowed only two earned runs in 27 innings.

Coveleski was also present on two noteworthy dates. On August 16, 1920, he watched as teammate Ray Chapman was knocked unconscious by a pitch from Carl Mays. Chapman died the next day, becoming the first and only player to die from an on-field incident. On October 10, 1920, during Game Five of the World Series, Covey witnessed the first and only unassisted triple play in Series history when teammate Bill Wambsganss turned the trick. The same game also produced the first grand slam in the history of the Fall Classic when in the first inning Cleveland teammate Elmer Smith went deep.

While the 1925 Series may not have been a memorable one, the 1925 season was. Coveleski had 13 consecutive wins en route to a 20-5 season, and led the league in winning percentage (.800) and ERA (2.84). According to *Total Baseball,* if there had been a Cy Young Award in 1925, Stanley Coveleski would have won it.

A report dated June 20, 1927, stated that the Senators very recently released Coveleski, as he could not get into shape due to various injuries. Coming off his abbreviated and injury-plagued 1927 season with Washington in which he went 2-1 and was released on May 8th, Coveleski was invited by the Yankees to try out for the team in spring training. Six other teams passed on Coveleski before New York gave him a chance.

A couple of *Sporting News* columns in early 1928 reported on Stan's progress. In "Training Camp Notes" on March 22 it was reported that Coveleski was making a good showing. Columnist Joe Vila reported on April 5 that ". . . the veteran spitball expert deserves success. No player has ever toiled so faithfully in an effort to come back after a year's absence from the game. When Huggins agreed to give Coveleski a trial last season the latter discovered that he needed a long rest and asked to be released. He didn't try to obtain money under false pretenses."

Coveleski developed boils at the beginning of the 1928 season, which delayed his Yankee debut. With 60,000 in attendance the veteran spitballer won his first start with the Yankees on May 6 when he beat Chicago 4-2 at Yankee

Stadium. He pitched 6⅓ innings and allowed seven hits as Gehrig and Joe Dugan hit home runs to lead the way.

On May 12, in an 8-7 New York win highlighted by home runs by Ruth and Gehrig, he received a no-decision. Ruth and Gehrig continued their one-two punch on May 17 as they both homered in Stan's 4-3 six-hit, complete-game victory over the Browns. In a Joe Vila column dated May 21, he noted that "Stanley Coveleski appears to have achieved a real comeback."

For his third consecutive start, Ruth and Gehrig hit home runs in support of Coveleski on May 22 as he threw a complete game en route to a 14-4 pounding of Boston. Four days later he beat the A's, this time on the strength of a Tony Lazzeri home run.

In a game on June 10, although he had the support of two Ruth home runs, Coveleski received a no-decision as the Yankees fell to Chicago 8-6. Stan would record his last victory with the team when he beat Boston on June 30.

After leaving the team to attend to his sick mother in early July, Coveleski was back on the mound against the Red Sox on July 23 as he pitched two innings of relief in an 8-3 loss. Babe Ruth hit his 40th home run of the season in the game.

Coveleski made his final appearance with the team on August 3 and received a no-decision in 1⅔ innings of relief.

In a *Sporting News* column dated August 28, 1928, it was reported that Covey was given his release. He would finish his major league career with the Yankees as he went 5-1 in eight starts, including a win over the A's on May 27. Coveleski helped the Yankees hold off the Athletics as they captured the 1928 pennant, their third straight and sixth of the decade.

In 1969 Stanley Coveleski was inducted to the Baseball Hall of Fame along with his 1928 teammate Waite Hoyt. Forty-one years earlier, Coveleski traveled with Hoyt from Hot Springs, Arkansas, to his first and only spring training with the Yankees.

That same week in 1969, baseball celebrated it's centennial while Neil Armstrong was taking "one small step for man and one giant leap for mankind."

Stan Coveleski settled and died in South Bend, Indiana. But not before he encouraged the kids of the community to develop their talent and keep baseball alive. As a tribute to a great athlete, the South Bend Silver Hawks would be playing in Stanley Coveleski Regional Stadium at the turn of the twenty-first century.

CHARLES HERBERT RUFFING
"RED"

BOSTON, A.L. 1924-1930
NEW YORK, A.L. 1930-1946
CHICAGO, A.L., 1947

WINNER OF 273 GAMES.
WON 20 OR MORE GAMES IN EACH OF FOUR
CONSECUTIVE SEASONS. LED IN COMPLETE
GAMES 1928. TIED IN SHUTOUTS 1938-1939.
WON 7 OUT OF 9 WORLD SERIES DECISIONS.
SELECTED FOR ALL STAR TEAMS
1937-1938-1939

Red Ruffing
(Elected 1967)

Few players in baseball history have experienced a reversal of fortune quite as dramatic as 26-year-old Red Ruffing did after being traded from the lowly Red Sox to the power-laden Yankees.

During the seven years he played for the Red Sox, they finished in last place every year except one—his first, in 1924. That year they escaped the cellar by one game. Ruffing compiled a 39-96 record over that span. The Red Sox were a pitiful franchise after team owners sold off most of their stars throughout the 1920s.

Playing on such a woeful team may have unnerved some people. Not Red, as he was just happy to be playing at all. Ruffing quit school at the age of 15 and like many Midwestern kids he began a life in the coal mines of Nokomis, Illinois. Ruffing worked with his father in the mines and was managed by him on the company baseball team. He played first base and outfield until an accident sidelined his playing for a year. After being nearly decapitated and getting his foot caught between two mining cars, he lost four toes on his left foot. When he returned to playing he took up pitching for his father's team. The soft-spoken Ruffing was quoted as saying, "The foot bothered me the rest of my career and I had to land on the side of my foot in my follow-through."

It would have been all but impossible to have won many games on those Boston teams and the team even considered converting Ruffing to an outfielder, a la Babe Ruth. The great Yankee manager Miller Huggins may have changed the course of history in a conversation with Red one day. Huggins said to Ruffing, "You will never be more than a fair outfielder, and you could be a great pitcher . . . I'm going after you."

Huggins died on September 25, 1929, before he could bring Ruffing to New York. Fortunately for Red the Yankee brass must have shared Huggins's high opinion of him and on May 6, 1930, they acquired him in a trade with Boston. New York sent Cedric Durst and $50,000 to the Red Sox in exchange for Ruffing.

The turnaround was immediate for Ruffing as he posted a 15-5 record the rest of the season. Always known as a great hitting pitcher, he also hit .364 with 17 runs scored, eight doubles, two triples, four home runs, and 22 RBIs. On September 18 he hit two home runs in a game. Ruffing would repeat this feat again six years later. Although the Yankees failed to capture the pennant, Ruffing had just laid the groundwork to what would eventually become a Hall of Fame career.

Throughout his career Ruffing was one of the best hitting pitchers of all time. Finishing with a career .269 batting average, he hit over .300 eight times, with a high of .364 in 1930. This average ranks as the second best ever for a pitcher, trailing only Walter Johnson's .433 in 1925. His 36 home runs ranks him third all time and his 520 hits ranks him second. So good was Red's hitting ability that he pinch-hit 258 times during his career.

As the Yankees crept closer to the top in 1931 Ruffing won a then-career-high 16 games. While the Yankees would once again fail to capture the crown, the year was not without its noteworthy incidents. On April 26 the injury-plagued Yankees found themselves in a jam when right fielder Dusty Cooke, who had replaced the injured Babe Ruth, was also hurt. The shorthanded Yankees sent Ruffing to the outfield. This would be the third and final time Red played the outfield in his major league career. On June 4 Ruffing halted the eighth longest consecutive at-bat hitting streak in American League history. He stopped Oscar Melillo of the Browns after he hit safely in eight consecutive plate appearances. Ruffing pitched on August 2 and won Game One of a doubleheader against the Red Sox 4-1. In Game Two he is witness as his team loses 1-0. The Yankees would not be shut out again for the next 308 games.

The 1932 season brought continued improvement from Ruffing. He finished the year at 18-7 with a team best 3.09 ERA as he led the Yankees to the pennant and the World Series. He littered the league-leader board while finishing first in strikeouts with 190 and most strikeouts per nine innings with 6.60. Red also finished second in ERA and fewest hits per nine innings, and third in winning percentage and complete games.

On May 16, 1932, the Yankees matched a feat accomplished by only two other teams, Cleveland in 1903 and Boston in 1909, throwing four straight shutouts. Ruffing, along with Johnny Allen, George Pipgras, and Lefty Gomez turned the trick.

Ruffing struck out 10 and hit a home run in a game on August 13 to beat the Senators 1-0. It was the first extra-inning, game-winning home run by a pitcher since 1906 when Tom Hughes accomplished the feat. Ruffing later said this was one of his greatest achievements in baseball.

In Game One of the Fall Classic Red struck out 10 and threw a complete-game 12-6 victory. He never got another start, as New York swept the Chicago Cubs in four straight. This was his first win en route to a 7-2 World Series career record.

Ruffing struggled to a 9-14 record in 1933 as the Yankees lagged eight games behind Washington. It was Red's only losing season of the 1930s. He finished third in the league in strikeouts (122) and most strikeouts per nine innings (4.67) while finishing fourth in complete games with 18. His ERA was a respectable 3.91 and his three saves were the highest single-season total of his career. In a game against Boston Ruffing shined against his former club as he hit a grand slam.

Red rebounded in 1934 as he posted a 19-11 record and finished first in the league with 5.23 strikeouts per nine innings. Ruffing also finished third in the league in strikeouts and shutouts, and fifth in the league in wins. In a game on April 30 he helped his own cause by hitting a home run in the ninth to defeat Washington and propel the Yankees into first place. In a season that marked the end of the Babe Ruth era in New York the Yankees would finish the season at 94-60, seven games behind the Tigers.

At the second annual All-Star Game on July 10, 1934, Ruffing pitched as the American League captured a 9-7 win. During this game Carl Hubbell amazed all who were witness as he struck out five future Hall of Famers in a row. The victims were Babe Ruth, Lou Gehrig, Jimmie Foxx, Al Simmons, and Joe Cronin.

Although Ruffing put up a 16-11 record with an impressive 3.12 ERA, the Yankees could do no better than second place in 1935. Red led the team in wins and helped his team lead the league in ERA at 3.60. None of this mattered as, with the exception of Lou Gehrig, most of the Yankees lineup lacked its usual punch.

In 1936 Ruffing began a string of four consecutive seasons of at least 20 wins. This was a far cry from Boston when he struggled to win just 10. He would finish the season 20-12 as the Yankees won the pennant by 19½ games. He led the team in wins—pretty good for a guy who was unsigned as late as March 25. On March 26 Ruffing signed a contract to play the season for $12,000. He finished third in the league in complete games and fourth in wins.

On June 7 the Yankees beat the Indians 5-4 in 16 innings. Ruffing had three hits including a home run to lead the Yankees. On June 17 Red hit two home runs in a game for the second time in his career.

Red led the Yankees into their first ever World Series without Babe Ruth. In the Series Ruffing finished with an 0-1 mark as the Yankees rode two wins by Lefty Gomez to a four-games-to-two victory over their crosstown rivals the Giants. It was their first ever World Series Championship in the post–Babe Ruth era.

Ruffing won 20 games for the second straight year in 1937 as he went 20-7. The Yankees rolled through the league again to capture the crown by 13 games. He finished second in the league in wins as teammate Lefty Gomez bested him by one. Red also finished third in the league in winning percentage, complete games, and fewest walks per nine innings. For all his hard work Ruffing finished eighth in the MVP voting.

Red usually started the opening game of the season and when the Yankees made it to the World Series he usually started that too. This year was the only time in his seven different World Series that Ruffing didn't start Game One. After teammate Lefty Gomez won Game One, Red followed up with a complete-game 8-1 victory in Game Two. In that game Red beat the Giants from the mound and from the plate. While striking out eight, offensively he contributed two hits and three RBIs to aid the cause. The Yankees rolled in five games to win their second consecutive World Series Championship and seventh overall.

Ruffing won at least 20 games in 1938 for the third consecutive year as he posted a 21-7 record. The Yankees won the pennant by 9½ games over Boston. Red finished first in the league in wins, winning percentage, and shutouts. He also finished second in ERA and complete games while finishing fourth in innings pitched and fifth in strikeouts. He finished fourth in the MVP voting and if the Cy Young Award had existed *Total Baseball* speculated Ruffing would have won it. Red was also selected to his first All-Star team.

In a game on May 30 the largest crowd in Yankee Stadium history (83,533) witnessed Ruffing end Lefty Grove's eight-game winning streak in a 10-0 romp of the Red Sox. Six thousand fans were turned away and 511 were given refunds because there was no place to sit.

In the Series the Yankees beat the Chicago Cubs four straight to become the first team in Major League history to win three consecutive World Series Championships. Red opened the Series with a 3-1 victory and closed it out four days later with an 8-3 win. Ruffing became one of the very few pitchers to win two decisions in a four-game Series sweep. In Game Four Lou Gehrig had his final World Series hit, a single in the eighth inning.

In 1939 Red became one of the few players to win 20 games and bat over .300 as he was selected to his second consecutive All-Star team. He compiled an identical 21-7 mark of a year earlier and finished fifth in the MVP voting. Although things seemed the same as they had a year earlier, many things would be quite different in 1939. In January longtime team owner Jake Ruppert had died of phlebitis and on May 2 the "Iron Horse" Lou Gehrig removed himself from the lineup after 2,130 consecutive games. Even without Gehrig the Yankees ran away with the pennant by 17 games over Boston and rookie sensation Ted Williams.

In a 21-0 win over the Athletics on August 13 the Yankees tied the record for the most lopsided victory in major league history. Ruffing collected four hits to go along with the victory as DiMaggio and Babe Dahlgren homered twice each.

Playing against the Cincinnati Reds in the World Series the Yankees were heavy favorites. In Game One Ruffing won a duel against Reds pitcher Paul Derringer. The tense, low-scoring game remained tied 1-1 until the last of the ninth when Bill Dickey knocked in the winning run. New York went on to sweep and won their unprecedented fourth consecutive World Championship in a row.

Ruffing finished 15-12 in 1940 as the Yankees finished in third place—two games behind the Tigers. Red led the team in wins while posting a 3.38 ERA and was picked for his third All-Star team.

While winning 15 games in the summer of 1941, Ruffing had a front row seat to one of the greatest feats in sports history. When he wasn't pitching, Red sat back and witnessed Joe DiMaggio's remarkable 56-game hitting streak. Ruffing also witnessed some of Ted Williams's ultimately successful quest to hit .400. Years later in his book *My Turn at Bat* with John Underwood, Williams recalled the following story about Red. In a game with the Yankees, Ruffing and Lefty Gomez would ring cowbells every time Ted came to the plate. Even though the umpire warned them to stop they kept doing it and were eventually thrown out of the game.

Red led the team in wins and finished third in the American League with a .714 winning percentage. Offensively he batted .303 with two home runs and 22 RBIs. Ruffing was selected to his fourth consecutive All-Star team and the Yankees were on top again as they finished 17 games ahead of Boston.

Ruffing would once again open a Subway Series, this time against the Dodgers. In Game One he beat Brooklyn 3-2 in his only Series appearance and propelled the Yankees to their ninth World Championship. It was Red's third World Series Game One start in the last four years.

Although Red's record slipped to 14-7 in 1942 it mattered little as the Yankees won the pennant by 10 games. Even though three teammates won more games in the regular season, it was the experienced five-time All-Star Ruffing who was given the ball to open up the Fall Classic against the Cardinals. Appearing in his last World Series, Red gave the fans something top remember in Game One. For 7⅔ innings Red toiled at his craft without allowing a single hit. In the eighth however it was Cardinal center fielder Terry Moore who stopped the bid, but the Yankees went on to win the game 7-4. After dropping Games Two, Three, and Four, the desperate Yankees sent Red to the mound in Game Five. Ruffing took the game into the ninth tied at two but the tired 39 year old couldn't hold on as he gave up a two-run home run to Whitey Kurowski. Slim as it was, the Yankees still had hope as they batted in the bottom of the ninth. With one on and two out and Ruffing due to come up, manager Joe McCarthy made an interesting move. McCarthy chose to pinch-hit for Ruffing and sent up seldom-used outfielder George Selkirk. On the season Selkirk had batted .192 with 15 hits in 78 at-bats. Selkirk promptly grounded out to second to end the game and the Series. Ironically, that season Ruffing's offensive production was better than Selkirk's as he batted .250 with 20 hits in 80 at-bats. Incidentally, it was Ruffing who was called upon to pinch-hit for Ernie Bonham in Game Two as the Yankees trailed 4-3 in the top of the ninth.

On January 4, 1943, Red Ruffing was drafted into the Army just four months shy of his 39th birthday. Red missed the entire 1943 and 1944 seasons before returning on July 11, 1945. He finished the season with a 7-3 record as the Yankees finish 6.5 games back. After starting the 1946 season 5-1 with a 1.77 ERA Ruffing suffered a broken kneecap that ended his season. The Yankees released the 42-year-old pitcher that September and he finished out his career with the White Sox in 1947. In 1962 Ruffing became the first ever pitching coach of the expansion New York Mets.

Upon his retirement Red Ruffing held World Series records for most strikeouts, games, and wins. To this day he still ranks second all time in Series wins, third in innings pitched and complete games, and fourth in strikeouts. He also held the record for the most consecutive games started with 241 until Bob Gibson broke it in 1973.

After starting his career with a 39-96 record, Ruffing put up a 231-124 record with the Yankees and finished at 273-225 in 536 starts. He was 7-2 with a 2.63 ERA in the World Series and had four straight 20-win seasons. He drove in more runs than any other major league pitcher in history and finished as arguably one of the greatest hitting pitchers of all time.

On February 16, 1967, in a special run-off election, Red Ruffing was elected to the Baseball Hall of Fame.

After suffering a stroke in 1973, Red remained confined to a wheelchair the rest of his life. He continued to attend many induction ceremonies until his death in 1986.

CHARLES DILLON STENGEL
"CASEY"

MANAGED NEW YORK YANKEES 1949-1960.
WON 10 PENNANTS AND 7 WORLD SERIES WITH
NEW YORK YANKEES. ONLY MANAGER TO WIN
5 CONSECUTIVE WORLD SERIES 1949-1953.
PLAYED OUTFIELD 1912-1925 WITH BROOKLYN,
PITTSBURGH, PHILADELPHIA, NEW YORK AND
BOSTON N.L. TEAMS. MANAGED BROOKLYN
1934-1936. BOSTON BRAVES 1938-1943.
NEW YORK METS 1962-1965.

Casey Stengel
(Elected 1966)

A quarter of a century before he donned the Yankee pinstripes for the first time, Casey Stengel was already making history in "The House that Ruth Built."

Playing center field for the New York Giants in 1923, he appeared in that year's World Series against the Yankees in their brand new ballpark in the Bronx. In the opening game, Stengel hit what was the first World Series home run in the history of Yankee Stadium. In the ninth inning with the score tied at four, Stengel's solo inside-the-park home run gave the Giants a 5-4 victory. He would add another home run in Game Three, however, the Yankees ultimately won the Series in six games for their first World Series title. But of course, Stengel would be a big part of many of their Fall Classic triumphs in decades to come.

Born in Kansas City, Missouri, in 1890, Charles Dillon Stengel went on to attend Western Dental College there after high school. Being left-handed was considered a handicap for aspiring dentists, and he ultimately abandoned the profession. Years later, he would declare that his decision was one of the best things that ever happened to dentistry. Turning his attention to baseball, he spent three seasons in the minors before breaking in with Brooklyn in 1912.

It wasn't long before Casey developed a reputation as a colorful, rather eccentric character, and there are no shortage of oft-told anecdotes. One of the more noteworthy stunts came in 1918 after Brooklyn had traded him to Pittsburgh. During his first game back at Ebbets Field with the Pirates, he came up for his first at-bat and was greeted by a chorus of hearty boos. As he mockingly tipped his cap to the crowd, a small bird flew out from underneath.

After stints with the Pirates and then the Phillies, Stengel moved to the Giants in 1921, and ended his major league playing career with the Boston Braves early in the 1925 season. He finished with a respectable .284 batting average over his 14-season stay in the big leagues, and had enough speed to have double figures in stolen bases seven times. Having been managed by Hall of Fame managers such as Wilbert Robinson with Brooklyn and the legendary John McGraw with the Giants demonstrated for him the qualities helpful to his future profession.

Stengel left the Braves in 1925 to become a player/manager as well as team president of the minor league Worcester team of the Eastern League. As the frustrating season concluded, Stengel made a few interesting managerial decisions. As field manager, he released Stengel the player. As team president he fired Stengel from his managerial position. Then in a clean sweep, Stengel resigned as team president. He did make one important contact in his brief time in the Eastern League when he became acquainted with the New Haven team's George Weiss, who would be an important figure in Stengel's baseball future.

Casey moved on to manage Toledo of the American Association starting in 1926, and brought a pennant to the team the following year. After six years in Toledo he made his return to the majors when he was hired as a coach for his original Brooklyn team under new manager Max Carey.

Two years later, in 1934, Stengel took over as Dodgers manager. In his three-year stint, he was handicapped by a serious lack of playing talent and never finished higher than fifth place. He was relieved of his duties after the 1936 season, and after one year out of uniform, Stengel was hired to manage the Boston Bees, as the Braves were known at the time. Unfortunately, the Bees were not much better off than the Dodgers, and in his six seasons as field boss, they finished just barely above .500 only once. In the nine seasons Stengel had managed in the major leagues to that point, he had compiled a combined record of 581-742.

Beginning in 1944, Stengel found himself back in the American Association as manager of the Milwaukee team, taking them to the pennant right away. Staying in the same circuit, he then moved on to manage the Kansas City team in 1945, then moved yet again in 1946, this time out to Oakland in the Pacific Coast League. Stengel created more positive attention for himself within the game by leading the Oaks to the league pennant in 1948. He did so with such players as 40-year-old Hall of Fame catcher Ernie Lombardi, who had already concluded his major league career, and future Yankee infielder Billy Martin.

Stengel had been at the helm of Oakland for three seasons when his big break came in the fall of 1948. The Yankees had finished a disappointing third in the A.L., and Bucky Harris was let go as the team's manager after the end of the 1948 season. On October 12, Yankees new general manager George Weiss reached back to his Eastern League days from the 1920s and announced Stengel as his selection as the 15th man to guide the New York team on the field of play since their beginning in 1903.

Some wondered that with Stengel's reputation and image if his hiring was mainly for comic relief while the team was rebuilding. Much later it would be said that it was at this time that the clown became a genius. He amazed all whom he regaled with his form of speech, in time known as "Stengelese," which would be described as "circuitous doubletalk laced with ambiguous antecedents, dangling participles, a lack of proper names and a liberal use of adjectives like 'amazing' and 'terrific.'"

Though the Yankees got off to a great start in 1949, age and injuries to key players plagued them. A bad heel caused Joe DiMaggio to miss the first half of the season, and a broken finger kept Berra out of the lineup a month. Stengel was forced to constantly juggle the lineup, as evidenced by the fact that he used seven different players at first base, and six outfielders played at least 60 games in the outfield. He somehow found the knack of plugging in the most effective replacement parts, pulling all the right strings, and making just the right moves. In the end it all came down to the final series of the season with Boston, and when the dust had settled, the Yankees finished with a one-game lead in the A.L. Stengel had proven many wrong with his ability to return the Yankees to the top, and his place was further solidified with a World Series defeat of Brooklyn in five games.

The 60-year-old manager, celebrating his 40th anniversary in professional baseball in 1950 faced the task of proving he was not just a fluke. The Yankees pursuit of the pennant in 1950 was aided by several key performances, some of which were not totally expected. DiMaggio returned to play a full season and had what would be his last truly big year with 32 home runs and 122 RBIs; Vic Raschi led the pitching staff again, duplicating his win total from 1949 with 21; Phil Rizzuto came through with his career-year, which earned him league MVP honors; and 37-year-old Johnny Mize, acquired from the Giants late in the 1949 season, chipped in with 25 home runs. The most unforeseen contribution came from rookie lefty Whitey Ford, who was called up from Kansas City in June and proceeded to win his first nine decisions and finished with a 9-1 record. Stengel's men went on to top second-place Detroit by 2½ games to earn the right to face the surprising "Whiz Kid" Phillies in the 1950 World Series.

Games One, Two, and Three were nail-biters, with the Yankees prevailing by just one run in each. Stengel then sent confident rookie Ford in Game Four at the Stadium and he surprisingly didn't allow a run until the ninth inning. With a little help from Allie Reynolds in closing it out for the 5-2 win, Stengel had become the first manager to win the World Series in his first two seasons with a given team.

In 1951 Stengel oversaw what would be somewhat of a landmark year for the Yankee franchise, ushering out the DiMaggio era as the Mickey Mantle era was beginning. While DiMaggio still had many key moments, it was clear that he wasn't quite the player he once was. Mantle was showing great potential in his rookie year after surprisingly making the jump at 19 years old all the way from Class "C" ball, but was experiencing growing pains in the process. Stengel got fine pitching from his top three starters, Lopat, Raschi, and Reynolds; an MVP season from Berra; and a rookie-of-the-year campaign from versatile Gil McDougald as they went on to defeat the neighboring Giants for their third straight title.

Few informed observers gave Stengel much chance of making it four in a row in 1952. DiMaggio had walked away at age 37 despite virtually being pleaded with by team ownership to play one more year. A few other regulars, including pitcher Tom Morgan and infielders Bobby Brown and Jerry Coleman, missed significant amounts of time due to serving in the military. An injury to Ed Lopat's pitching shoulder also complicated matters.

But Mantle emerged as an up-and-coming star replacing Joe D. in center, while Billy Martin filled in effectively for Coleman at second and McDougald took over for Brown at third. Allie Reynolds led the staff with an outstanding year, and despite Cleveland having three 20-game winners, Stengel's magic left New York on top by a margin of two games.

Matched up against Brooklyn in the Series of 1952, the Yankees overcame a great performance by Duke Snider and a three-games-to-two deficit to bring the trophy home to the Bronx for the fourth straight year. This equaled the feat of the 1936 to 1939 Joe McCarthy-led edition.

Stengel welcomed back Whitey Ford in 1953 after two years in the Army and the young lefty came through with an 18-6 record in his first full season. One of the most prominent highlights of the campaign was the Yankees' 18-game winning streak. With otherwise a very similar cast as in 1952, New York once again finished ahead of second-place Cleveland and third-place Chicago to earn a repeat in the Series with Brooklyn.

Billy Martin, one of Casey's favorites, delivered an MVP performance in the Series with 12 hits in 24 at-bats, leading the Yankees to the title four games to two. Stengel's team had now achieved what none had ever done in the major leagues before or since—win five consecutive World Championships. This would be viewed as Stengel's most lasting achievement in his long managerial career. He had also become one of the forerunners of platooning players, which was not always completely popular with the players themselves, and he was one of the first to increase the role of relief pitchers in the late innings.

That the 1954 Yankees won 103 regular season games and still finished eight games out was a testament to the dominance of the Cleveland Indians. The Tribe had tremendous pitching, while the Yankee staff had begun to show signs of age, yet it was the first time since Stengel took over that the team won over 100 games. He could hardly be faulted for not taking New York to its sixth consecutive World Series.

The Yankees hiatus from postseason play was short-lived, as they returned to the Fall Classic in 1955 against rival Brooklyn. Stengel was once again able to compensate for injuries and in some cases sub-par seasons, making the adjustments that landed New York three games above runner-up Cleveland. Things looked promising as the Yankees jumped out to a two-games-to-none lead over Brooklyn in the 1955 Series, but the Dodgers took four of the next five to capture the only World Championship Brooklyn would ever see. But Stengel and company would have the chance to gain revenge the next year in yet another Yankee–Dodger World Series.

It was in 1956 that 24-year-old Mantle emerged as a true superstar, winning the A.L Triple Crown and MVP Award. Stengel also managed to come up with two young pitchers who gave a big boost to the staff, Johnny Kucks and Tom Sturdivant, who contributed 18 and 16 wins, respectively. Stengel had the team in first place from May 16 on. It was Brooklyn however who jumped out to a two-games-to-none lead in the 1956 World Series.

The Yankees came back to win Games Three and Four at the Stadium, setting the stage for Don Larsen's historic perfect game on October 8. Two days later the Yankees' revenge over Brooklyn was complete with a 9-0 win in Game Seven in the last World Series game ever played at Ebbets Field.

Stengel's 1957 edition again received big offensive contributions from the likes of Mantle, Berra, and Bill Skowron. He had to make due however with a patchwork pitching staff that, although had six members with double figures in wins, only had Sturdivant with as many as 16. New York was still able to top second-place Chicago by eight games, and would be meeting the Milwaukee Braves in the Series. The Braves, fast becoming a National League powerhouse, had come a long way since Stengel had skippered them a decade and a half prior in Boston. Big, tough, right-hander Lew Burdette helped to spoil New York's October with three complete-game wins, including shutouts in Games Five and Seven to take the title.

Similar to when Stengel's men had the chance to gain revenge over Brooklyn in the 1956 Series after losing to them the year before, they found themselves in the same position in October of 1958 with Milwaukee. Once again the Yankees topped the second-place White Sox, this time by a full 10 games, and remarkably Stengel had his ninth pennant in 10 seasons with the team. New York then had to overcome a three-games-to-one deficit, and were aided in the cause by Bob Turley's five-hit shutout in Game Five. The Yanks managed to win the final two games in Milwaukee and were once again atop the baseball world.

By far the most forgettable year in Stengel's time with the Yankees was 1959. The team finished only four games above .500 at 79-75 and actually had fallen into last place for a short time in late May. The offensive woes were highlighted by the fact that Mantle only drove in 75 runs, Berra, 69, and Skowron, who missed half the season with a back injury, only 59. The team made a transaction in December of 1959 with the intention of bolstering the offensive attack by bringing in 25-year-old outfielder Roger Maris. It was thought that the lefty-swinging Maris might be well-suited to the short dimensions in Yankee Stadium's right field, and only history would tell just how much.

Things didn't look terribly optimistic for the team come the end of Spring Training 1960, and as they were floundering by the end of May, some wondered if the Stengel magic had run its course. But an MVP season from newcomer Maris and a very productive year from Mantle as well catapulted the Yankees into the thick of the race by August. They closed out their season by winning 15 straight games, topping a surprising second-place Baltimore team by a full eight games.

Stengel had turned 70 years old during the 1960 season, and the team's owners became concerned when he spent a week in the hospital in midseason. They began to wonder if the pressures and expectations that came with managing the Yankees might not be a bit much for a man of such an advanced age. Stengel was in the final year of a two-year contract and was telling the press that he would decide on his future after the end of the season, and his health would be a factor.

The Yankees went into the 1960 World Series favored to dispatch the upstart Pittsburgh Pirates, but few would predict the unusual occurrences that transpired, particularly the shocking conclusion. Over the course of the seven games, the Yankees outscored Pittsburgh by a combined total of 55 runs to 27, but Bill Mazeroski's home run made it academic. On October 18, 1960, five days after the Yankees loss in Game Seven, team owners Dan Topping and Del Webb announced that they would not be bringing Stengel back as manager in 1961. It was learned that the decision had been made largely due to concerns over Casey's health, and that he would not have been brought back even if New York had beaten Pittsburgh in the World Series. Ownership seemed intent on implementing a 65-year-old limit for its management staff.

Stengel's 12-season run with the Yankees had produced remarkable results. His 10 league pennants tied the legendary John McGraw in that category, and his seven World Championships is equaled only by Joe McCarthy. His combined regular season won-loss record with the Yankees was an impressive 1,149-696 for a winning percentage of .623. The New York baseball writers even threw a party in his honor at the Waldorf-Astoria shortly after his dismissal. Stengel had provided them with countless interesting and colorful quotes, and the scribes continually marveled at his stamina and amazing recall.

Stengel would, of course resurface with the newly formed Mets in 1962, but that experience turned out to be little more than a comedy until a broken hip forced his retirement in the middle of the 1965 season. The following year he became eligible for the Hall of Fame and sailed right in, gaining enshrinement that summer along with Ted Williams. Standing at the podium that warm July day, Stengel reflected back to his playing days, telling the crowd, "I chased the balls that Babe Ruth hit." He also took the opportunity to thank the man who brought him to the Yankees when he said, "Well, I fortunately met Mr. Weiss, who was running the New Haven club and after that it proved a very great acquaintance because whenever I was discharged Mr. Weiss found out and would re-employ me."

Stengel retired to his longtime home in Glendale, California, with his wife, Edna, making the occasional appearance back at Yankee Stadium. The couple lived in comfort due to shrewd investments in oil, real estate, and the banking business. In 1970, the Yankees made Casey's uniform number 37 the fifth number to be retired by the team.

Stengel passed away on September 29, 1975, in Glendale from complications of pneumonia at the age of 85. Upon his death, the *New York Times* wrote that he "had the baseball mind of a genius, the heart of Santa Claus and St. Francis, and the face of a clown." The following summer on what would

have been his 86th birthday, July 30, the team erected a plaque in Monument Park as a tribute to the "Ol' perfessor" that read:

CHARLES DILLON "CASEY" STENGEL
1890–1975
BRIGHTENED BASEBALL FOR OVER 50 YEARS
WITH SPIRIT OF ETERNAL YOUTH
YANKEE MANAGER 1949–1960 WINNING
10 PENNANTS AND 7 WORLD CHAMPIONSHIPS
INCLUDING A RECORD 5 CONSECUTIVE 1949–1953
ERECTED BY NEW YORK YANKEES
JULY 30, 1976

MILLER JAMES HUGGINS
1904–1929
MANAGER OF ST. LOUIS CARDINALS
AND NEW YORK YANKEES,
LED YANKEES TO 6 PENNANTS
IN 1921, 1922, 1923, 1926, 1927 AND 1928 AND
3 WORLD SERIES VICTORIES 1923, 1927 AND 1928.
SECOND BASEMAN IN PLAYING DAYS
WITH REDS AND CARDINALS, 1904-1916.

Miller Huggins

(Elected 1964)

Long before Casey Stengel was managing the Yankees to the World Series on almost a yearly basis, even before Joe McCarthy was filling out lineup cards well into many Octobers, diminutive Miller Huggins was the Yankee skipper who led them to the Fall Classic for the first six times.

Huggins was directing the team on the diamond at the onset of its first of many "golden ages" as field manager throughout the 1920s. He was there to welcome Babe Ruth, Lou Gehrig, and a tremendous supporting cast that truly created the Yankee dynasty.

The 5-foot 6-inch, 140-pound Cincinnati native had broken into the major leagues as a second baseman with his hometown Reds in 1904. Despite his small stature, he managed to play for 13 seasons, finishing as an active player with the Cardinals in 1916. The scrappy second baseman had actually spent three of his seasons with the Reds playing under manager Clark Griffith, one of the pioneers and original manager of the Yankee franchise. Huggins, considered a very smart player, had taken over as the St. Louis manager in 1913, serving as player/manager through 1916, and directing the team strictly from the bench in 1917. Though he had only finished as high as third place in the standings with St. Louis on two occasions, he was nonetheless regarded as a shrewd manager. One lasting effect he had on a future superstar was his encouraging a young Rogers Hornsby to alter his batting stance.

In 1917 the Yankees had finished a disappointing sixth in the A.L., and it had been years since they were among the elite teams in the league. American League president Ban Johnson felt the league would benefit far more with a strong team in New York City, particularly in competing for fans with John McGraw's Giants. Johnson strongly recommended to the Yankees that they consider hiring Huggins, who like Johnson had graduated many years earlier from the University of Cincinnati Law School.

Huggins ultimately accepted the offer in January 1918, and joined a team that included such sluggers as A.L. home run champ Wally Pipp, Frank "Home Run" Baker, fine defensive shortstop Roger Peckinpaugh, and quality pitcher Bob Shawkey. But while the pennants did not come right away, the team began to creep up in the standings. In Huggins's inaugural campaign in New York, they finished fourth, and moved up to third in 1919 and 1920. But of course, the addition of Babe Ruth as an offensive weapon in 1920 signaled the beginning of a new era. When the Ruth purchase was announced in January of 1920, it was Huggins who traveled out to California to meet with him and get his name on a Yankee contract.

The Yankees made many trades in the early 1920s that helped to transform them into the powerhouse they would become. Huggins provided his input on many of these acquisitions to front office chief Ed Barrow, having a say on the personnel he would oversee on the field.

Huggins finally led the team to the top of the A.L. standings in 1921, and while Ruth was a big factor, the pitching staff pulled its weight with the league lead in ERA and strikeouts. The 1921 World Series featured the two teams who called the Polo Grounds home, and the outcome could not have been much closer. Unfortunately, Huggins's men were on the short end in the deciding game by a slim 1-0 margin.

As defending American League Champions, the Yankees came back in 1922 and narrowly squeaked out another pennant over the very surprising St. Louis Browns by one mere game. Huggins had a chance at revenge over McGraw and his Giants, who were returning to the Series as well, but the excitement was short-lived. Aside from Game Two, which was declared a tie when called due to darkness with the score knotted at three, the Yankees were unable to win a game. The Series loss created a further rift between the two co-owners of the Yankees, Jacob Ruppert and Tillinghast Huston. They had disagreed on the choice of managers back in 1918 when Huggins was hired, as Huston wanted to bring in Brooklyn manager Wilbert Robinson. Ruppert went ahead and followed Ban Johnson's suggestion and hired Huggins. Huston wanted Huggins dismissed immediately after the 1922 Series loss, while Ruppert continued to support him and wanted him retained. Over the winter, Ruppert finally bought out Huston's share of the Yankees, and Huggins's job was safe. Once the deal was made in the spring of 1923, Ruppert called a team meeting at once to inform the players in no uncertain terms that Huggins was his manager.

The team responded with their best season to that point under Huggins, winning 98 games and topping second-place Detroit, managed by Ty Cobb, by 16 games in the standings. They featured a well-balanced attack that saw them lead the A.L. not only in home runs and slugging percentage, but fielding percentage and earned run average. Yet again, the Yankees were to face the New York Giants in the Fall Classic, for what would be the only time in the 20th century that the same two teams faced each other in three consecutive Series. One noteworthy difference in 1923 was that the Yankees had their new state-of-the-art facility in which to host the Giants.

It all added up to the first true occurrence of "Yankee magic," and the confidence in Huggins's ability to lead the team to the ultimate victory was justified as they disposed of McGraw's men in six games. There is no World Championship quite like the first one, and it should never be forgotten that it was under Miller Huggins's watch that it all occurred. Ruppert was quick to bestow much credit upon him for the title.

New York was unsuccessful at defending their A.L. Championship in 1924, finishing three games in back of the great Walter Johnson and the Washington Senators. And while 1925 was thought to represent a new chance to get back to the top, it quickly turned into a disaster for Huggins's men. It began when Ruth collapsed shortly before the season opened and required abdominal surgery, missing nearly the first two months of the season. In August, Huggins had begun to tire of Ruth's shenanigans and continually ignoring curfew. He was a very lenient man, forgiving almost to a fault, but continued offenses irked him and he finally laid down the law. Huggins informed Ruth he was suspended indefinitely and would be fined $5,000. Ruth thought he could likely get the punishment overturned by Ruppert, but he didn't realize that Huggins had the support of both the owner and Ed Barrow. In the end, Ruth had little choice but to apologize to the team as Huggins had ordered, and he promised the manager he would observe the rules in the future. Little Hug, sometimes referred to in the press as the "Mite Manager" or "Mighty Mite," had put his foot down on the biggest star in the game and come out on top.

But 1925 was a down year for other reasons as well. Aside from Ruth managing only 25 home runs and 66 RBIs in his limited time, they ranked next-to-last in runs scored, led the league in errors, and uncharacteristically finished below .500 and in seventh place. Yankee fans and the New York sports-writers alike were beginning to grow impatient with what they considered to be underachieving from Huggins's team.

But come 1926, Ruth had dedicated himself more to a training regimen, young Lou Gehrig was firmly entrenched in the lineup, and the Yankees were poised for an extended stay at the top of the A.L. They edged out Cleveland by three games and earned the right to face the St. Louis Cardinals in October. With a three-games-to-one New York lead, many felt a Yankee title was a foregone conclusion, however, they let the Cardinals get back in it. It came right down to the ninth inning of the seventh game, but Ruth getting caught stealing on an inexplicable attempt with two outs ended Yankee hopes.

The 1927 edition displayed considerably more dominance than any of Huggins's previous teams. In mid-July the manager predicted that they would win 100 games, and his men exceeded his projection by a full 10 games. They had moved into first place to stay on May 1, and clinched the pennant with three weeks to go in the season. In 22 games against the St. Louis Browns, the Yankees won all but one. Huggins acknowledged his team's superior offensive power, but argued that no team could dominate as they did without the terrific pitching that they also possessed.

Only the Pittsburgh Pirates stood in the way of Huggins and company quieting their critics and returning to the top of the baseball world. Terrific performances from Ruth, Mark Koenig, and pitcher Wilcy Moore helped New York administer a sweep, allowing them to bask in the glow of their second world title. Amid such celebrations, Huggins would always avoid the spotlight, as he was not one to mix or socialize with others. Never seeking attention or accolades, he was always quick to deflect praise to his players.

His efforts, however, earned him a sizable raise, and he was said to be the highest-paid manager in the A.L. in 1928, second in the majors to only John McGraw. Huggins would earn his money in 1928, as his team had many injuries and he was forced to utilize his bench on a fairly regular basis. He was also credited with getting the most out of players who had been discarded by other teams, such as Pat Collins, Gene Robertson, Cedric Durst, and Joe Dugan. New York writer Joe Vila wrote in his column dated July 9, 1928, "The wonderful success of Colonel Ruppert's team is largely due to the shrewd and brainy leadership . . ." of Huggins. *The Sporting News* of July 19, 1928, editorialized of the manager's value:

Huggins is a master mind in baseball in more ways than one. The credit often goes to Huggins associates on the New York Club, but it is a fact that the "Mite Manager" is the man whose opinion rules and whose word goes when a deal is made. Colonel Jake Ruppert has only to sign the papers.

New York was able to hang on to retain their A.L. crown over the Philadelphia Athletics by 2½ games. Going into the Series, a rematch of the 1926 Fall Classic versus St. Louis, many considered the Yankees underdogs because of their injuries. In Joe Vila's column of October 1, he again credited Huggins amid the adversity: "To Huggins belongs the lion's share of the praise. He wore his thinking cap night and day during the prolonged agony. . . ."

Injuries did not turn out to be a factor as the Yankees cruised in four games, outscoring St. Louis by a total of 27-10. Huggins got wonderful pitching from Waite Hoyt, nine RBIs from Gehrig, and a three-home-run game from Ruth. New York was able to atone for their Series loss to the Cardinals two years earlier, and Huggins finally began to receive the credit he deserved from the sporting press.

In the quest for a third straight pennant in 1929, it became clear early on that the heavily talented Athletics were ready to emerge as a powerhouse. By early September, it was obvious that New York would do no better than second place. Huggins had not been feeling well for some time, and on September 20 he came to Yankee Stadium and instructed his coach Art Fletcher to take over the team for a few days. He then checked himself into a local hospital and proceeded to deteriorate rapidly. Just five days later on September 25, 1929, Huggins passed away from a skin affliction known as erysipelas. The baseball world was stunned, and at Huggins's funeral several Yankees, including Ruth, served as pallbearers.

Charlie O'Leary, who for years served as Huggins's coach and right-hand man said, "Huggins was a great little fellow to work for. No one I ever came in contact with knew more baseball than Hug."

In early March 1931, the park in St. Petersburg, Florida, where the Yankees held spring training was renamed "Miller Huggins Field." A ceremony was held and a plaque unveiled.

The Yankees began their hallowed tradition of honoring great figures from their past with plaques in the deep center field area by dedicating a memorial plaque to Huggins on May 30, 1932. It read:

MILLER JAMES HUGGINS
MANAGER OF THE NEW YORK YANKEES 1918–1929
PENNANT WINNERS 1921–22–23–26–27–28
WORLD CHAMPIONS 1923, 1927, AND 1928
AS A TRIBUTE TO A SPLENDID CHARACTER WHO
MADE PRICELESS CONTRIBUTIONS TO BASEBALL
AND ON THIS FIELD BROUGHT GLORY TO THE
NEW YORK CLUB OF THE AMERICAN LEAGUE.
THIS MEMORIAL ERECTED BY COL. JACOB RUPPERT
AND BASEBALL WRITERS OF NEW YORK
MAY 30, 1932

In 1964, the Hall of Fame Veterans Committee took Huggins's managerial record and contributions to baseball into consideration. He had compiled a won-loss record in his 11 seasons with the Yankees of 1,067-719 for a .597 winning percentage, and had led the team to six pennants and its first three World Championships within one eight-season span. The committee determined at that time that a bronze plaque for Miller Huggins was well deserved and long overdue.

BURLEIGH ARLAND GRIMES
1916–1934

ONE OF THE GREAT SPITBALL PITCHERS.
WON 270 GAMES, LOST 212 FOR 7 MAJOR
LEAGUE CLUBS. FIVE 20 VICTORY SEASONS.
WON 13 IN ROW FOR GIANTS IN 1927.
MANAGED DODGERS IN 1937 AND 1938.
LIFETIME E.R.A. 3.52.

Burleigh Grimes
(Elected 1964)

On May 15, 1934, when major league teams were required to trim their rosters down to 23 players, 19-season veteran hurler Burleigh Grimes was among the victims of the numbers game. In order to make room for catcher Francis Healy, who had been claimed from the Giants, the St. Louis Cardinals gave the 41-year-old spitball artist his unconditional release. Grimes was taken by surprise by the move, as he thought he had pitched effectively in his relief role.

The following week, Joe McCarthy's Yankees were in St. Louis to play the Browns, and desperate for bullpen help, signed Grimes and took him with them. Though he had pitched for six teams to this point, this would be his first and ultimately only foray into the American League. It was suspected that while many believed Grimes could still be of use, some managers would not consider him because he was regarded as a potential managerial candidate and they were afraid that he could be appointed their successor. Joe McCarthy had no such fear, having a contract that extended through 1935.

Washington had actually offered more money than the Yankees, but having pitched for the Dodgers and Giants throughout most of the 1920s, he preferred New York. Grimes also was not anxious to pitch in another scorching, hot-weather city.

Burleigh had begun his major league career back in 1916 with the Pirates, and was one of only 17 spitball pitchers who were allowed to continue using the pitch after it was outlawed in 1920. By 1934, with Red Faber having retired the year before, Grimes was the last remaining legal spitball artist.

He had reportedly learned the subtle nuances of the moist delivery when he was 16 years old by observing a pitcher named Hank Gehring of St. Paul in the American Association. Young Grimes then went back to his job

at the Post Office in Clear Lake, Wisconsin, and began working on the pitch after work by throwing it to a fellow clerk. In the years that followed, it contributed to a stellar career on the mound that saw him win 20 games five times, and participate in four World Series. Grimes was 2-0 in the 1931 World Series as his Cardinals prevailed over the Philadelphia Athletics, and his final World Series appearance came the next year with the Cubs. It was in that Series that Burleigh and his teammates witnessed Babe Ruth hit his famous "called shot" in the Yankee sweep.

Beyond the sheer statistics, Grimes developed a reputation as an extremely tough competitor who was not afraid to include the brushback pitch as part of his repertoire. The addition of Grimes to the roster now gave the 1934 edition of the Yankees an incredible nine future Hall of Famers in uniform, including manager McCarthy. He would make his official A.L. debut on May 30, 1934, in the second game of the Memorial Day doubleheader versus Washington with 70,000 jammed into the stadium. In this particular game, Babe Ruth, in his final season with the Yankees, showed that he was still feared by pitchers despite his advanced age. He was issued three straight walks before being removed from the game with no official at-bats. Grimes then came on in relief of Johnny Murphy in the eighth inning and gave up two runs to tie the score at four. He then settled down and finished the game as the Yankees scored a run in the eleventh inning to win 5-4. Grimes recorded his 270th career victory, which would subsequently be his last in the major leagues.

A few of the games Grimes pitched for the Yankees seemed to include noteworthy happenings involving both Gehrig and Ruth. In Burleigh's second appearance in pinstripes, on June 1, Lou was celebrating the ninth anniversary of his streak, which now stood at 1,389 games. A week and a half later, Gehrig hit one of his record 23 grand slams against Philadelphia to help win 7-3. Grimes came in to pitch a hitless ninth inning in the victory at the Stadium. The game on July 14 in Detroit, in which Grimes pitched the final $1\frac{2}{3}$ innings and took the loss, was one of the most unusual of Gehrig's streak. Plagued with a nagging back injury, McCarthy listed Lou on the lineup card as the shortstop batting leadoff. He singled and was then removed immediately, keeping his streak alive. The game, which was to be the final loss of Grimes's career also featured the 701st career home run for Ruth.

A 12-5 Yankee loss in Cleveland turned out to be the final official appearance of Grimes in a New York uniform. He came on in relief for the final inning of a game in which the main highlight for New York was the 2,000th walk of Ruth's illustrious career.

Ten days later, after having pitched in 10 official games for the Yankees, Grimes appeared in an exhibition game against Wheeling of the minor league Middle Atlantic League. He surrendered nine hits as New York was upset 6-4, and was given his unconditional release a few days later. In early August he signed with Pittsburgh, with whom he had made his major league debut. By the end of the 1934 season, Grimes's playing career had reached its conclusion. Thirty years later, the Hall of Fame Veterans Committee rewarded him for his outstanding career on the mound. Burleigh lived to the age of 92, passing away in his hometown of Clear Lake, Wisconsin.

JOSEPH VINCENT McCARTHY
CHICAGO N.L.1926-1930
NEW YORK A.L.1931-1946
BOSTON A.L.1948-1950
OUTSTANDING MANAGER WHO NEVER PLAYED
IN MAJOR LEAGUES.THE MAJOR LEAGUE
TEAMS MANAGED BY HIM DURING 24 YEARS
NEVER FINISHED OUT OF FIRST DIVISION.
WON PENNANTS CHICAGO N.L.1929,
NEW YORK A.L.1932-6-7-8-9-41-2-3.
WON SEVEN WORLD'S CHAMPIONSHIPS WITH
NEW YORK YANKEES-FOUR OF THEM
CONSECUTIVELY 1936-7-8-9.

Joe McCarthy

(Elected 1957)

fter the death of longtime Yankee manager Miller Huggins in 1929, and missing the World Series for the second straight year in 1930, the team was seeking a leader who could return them to their glory days. At the same time, Cubs owner William Wrigley impatiently fired his manager Joe McCarthy right at the end of the 1930 season for not taking the team to the World Series as he had in 1929. McCarthy's Cubs finished in second place, just two games behind St. Louis.

Realizing that an established manager such as McCarthy might just be the answer, general manager Ed Barrow of the Yankees wasted little time and signed him for the job in October of 1930. So McCarthy, essentially, was fired from one team because they didn't make it to the World Series, and almost immediately hired for another because they didn't make it to the World Series!

While he had never made it to the major leagues as a player, McCarthy had several years of experience as a manager in professional baseball. He had run the Louisville team of the American Association from 1919 through 1925, winning two league pennants. In 1926 he was hired to take over a Cubs team that was in shambles and built them into contenders in just a few short years. In taking over a Yankee team that had just finished in third place, it did not appear that a major overhaul was necessary. Colonel Ruppert agreed to hire McCarthy partly because Joe gave him the impression that he was willing to fight for every win. The Colonel also knew that the manager was taking on a big challenge because there were such high expectations for the team, but he was willing to be patient.

McCarthy held his first Yankee training camp in St. Petersburg in 1931, and he was quoted early on, "I'm like a man groping around in a dark room. It will take me a while to find the key hole, and in the meantime, I may stub my toe a few times." He also recalled for the assembled media that he played against Babe Ruth in the International League back in 1914. A second baseman in his playing days, McCarthy played for Buffalo while Ruth was appearing for Baltimore, then Providence in that circuit. Famed Yankee scout Paul Krichell, who discovered Lou Gehrig and several others, was also a catcher on Joe's Buffalo team that season.

When McCarthy reacquainted himself with Ruth at camp, he only requested that Babe be prompt. When Ruth was asked before the start of the season his opinion of McCarthy, he showed his support by saying simply, "He tells you what to do, and we are going to play our heads off for him." Joe would also be back together with one of his former players, as leadoff hitter and center fielder Earle Combs played for him for two years in Louisville.

McCarthy immediately instilled discipline on the team and insisted the players wear sport jackets and ties on the road. He belief was that they should look like champions both on and off the field. Ruppert was impressed with what he saw in camp and believed his new manager had inspired the team with his will to win. When the Yankees issued their published program in the spring of 1931, it had McCarthy on the cover instead of Ruth, whom it had featured for many years.

He got his Yankee managerial career off on the right foot on Opening Day, April 12, 1931, at the Stadium. Behind the complete game thrown by Red Ruffing and a Ruth home run, McCarthy's men beat the Red Sox by a score of 6-2. But in the end, Philadelphia was again just too powerful and won their third straight A.L. pennant, relegating New York and their 92 wins to second place.

The 1932 season turned out to be quite a different story for McCarthy and his Yankees. They switched places with the Athletics by winning 107 games and running away with the flag by 13 games. The potent offense with Ruth and Gehrig combining for 288 RBIs scored a major league-high total of 1,002 runs, while the pitching staff led the league in team ERA. McCarthy got terrific pitching performances from Lefty Gomez and Ruffing, but was also pleasantly surprised with rookie Johnny Allen's 17-4 record. Joe had now become the first manager to win pennants in both the National and American Leagues.

With his former team the Cubs topping their league in 1932, McCarthy would have the opportunity to gain a bit of revenge on the team that dismissed him two years prior. This was just one reason for tension between the two teams, as barbs were being hurled freely from bench jockeys in both dugouts. But on the field the Yankees were just too much for the Cubs, with Gehrig hitting .529 and Ruth hitting his most famous home run in what would be his final World Series. A four-game sweep left no doubt as to who had the greatest team.

The patience that owner Ruppert said he was willing to extend back in 1931 would be sorely needed over the next three seasons. The Yankees could not rise above second place, acting as bridesmaids to Washington in 1933 and Detroit in 1934 and 1935. February 1935 saw Ruth officially severing his ties with the team, but not before he inquired about the possible availability of the manager's job. Ruppert and Barrow assured him that they were perfectly satisfied with McCarthy.

By 1936, McCarthy had worked many new faces into the lineup, giving the team a slightly different look from the "Murderer's Row" days. Frankie Crosetti was firmly entrenched as the starting shortstop, with Red Rolfe next to him at third. George Selkirk was new in right field, sporting Ruth's uniform number 3. Monte Pearson and Bump Hadley were acquired for the pitching staff. But the most significant addition turned out to be the 21-year-old outfielder from San Francisco, Joe DiMaggio.

DiMaggio had a tremendous rookie season in 1936 and was one of five Yankees to drive in over 100 runs. Six New York pitchers recorded double figures in wins, and the team would be breaking a three-season World Series drought just as they had in 1932.

Their neighbors across the Harlem River, the New York Giants, would be their October opponents, as the city would enjoy its first inner-city Series since the three-year span from 1921 through 1923. The Yankees came out flat and dropped the opener at the Polo Grounds 6-1. But they responded in a big way in Game Two by embarrassing the National Leaguers on their home turf by the lopsided total of 18-4. Moving to Yankee Stadium, McCarthy's men captured the next two to take a commanding three-games-to-one lead.

Game Five, the Yankees' potential clincher, went into the tenth inning tied at four, but the Giants managed to put one across that inning when player/manager Bill Terry hit a sacrifice fly. The Series survived one more day, but back at the Polo Grounds the Yankees posted another one-sided victory, 13-5, to reign as champions for the fifth time.

McCarthy oversaw a Yankee team in 1937 that was led by a terrific sophomore season from DiMaggio and a dominating performance from Lefty Gomez, cruising to the pennant over Detroit by 13 games. Awaiting them was a rematch from the previous year's World Series with their former landlords from the Polo Grounds. The domination the Yankees showed was apparent as the combined score after three games was 21-3 in their favor. Carl Hubbell pitched a fine game to beat the Yankees 7-3 in Game Four, but it only served to delay the inevitable. On October 10 in the park they used to share with the Giants, McCarthy and his squad celebrated back-to-back Series titles.

McCarthy opened up training camp of 1938 without his young star center fielder DiMaggio, who was engaged in a long contract holdout. The dispute dragged on and Opening Day came without a resolution. The Yankees clearly missed him and with a deal finally reached, McCarthy was able to insert him back into the lineup two weeks into the season. As the season wore on and with Joe D. back in place it became clear that New York would again rule the roost in the American League. Again their balance showed by leading the league in both runs scored and earned run average. And one more time, McCarthy had the opportunity to compete in October against the team that had dismissed him many years prior, the Cubs. With two fine games from ace Red Ruffing and significant production from Frank Crosetti and new second baseman Joe Gordon, the outcome never really seemed in doubt. McCarthy, with another four-game sweep over the Cubs, as in 1932, gained another measure of satisfaction. He would say years later that he thought the 1938 edition was his best Yankee team.

Somewhat unusual in the 1938 Series was the lack of power shown by Gehrig, who contributed only four singles. The following spring it became clear that something was terribly wrong, and McCarthy had to make the painful move of writing Babe Dahlgren's name on the lineup card as his replacement. Two months later, McCarthy was standing by Gehrig's side as he made his famous farewell speech at home plate at Yankee Stadium.

One week later, McCarthy was managing the American League All-Stars to a 3-1 win over the Nationals at the Stadium. Years before, early in 1934, McCarthy was asked by A.L. officials to manage the All-Star team in the upcoming Mid-Summer Classic. He said he would be honored, but suggested that the managers of the previous year's pennant winners annually perform the privilege. His suggestion was adopted shortly after.

The 1939 Yankees experienced a rash of injuries to their pitching staff, making it difficult for McCarthy to use a set rotation. Aside from Ruffing's 21 wins, he had six pitchers who won between 10 and 13 games. But they got a hold of first place early, and never lost it after May 11. In the end, they would win by a margin of 17 games over the second-place Red Sox.

Only the Cincinnati Reds stood in the way of McCarthy extending his unmatched string of world titles to four. The team allowed Gehrig to don his uniform and sit on the bench with the players, acting as an honorary captain. His presence may have inspired a bit of "Yankee Magic." In the four-game

Yankee sweep, they had broken a tie and won with an RBI single in the ninth inning of Game One, and in the clincher, they came back with two to tie in the ninth and three in the bottom of the tenth to win. McCarthy's team had now set a record for consecutive World Championships that would stand until a Yankee team of a later generation would break it.

New York got off to a very slow start as the 1940 season got underway, in part due to a knee injury to DiMaggio, and also the collective slumps of many regulars. They found themselves in last place in mid-May, and a great stretch in August and early September could not get them beyond third place by season's end. For the first time since 1935, McCarthy headed home at the conclusion of the regular schedule.

He brought his squad back in 1941 in a big way. Although they got off to another slow start and didn't really turn things around until late May, they managed to clinch the pennant on September 4, the earliest a pennant was ever won in a season of regulation length. Among the changes McCarthy made this season were bringing up Phil Rizzuto from the minors and giving him the shortstop job, and making Tommy Henrich his regular right fielder.

The Brooklyn Dodgers had risen from the depths of the National League and were set to challenge the Yankees for the title that October. Two teams from New York facing off for the title would always have potential for drama, and the big turning point came in Game Four with the Yankees up two games to one. Brooklyn catcher Mickey Owen's passed ball in the ninth paved the way to four Yankee runs and a come-from-behind win. New York pitcher Ernie Bonham finished Brooklyn off the next day with a four-hitter, and McCarthy's team was tasting victory champagne for the fifth time in six years.

With the United States becoming involved in the world conflict, the 1942 season would be the last go-round for McCarthy with this particular lineup. Anxious to get back to the World Series, they grabbed hold of first place early and were never seriously threatened, closing with a 103-51 mark. The St. Louis Cardinals came on late and passed the Dodgers to earn their first Series invitation in eight years. But as the youngest team in the major leagues, few gave them any chance over the experience of McCarthy's champions.

Game One started as expected, with veteran Ruffing topping the Cards 7-4. But Yankee fans were shocked when St. Louis took the next four games, with the indignity of the final three coming at Yankee Stadium. It would be the only World Series McCarthy would lose in a Yankee uniform.

With DiMaggio, Rizzuto, Henrich, and Ruffing gone to military service by the spring of 1943, McCarthy had the task of molding several new faces into champions. The Senators gave them a run, but New York pulled away in

the second half of the season. With St. Louis repeating in the N.L., McCarthy had a chance to atone for the previous year's embarrassment. In the end it was familiar faces such as Bill Dickey, Frank Crosetti, and Spud Chandler who helped to turn the tables on St. Louis by putting them away in five games. The 56-year-old McCarthy would celebrate his seventh World Series Championship since donning pinstripes, the sixth in eight years, but it would be his last. Losing still more regulars to the service, the Yanks could do no better than third place in 1944, and fourth in 1945. Citing health reasons, McCarthy considered resigning in 1945, but hung on as most of his regulars returned to the team from the military in the spring of 1946. But in late May, 35 games into the season, McCarthy had a falling out with team owner Larry MacPhail and finally did step down. He would resurface in 1948 to manage the Red Sox for two-and-a-half seasons before concluding his managerial career.

But the legacy he had built up as a manager would be difficult to top. His Yankee years alone included seven World Championships, eight pennants, four second-place finishes, and a record of 1,460-867 for a spectacular .627 winning percentage. His overall managerial winning percentage including his

Chicago and Boston years at .615 is number one on the all-time list. Aside from the numbers, McCarthy was considered a calm and dignified man who had the admiration of his players. Phil Rizzuto regarded him as the best manager he ever saw, and said, "He would never say anything bad behind a player's back and he would never second-guess his men." Said DiMaggio, "There wasn't a day that someone on the Yankees didn't learn something from McCarthy."

He became only the fourth man elected to the Hall of Fame as a manager upon his enshrinement in 1957, joining John McGraw, Connie Mack, and Wilbert Robinson.

"Marse Joe" as he was called, passed away in Buffalo, New York, on January 13, 1978, at 90 years of age.

JOSEPH PAUL DI MAGGIO
NEW YORK A.L. 1936 TO 1951

HIT SAFELY IN 56 CONSECUTIVE GAMES
FOR MAJOR LEAGUE RECORD 1941. HIT 2
HOME-RUNS IN ONE INNING 1936. HIT 3
HOME-RUNS IN ONE GAME (3 TIMES). HOLDS
NUMEROUS BATTING RECORDS. PLAYED IN
10 WORLD SERIES (51 GAMES) AND 11 ALL
STAR GAMES. MOST VALUABLE PLAYER
A.L. 1939, 1941, 1947.

Joe DiMaggio
(Elected 1955)

T o simply review the statistics of Joseph Paul DiMaggio, as impressive as
they are, is to overlook a large part of his true gifts. Virtually all those
who played with him, against him, or observed him for any length of
time agree that he did it all on the field with a style and grace unmatched.

And then there is that unmistakable mystique in the manner in which he
carried himself both on and off the field that has inspired reverence from very
early in his career. It has been said that when he walked into the New York
clubhouse it was as if a senator, or even a president had walked in. Indeed, as
the years went on, Joe DiMaggio was accorded the type of admiration and
respect that was generally reserved for dignitaries, popes, and heads of state.

As was true with the other few top Yankee legends, DiMaggio rose to legendary status from humble beginnings. The son of Italian immigrants whose
father worked as a fisherman off the shores of San Francisco to support eight
children qualifies as a classic American success story. Rising from success as an
amateur ballplayer on the San Francisco sandlots at the beginning of the
depression, to his status as an American icon in little more than a decade is
more than just Hollywood movie material, it is the stuff of fairy tales.

Young DiMaggio had signed as a shortstop with the nearby San Francisco
Seals of the Pacific Coast League late in the 1932 season, shortly before he
turned 18. By the following summer, now playing outfield full-time for the
Seals, he began to capture the attention of baseball observers with his unprecedented 61-game hitting streak. As a result he became a legitimate celebrity on
the west coast circuit and attracted the attention of major league scouts.
DiMaggio also got the first taste of hero worship that would in a few short
years become the norm.

Several teams were expressing interest in purchasing him from San Francisco early in the 1934 season, including the Pirates, Red Sox, and Yankees. But in late May, DiMaggio suffered an off-the-field knee injury. After hobbling through June and July, playing off and on, he finally could not put weight on the knee and his season was over by early August. Yankees west coast scout Joe Devine had Joe examined by a specialist in Los Angeles, and the doctor concluded that with rest he should return to 100 percent the following spring.

The Yankees decided at that point to make a serious offer. On November 23, two days before Joe's 20th birthday, the deal between New York and the Seals was completed. San Francisco would receive $25,000 and five minor players in exchange for DiMaggio. The interesting aspect of the deal was that the Seals were allowed to retain the services of Joe for one more season.

That 1935 season was a spectacular one for DiMaggio, as he hit .398, 32 home runs, and 154 RBIs in 679 at-bats. He was voted the Pacific Coast League's Most Valuable Player and as would become a habit, his team won the league championship.

DiMaggio arrived in St. Petersburg for Yankees training camp of 1936 ready to meet the challenge and conquer new worlds. He had actually turned down New York's initial contract offer and finally settled for $8,500, a very high figure for a rookie in those times. With that came great expectations for the phenom, as the Yankees hadn't been to the World Series since 1932 and attendance had started to decline.

DiMaggio wasted no time in living up to his billing as a potential superstar as he proceeded to tear the cover off the ball in the early going. New York writers were wild about him and devoted considerable space in their columns to his every move. Noted New York writer Dan Daniel proclaimed in March, "Here is the replacement for Babe Ruth." They were well on their way to creating the legend of DiMaggio before he even had a chance to do it himself in an official Yankee game.

In late March, early in the spring training schedule, DiMaggio was spiked on his left foot while sliding into second base. While receiving heat therapy treatment on the injured foot he received a bad burn that sidelined him for weeks, causing him to miss the first 16 games of the season.

He was finally able to make his major league debut on May 3, 1936, versus the St. Louis Browns at Yankee Stadium. DiMaggio was wearing a number on his uniform that he would not be associated with later on—number 9. And he was also playing left field rather than what would become his home, center field. He gave the fans a glimpse of his potential by going three for six including a triple, three runs scored, and an RBI in the Yanks 14-5 pounding of the

Browns. One week later he reached an important milestone—his first career home run, coming in a 7-2 win against Philadelphia.

DiMaggio was becoming very popular around the league and was even among the leading vote-getters for the All-Star team in the public poll. He made his first All-Star Game appearance that year in Boston and ultimately would be named to the team every year of his career. A couple of weeks after the 1936 All-Star Game, Joe appeared on the cover of *Time* magazine.

It took DiMaggio a while in his rookie year before he settled in to his regular position in the field. In mid-June he was switched from left field over to right, then in early August he was finally moved to center to stay. By season's end Joe had thrown out a total of 22 runners from his three positions to lead all American League outfielders.

The powerful Yankees went on to win 102 games and clinched the pennant by September 9 with nearly three weeks to go in the season. DiMaggio had contributed 29 home runs and 125 RBIs to the cause, batting .323. His 15 triples led the league and his rookie season was generally regarded as the finest all-around inaugural campaign any youngster had to that point. Many attributed the addition of DiMaggio as being the piece of the puzzle needed for the Yankees to recapture the pennant.

The Giants from across the river had topped the N.L., creating the first all-New York World Series since the two teams met 13 years prior. DiMaggio made the first of his nearly annual Series appearances in the opening game on September 30 at the Polo Grounds. In the third inning batting third in the order, he struck a single off Giant ace lefty Carl Hubbell for his first of many hits in Series competition. The Yankees didn't fare too well in that game, losing 8-1, but came back very strong the next day. In their 18-4 explosion, Joe added a double, two singles, a sacrifice fly, two runs scored, and two RBIs.

The Yankees had built up a three-games-to-one lead going into Game Six at the Polo Grounds on October 6. Still more than one month shy of his 22nd birthday, DiMaggio capped off his tremendous rookie season with three hits in the Yanks' Series-clinching 13-5 win. They had returned to the top of the baseball world, and Joe had become immensely popular with the New York fans, particularly within the Italian community. New York City had the largest Italian population of any city in the United States, and while many major league teams were reluctant to sign ballplayers of that nationality, the Yankees showed no such prejudice. They had signed Tony Lazzeri and Frank Crosetti years before.

Joe almost certainly would have added the Rookie of the Year Award to his trophy case in 1936, however, the award was not created until 1947. But there would be no shortage of honors over the course of his distinguished career.

DiMaggio's finances were handled by his older brother Tom, who was nine years his senior. Tom convinced him that he was worthy of a considerable raise in pay after his impressive rookie campaign, and after much haggling over the winter Joe signed for $17,000, double his pay of 1936.

A minor shoulder injury in early April and having his tonsils removed prevented DiMaggio from opening the 1937 season with the team. He didn't start a game until May 1st, but sporting his now familiar number 5, he started right off strong with three hits in a 3-2 win. Over the course of his sophomore season he saw improvement in almost every offensive category, including home runs as he led the entire major leagues with 46. One of his biggest days came on June 13 when he slugged three homers in a game versus St. Louis. It was being speculated as the season concluded that DiMaggio could have even surpassed Ruth's record of 60 if the left field dimensions of Yankee Stadium were not so cavernous.

Among his other superb batting figures included leading the A.L. in runs with 151 and slugging percentage at .673; being second to only Hank Greenberg with 167 RBIs; and stroking 215 hits to compile a .346 average. He was now the most potent offensive force on a dominant Yankee team that again won 102 games, this year beating out second-place Detroit by 13 games.

The 1937 World Series would again feature the Yankees and Giants, and the perception that the National Leaguers were overmatched did not take long to be proven correct. In Game One at the Stadium, DiMaggio singled in the Yankees first two runs in a game they would win 8-1. They took the next two games by scores of 8-1 and 5-1, but the Giants put off elimination with a 7-3 victory in Game Four. The next day at the Polo Grounds Joe helped drive a nail in the Giants' coffin with a solo home run in the 4-2 win to give the Yankees their first back-to-back titles since 1928.

In just two seasons, DiMaggio had become a major celebrity, due in large part to his performance on the field with baseball's greatest team. But it was aided in part by the New York sporting press and the incredible mystique they had helped foster. He was beginning to become a regular at Toots Shor's restaurant/nightclub, which had become a haven for the sports world's elite. It was there that he was insulated, isolated, and even protected from those who sought to encroach on his privacy.

Over the winter of 1937–1938 DiMaggio engaged in a holdout more serious than the year before. In light of the season he had in 1937, he was seeking a $40,000 contract, while Ed Barrow was offering $25,000. The stalemate went on, and not only did DiMaggio miss all of spring training, he was still unsigned come Opening Day. When it didn't appear that either side would budge, Joe relented and signed the $25,000 contract on April 25. He was back in the Yankee lineup on April 30.

It was early in the season that manager McCarthy shuffled the batting order and began utilizing DiMaggio in the cleanup spot, where he would spend virtually the rest of his career. The Yankees trailed Cleveland in the first half of the season, but overtook them for good by August. In the end, New York's 99 wins prevailed over the second-place Red Sox by 8½ games. One prominent highlight for DiMaggio during the season was tying a major league record by slugging three triples in a game in Monte Pearson's 13-0 no-hitter versus Cleveland on August 27. With the team heading to its third consecutive World Series, Joe reigned as their triple crown leader, pacing the Yanks with 32 homers, 140 RBIs, and a .324 average.

The Series commenced on October 5 against the Cubs at Wrigley Field, but it was the following day in Game Two that DiMaggio made his biggest impact. In his first at-bat Joe singled and eventually scored the Yankees' first run on a ground ball. Then in the top of the ninth with New York clinging to a one-run lead, he hit a two-run home run to make it 6-3, which stood as the final score. The Cubs offered little resistance in the Yankees four-game sweep.

DiMaggio settled for a modest raise in pay up to $27,500 for 1939, signing early and arriving in camp as it began. He suffered a calf injury running to field a ball in late April, and was sidelined for the entire month of May. When he was able to rejoin them in early June, the team had hit its stride and was dominating the league with relative ease.

DiMaggio had a front row seat on July 4, 1939, to one of baseball's most poignant moments. He was deeply touched as his elder teammate and hero Lou Gehrig was honored at a ceremony at home plate just after the diagnosis of his incurable disease.

Throughout the summer of 1939, DiMaggio was hitting at a frantic pace, even flirting with .400 into September. He went on to win his first A.L. batting title at .381, beating out runner-up Jimmie Foxx's .360. Joe also experienced a thrill by hitting a home run in that year's All-Star Game held at Yankee Stadium on July 11, which helped the A.L. win 3-1.

With the Yankees capturing the A.L. flag yet again, this time by 17 games, they were set to take on a new opponent, the Cincinnati Reds in October. DiMaggio would be appearing in the fourth World Series in his four years with the club. The heavily favored Yankees jumped out to a two-games-to-none lead in the first two games at New York, then moved on to Cincinnati.

At Crosley Field in Game Three, DiMaggio drove a two-run home run to straightaway center field to give the Yankees a 4-3 lead in a game that they went on to win 7-3. The next game, October 8, the Reds tried to hold off elimination as the game was tied 4-4 going into extra innings. DiMaggio singled in the go-ahead run in the tenth, then scored that same inning as the Yankees clinched a record fourth straight world title.

A few weeks later Joe learned that he had been named the Most Valuable Player of the American League for 1939. Although it was widely accepted that he was one of the truly elite players in the league, the award served as an official recognition of his status. He added a personal milestone to his remarkable year by marrying actress Dorothy Arnold in what turned out to be a major social event in Joe's San Francisco neighborhood.

As the Yankees were just a couple of days away from opening their 1940 season, DiMaggio strained ligaments in his right knee in a final exhibition game against Brooklyn. As had happened in three of the previous four seasons, he would not be available for opening day. He returned to action in early May only to find the Yankees struggling. As the season went on they found themselves flirting with first place in August and early September, but ultimately couldn't keep pace and finished third behind Detroit and Cleveland. Despite winning his second straight batting title and driving in 133 runs, Joe faced the unfamiliar prospect of going home at the end of the regular season.

Likely no player in history had performed more impressively overall in his first five seasons than DiMaggio had, yet his sixth season, 1941 would forever stand as his defining year. It is somewhat ironic that just prior to embarking on the incredible streak that would be his most enduring achievement, he was mired in the worst slump of his major league career to that point. The Yankees as a team were underachieving as well.

But on May 15, DiMaggio began hitting and very shortly after, the team began winning. By the time he had hit in his 37th straight game on June 25, the Yankees had climbed back into first place for the first time since April. Joe's streak didn't start to receive a lot of attention in the press until early June, but as the weeks went on it almost became a national obsession. Fans across the country began following the progress of the streak on a daily basis. He passed George Sisler's American League record of hitting in 41 straight games on June 29 in Washington, and only Wee Willie Keeler's major league mark of 44 was left to pass.

It came in grand fashion three days later on July 2, as DiMaggio slugged a three-run homer to help beat Boston 8-4. For more than two weeks he would continue to add to his own remarkable feat. On July 16 against the Indians in Cleveland, Joe extended the streak to the now-fabled 56 with a double, two singles, and three runs scored in New York's 10-3 win.

The next night, more than 67,000 fans filed into Cleveland's Municipal Stadium to see if the amazing run could be extended further. But three groundouts, two of them fine plays by Ken Keltner at third base, and one base on balls meant that the streak was finally over. Remarkably, after going hitless on that July 17, Joe began a new streak that lasted 16 games. DiMaggio said later that stopping at 56 instead of 57 may have cost him thousands of dollars because the Heinz-57 Varieties company would have given him an endorsement deal.

During the streak, DiMaggio batted .408 and the Yankees went 41-13, climbing from fourth place to first. With Joe leading the way, New York opened up a huge lead and managed to clinch on September 4, three-and-a-half weeks before the season closed. In the National League, the Brooklyn Dodgers had risen from years in the depths of the standings to claim their first pennant in 21 years. The year 1941 marked the first of seven meetings of Brooklyn and the Yankees in the World Series.

The teams split the first two games at Yankee Stadium and moved on to Ebbets Field. There, DiMaggio broke a scoreless tie in the eighth inning when he singled to center, scoring Red Rolfe, and New York squeaked out a 2-1 win. The next day with Brooklyn trying to even the Series, a play that would stand for all time as this Fall Classic's signature moment occurred with two out in the Yankee ninth.

With a 4-3 lead, Brooklyn pitcher Hugh Casey retired the first two Yankee batters in the ninth. Tommy Henrich swung at strike three for what would have ended the game, but catcher Mickey Owen couldn't handle it and Henrich was safe at first. DiMaggio then singled, and both he and Henrich scored on Charlie Keller's double to take the lead. The Yankees had a four-run inning to make it 7-3, and the Dodgers went quietly in the bottom of the ninth inning as New York took a commanding three-to-one lead in the Series. They made it official at Ebbets Field the following day, October 6, capturing the title on the strength of a 3-1 win. DiMaggio could call himself a World Champion for the fifth time in six years in the major leagues.

Six weeks later he learned that he had won his second straight A.L. MVP Award. DiMaggio had edged out Ted Williams, who had also garnered a great deal of attention for his .406 batting average. The two men developed a mutual respect and admiration and would be linked together for the rest of their lives.

At the dawn of 1942, the United States had already become fully engaged in World War II, but DiMaggio at this time was not subject to the draft due to his marital status. He reported to training camp in St. Petersburg and had agreed to a contract that would pay him $42,000 for that season. Though he would have one of his healthiest seasons that year, appearing in all 154 Yankee games, he slumped badly in the first half of the season. After what he had accomplished the previous year, expectations were extremely high and a .305 average, 21 home runs, and 114 RBIs seemed sub-par for DiMaggio. Luckily, very solid seasons from Joe Gordon and Charlie Keller, as well as a pitching staff that led the league in ERA, contributed to 103 wins and another A.L. pennant.

The St. Louis Cardinals would be providing the opposition in the World Series, and the Yankees were heavily favored over the much younger National Leaguers. Game One at Sportsman's Park only served to justify the expert's opinions as old pro Red Ruffing held the Cardinals scoreless until the ninth inning in the Yankees 7-4 win. DiMaggio stroked three singles and scored two runs in the win.

But somehow the tide turned. St. Louis came back and shocked the Yankees and their fans by winning the next four games to take the Series. The final indignity was watching Cardinal rookie Whitey Kurowski hit a two-run home run in the ninth inning of the final game to break a 2-2 tie. DiMaggio was on the losing end of a World Series for the only time in his career.

Believing he would eventually be drafted, Joe enlisted in the Army in mid-February of 1943. He was stationed in California and was promoted to the rank of sergeant later that fall. DiMaggio was transferred to Hawaii in 1944, and after a couple of hospitalizations for a serious ulcer problem, he was reassigned to Atlantic City. He was finally discharged in mid-September 1945, but the Yankees were just about out of the race and Joe was encouraged to rest up for 1946.

As the 1946 season was set to begin, baseball observers were curious as to how a player like DiMaggio would be affected by the loss of three seasons to military service. Joe created positive attention on Opening Day as he homered in the Yankees' 5-0 win over the Athletics. He appeared to have not missed a beat as he had 20 home runs by the end of May. He then fell into a bit of a slump, and then in early July he injured his knee and ankle sliding into second base. He was out of action for a month, and when he returned in early August it was clear that Boston and Detroit were forces to be reckoned with in the American League. New York couldn't quite get past them and ended up finishing in third place, 17 games behind the pennant-winning Red Sox. DiMaggio's numbers did not equal his prewar performance, ending with a .290 batting average, 25 home runs, and 95 RBIs. Unknown at the time was that Joe was suffering from heel spurs for the first time and surgery would be performed in January 1947. This would be a nagging problem in the later years of his career.

Due to a slow recovery, DiMaggio was not able to appear in the first few games of 1947. When he finally made his first start on April 20 in Philadelphia he hit a three-run home run to help beat the Athletics 6-2. Throughout the season he suffered from a variety of physical woes that included not only his heel, but his shoulder, neck, and right elbow. DiMaggio compiled a .315 batting average, and though his 20 home runs and 97 RBIs seem relatively modest by his standards, there were numerous games in which he delivered key hits and played a large role in victories. Under new manager Bucky Harris, the team's balanced attack returned them to the top of the league as they clinched the flag on September 15.

Despite the ailing right elbow which made throwing difficult, DiMaggio excelled in center field as usual. Remarkably he committed only one error all season, when after catching a fly ball he threw to first base to double off the runner but no one was covering the base.

Most importantly, DiMaggio was heading back to the World Series for the first time since the loss to the Cardinals in 1942. The Yankees would be facing their crosstown N.L. rival Dodgers, featuring rookie Jackie Robinson.

New York hosted the opener on September 30, and in the fifth inning down 1-0, DiMaggio singled for the first Yankee hit. A few batters later, he scored the first New York run on a Johnny Lindell double, and by inning's end the Yanks were up 5-1 and hung on to win 5-3. New York also captured Game Two and went to Brooklyn for what would be a wild affair in the third game.

Down 6-0 going into the top of the third, DiMaggio singled in the first Yankee run. Then in the fifth he hit a two-run home run to pull New York to within one run. The Dodgers hung on to win 9-8, preventing the Yankees from taking a 3-0 Series lead.

Brooklyn evened up the Series the next day when they spoiled Bill Bevens's no-hitter in the ninth, and Game Five would be held at Ebbets Field on October 4. DiMaggio slugged a solo home run in the fifth to make it 2-0, and though the Yankees only got five hits, they prevailed 2-1.

The Series moved back to Yankee Stadium for Game Six and DiMaggio was involved in one of the more noteworthy plays in Fall Classic history. Trailing 8-5 in the bottom of the sixth with two runners on, he hit a long fly ball to left that Al Gionfriddo caught up to, taking away what would have been a game-tying home run. Brooklyn would force a Game Seven with an 8-6 win.

Fine Yankee pitching the next day, including a great five-inning stint by Joe Page, gave New York a 5-2 win and their first world title in four years. DiMaggio was enjoying his first time back on top since the defeat of Brooklyn back in 1941.

A month after the conclusion of the Series, DiMaggio had surgery to remove bone chips from his throwing elbow. It was at that time that he learned that he had won the American League MVP Award for the third time in his illustrious career. Early in 1948, the team rewarded him for his performance with a new contract that called for him to earn $65,000, one of the highest figures in baseball at the time.

DiMaggio set out to prove he was worth every penny. He was slugging the ball at an extraordinary clip, even carrying the team almost single-handedly with his bat at times. He hit for the cycle on May 21 versus Chicago, then hit three home runs two days later, two of them coming off of the great Bob Feller. He reached the 300-homerun plateau against Detroit on September 16.

In the off-season DiMaggio had surgery to remove spurs from his right heel, very similar to the surgery he had on his left heel two years prior. The nagging, bothersome injuries were beginning to add up, making it extremely difficult for him to perform at his top level. But through it all, he showed tremendous heart by giving it his all every time he took the field. No one ever accused Joe DiMaggio of ever giving less than everything he had once the game began. The Yankees continued to be so appreciative of his efforts that a few weeks before Spring Training of 1949 began he was given the largest yearly salary in Yankee history. He would earn $100,000 for the season.

Joe reported to Spring Training in St. Petersburg and new manager Casey Stengel in early March, but began experiencing pain in his right heel early on. He tried to play through it, but the pain became too much. He continued to test the heel, but the pain would return the following day, until he finally saw an improvement by late June. He made his season debut at that time in Boston. DiMaggio showed with a vengeance that he was ready by hitting a total of four home runs in the three-game sweep over the Red Sox. He was also present as his younger brother Dominic established a Red Sox consecutive game hitting-streak record of 34, but also saw the Yankees end that streak during the series.

DiMaggio had performed extremely well during the second half of the season, but came down with pneumonia in mid-September as the Yankees were battling Boston for first place. He didn't return to action until October 1 against Boston in the final series of the season. That day at Yankee Stadium, "Joe DiMaggio Day" was held, and the guest of honor was presented gifts with a total value of more than $50,000.

With two games left to play, the Yankees trailed Boston by one mere game, and a New York sweep would leapfrog them over the Red Sox and into the World Series. Though DiMaggio was clearly not physically able to perform at his very best, his mere presence was an inspiration to the team. A pair of 5-4

Yankee wins did the trick, and the World Series shaped up as a repeat of the matchup from the 1941 and 1947 Series with the Brooklyn Dodgers serving as the opposition.

Each game would be hard-fought, but the Yankees managed to put the Dodgers away in five games. DiMaggio's big highlight came in the clincher, as he hit a sacrifice fly to start the scoring in the first inning and hit a solo home run in the fourth of the 10-6 win.

Things had appeared bleak for Joe at the beginning of the season, but it all concluded in the most positive manner. He was approaching his 35th birthday and was able to appear in only 76 games, but hit a respectable 14 home runs and had 67 RBIs. His batting average for his abbreviated season at .346 indicates that he was still an extremely skillful batsman. Through a combination of his performance and the inspiration he provided, he had given his team what they needed and, in the end, celebrated his seventh World Championship with the Yankees.

A month before Spring Training 1950 was to begin, DiMaggio signed another contract that would pay him $100,000 for the season. He reported to camp in reasonably good health and Stengel allowed him to play when felt well enough. He was still regarded as a crucial part of the Yankee success.

On Opening Day, New York came back from a 9-0 deficit to beat Boston 15-10, with DiMaggio contributing a triple, double, and single. Although he was not maintaining a very high batting average over the first couple months, he had amassed 16 home runs by the end of June.

For the final month and a half of the 1950 season, DiMaggio was pounding the ball the way fans had become accustomed. On September 10, with the Yankees making a gallant run at the pennant, Joe hit three home runs at Griffith Stadium in Washington against the Senators. No one had ever hit three homers in one game in the cavernous park.

With a fight down to the wire with both the Red Sox and Tigers, New York finally clinched the pennant on September 29, finishing three games in front of Detroit. Joe D. had his last "DiMaggio-like" season, leading the league in slugging percentage, finishing third in home runs with 32, and fifth in RBIs with 122. He narrowly missed leading the Yankees in both runs scored and RBIs, falling just two in each category behind Yogi Berra.

The young Philadelphia Phillies earned the right to their first World Series in 35 years by beating the Dodgers on the last day of the season and would host the opener on October 4. The Yankees took the first game 1-0, and were engaged in a pitcher's duel between Allie Reynolds and Robin Roberts in Game Two. With the score tied at one in the tenth inning DiMaggio hit a solo home run off Roberts that stood as the game-winner and sent the teams to Yankee Stadium for Game Three.

New York won the third game by one run also, and looked to clinch the Series on October 7. DiMaggio singled in the first inning of Game Four to drive in their second run; was hit by a pitch in the sixth and scored on a Bobby Brown triple; and singled in the eighth in his final at-bat. The heavily favored Yankees had done what most had expected by sweeping the Phillies for their second straight world title.

DiMaggio signed what would be his final $100,000 contract in February 1951, and reported to training camp that was held in Phoenix that spring. He mentioned to a reporter during an interview that first week that he was considering retiring after the season, particularly if he was unable to maintain his former level of play. He simply was not interested in merely hanging on. After that interview he was reluctant to discuss the matter, remaining noncommittal with the press for the rest of the season. This caused a great deal of speculation on DiMaggio's future throughout the duration of the year. Also, with young right fielder Mickey Mantle garnering a significant amount of attention in his rookie season, many saw him as a potential replacement for Joe.

DiMaggio's first home run of the season on April 27 versus Boston was the 350th of his career. The next day a home run and an RBI single helped to beat Washington 6-4.

But he was being plagued by an aching shoulder and bothersome neck, and also lost playing time with a leg injury in June. It was also in mid-June that his mother passed away, causing him to return home for a few days. He went on a modest streak upon his return and was named to his 13th All-Star team by Stengel, but missed that game as well as two weeks of regular games with an injury to his left calf.

Shortly after his return in late July he hit a home run to help beat Chicago, then hit two more to beat them again two days later. There were still good days ahead, such as his three-hit day in August to help beat the Tigers, or a week later when he homered and tripled in a 6-4 win over the Senators. Despite his injury-plagued season of ups and downs, he contributed to the Yankees pennant-clinching game on September 28 against Boston by hitting the 361st and final home run of his career.

With 12 home runs, 72 RBIs, and a .263 batting average for 1951, his name certainly wouldn't appear among any leaders. Much more importantly, it would appear on the World Series roster of the American League champions. Winning was always a priority with DiMaggio, and he would have one more chance to shine under the bright lights of October baseball and experience the satisfaction of yet another Yankee World Championship.

The Yankees had to wait a few days to find out which team they would be facing, and when the nearby New York Giants shocked Brooklyn in their three-game playoff, the stage was set. After splitting the first two games at Yankee Stadium, the Giants took Game Three across the river at the Polo Grounds.

The fourth game became crucial to the Yankees, hoping to avoid going down three games to one. It was times such as these that DiMaggio so often rose to the occasion. He had been hitless so far in the Series, but singled in his second at-bat this game. Then in the fifth inning he hit a two-run home run that put the Yankees ahead 4-1, on their way to a 6-2 win. It would be his eighth and final home run in World Series competition.

The next day, DiMaggio had a double, two singles, and three RBIs as the Yankees embarrassed the Giants 13-1 in front of their home crowd. They now were looking at a chance to wrap up the Series back in Yankee Stadium in Game Six on October 10.

Joe had been intentionally walked twice and scored a run as the Yankees had a 4-1 lead after six innings. He led off the eighth inning by slugging a double to right field, and the 61,711 fans at the Stadium had just witnessed DiMaggio's final swing in a major league game. The Giants rallied in the ninth, but the Yankees hung on to win 4-3 and Joe DiMaggio sat atop the baseball world for the ninth time in his 13-year career.

Speculation in the press was still rampant as to whether or not Joe would be in a Yankee uniform in 1952. Owners Dan Topping and Del Webb tried to convince him to come back one more year on any basis he desired for the same $100,000 he had been paid the previous three years. But DiMaggio had the wisdom to recognize the time was right to walk away. On December 11, 1951, he made the official announcement at a press conference at the Yankee executive office. He explained that his all-too-frequent injuries had taken away his ability to produce at a level that the team and the fans deserve. DiMaggio stated sadly, "I've played my last game of ball."

His accomplishments could now be written in stone for all time—the .325 lifetime batting average; the three MVP Awards; the nine World Championships; and maybe most remarkably of all, the 56-game hit streak. He would be remembered as the model of perfection on a baseball field, a hero to a gener-ation of fans, and an icon for as long as baseball is played.

In 1955, less than five years after he gracefully strode off a major league field for the final time, he stood at the podium in Cooperstown and accepted the bronze plaque that symbolized his lofty place in the game's history.

On June 8, 1969, the Yankees dedicated a plaque appropriately placed in the center field area of the Stadium honoring the great DiMaggio. It read:

JOE DIMAGGIO
NEW YORK YANKEES 1936–1951
THE YANKEE CLIPPER
HIT IN 56 CONSECUTIVE GAMES
"GREATEST LIVING PLAYER" IN BASEBALL'S
CENTENNIAL YEAR
IN RECOGNITION OF HIS SINGULAR EXCELLENCE
AND FOR HIS LEGACY OF GREATNESS
THIS PLAQUE DEDICATED TO JOE DIMAGGIO
BY MICKEY MANTLE IN A CEREMONY AT
YANKEE STADIUM ON JUNE 8, 1969

He had earned his stature in the world of sports, but Joe was always appreciative of the circumstances that allowed him to achieve such a position. Back on "Joe DiMaggio Day" at Yankee Stadium on October 1, 1949, he said, "I'd like to thank the good Lord for making me a Yankee."

Yankee fans are grateful for that fact as well.

JOHN FRANKLIN BAKER
PHILADELPHIA A.L. 1908-1914
NEW YORK A.L. 1916-1922

MEMBER OF CONNIE MACK'S FAMOUS
$100,000 INFIELD. LED AMERICAN LEAGUE
IN HOME-RUNS 1911-12-13, TIED IN 1914.
WON TWO WORLD SERIES GAMES FROM
GIANTS IN 1911 WITH HOME-RUNS THUS
GETTING NAME "HOME RUN" BAKER. PLAYED
IN SIX WORLD SERIES 1910-11-13-14-21-22.

Frank Baker

(Elected 1955)

The *American Heritage Dictionary* defines a home run as "a hit that allows the batter to make a complete circuit of the diamond and score a run." In the last 11 years of the "deadball era" no one in the American League accomplished this feat more than Frank Baker.

Playing the bulk of his career, including his prime, during the deadball era the 5-foot 11-inch, 173-pound Baker needed every bit of his 52-ounce bat to lead the American League in home runs. He led for four consecutive years (1911–1914), with a high of 12 in 1913. Ironically, although he was not the most proficient home run hitter of his day (he never led the majors) he will forever be remembered as "Home Run" Baker.

In 1911 Baker played third base in Connie Mack's famed $100,000 infield. Batting cleanup, Baker led the American League with 11 round-trippers that season, but he didn't earn his nickname until his heroics in the World Series. In the bottom of the sixth inning of Game Two with the score tied 1-1 Eddie Collins doubled. Baker was up next and deposited an inside fastball from future Hall of Famer Rube Marquard into the right field bleachers to put Philadelphia up for good 3-1. The scene switched the next day as the A's traveled to New York for Game Three. The morning paper quoted Christy Mathewson as saying that Marquard's pitch selection was bad and that the correct way to pitch to Baker was outside. Later that day Mathewson, another future Hall of Famer, would pitch and carry a 1-0 shutout into the ninth. With one out Baker stepped up and deposited another homer to right field to tie the score—so much for Mathewson's theory. Philadelphia would go on to win the game in eleven innings and Baker's heroics will always be remembered in baseball folklore, for at that moment he became "Home Run" Baker.

After losing the 1914 Series to the "Miracle" Boston Braves, Connie Mack decided to sell off his stars rather than pay them more or lose them to the rival Federal League. Although Baker stayed he would never again play for Philadelphia. Following a contract dispute Baker announced his retirement on February 16, 1915, and sat out the year. In what was the transaction of the winter, Mack eventually sold Baker to the Yankees for a sum reportedly between $35,000–$37,500.

Baker came to the Yankees in 1916 having led the league in triples once, RBIs twice, and home runs four times. He had played in four World Series resulting in three championships and had earned an unforgettable nickname. Although he never led the league in an offensive category again, Baker became the Yankees best offensive player and their biggest drawing card prior to Babe Ruth's arrival. While with the Yankees he was in the top five in the league in home runs from 1916–1919, finishing second twice and no worse than fourth. In 1916 he finished fifth in slugging percentage while in 1918 he finished in the top five in batting average, at-bats, hits, doubles, total bases, and extra base hits. That year Baker also finished in the top 10 in slugging percentage, runs scored, and RBIs. The 1919 season was much of the same as he finished second in at-bats and in the top 10 in hits, total bases, and RBIs. While he was no longer a league leader, Baker's name littered the Yankee team leader board. In the four years between 1916 and 1919 he led the team in batting average and hits three times each. Twice he led the team in doubles, RBIs, games, total bases, and home runs. He also led once in at-bats and extra base hits.

From 1909 through 1919 Frank Baker's 80 home runs led the American League. Proving he was more than just a power threat during that span he was also second behind Ty Cobb in RBIs and fourth in hits behind Cobb, Tris Speaker, and Eddie Collins, all future Hall of Famers.

Baker sat out the 1920 season to care for his young children when his wife became ill and died. While he was out the new Yankee drawing card and home run king was just getting warmed up, as he hit 54 home runs to welcome in the "live ball" era. Ruth's 1920 total was more than half of Baker's career total of 96. A few years earlier, when Babe was a youthful Boston pitcher, the current home run king singled off the future home run king. Years later, when asked how many home runs he would have hit with a "lively" ball, Baker answered, "I'd say 50 anyway, the year I hit 12 I also hit the right field fence at Shibe Park 38 times."

Baker returned to the game in 1921 to help the Yankees capture their first pennant, playing 83 games at third base in a platoon role. He had two hits in eight at-bats as the Yankees fell to the crosstown rival New York Giants in the

World Series. Baker's platoon role continued in 1922 as he split time at third with Joe Dugan in what would be his final season. His final at-bat was a ground out in the World Series as the Yankees fell again to the Giants. Baker finished his career as one of the best World Series performers of all time. In 25 games he batted .363, had 18 RBIs, and hit three home runs.

During his career Frank "Home Run" Baker established 41 records (15 American League records, two major league records, and 24 World Series records). Although most of these have been tied or broken, Baker retired as one of the best offensive powers of his time and the greatest World Series performer up to that point.

After he retired Baker managed Easton, Maryland, of the Eastern Shore League to two last-place finishes. While managing, he discovered and signed a burly kid whom he would eventually send to Philadelphia. The kid, who went on to become one of the greatest sluggers of all time, was future Hall of Famer Jimmie Foxx.

Frank Baker was elected by the Veterans Committee and inducted into the Hall of Fame in 1955. Baker raised horses on his Maryland farm until his death in 1963.

ARTHUR CHARLES (DAZZY) VANCE
BROOKLYN N.L. 1922 TO 1932, 1935
PITTSBURGH N.L. ~ NEW YORK A.L.
ST. LOUIS N.L. ~ CINCINNATI N.L.

FIRST PITCHER IN N.L. TO LEAD IN
STRIKEOUTS FOR 7 STRAIGHT YEARS, 1922 TO
1928. LED LEAGUE WITH 28 VICTORIES IN
1924; 22 IN 1925. WON 15 STRAIGHT IN 1924.
PITCHED NO-HIT GAME AGAINST PHILLIES,
1925. MOST VALUABLE PLAYER N.L. 1924.

Dazzy Vance
(Elected 1955)

Though his main claims to baseball fame came while wearing other uniforms, it was the several formative pitching years that he spent in the Yankee organization that helped Dazzy Vance go on to achieve that success.

The native of Orient, Iowa, with a "dazzling" fastball had made his major league debut with the Pittsburgh Pirates in the spring of 1915. Large for those times at 6 foot 2 inches and 200 pounds, the right-hander distinguished himself enough in training camp that the team gave him the assignment of starting the third game of the regular season in Cincinnati on April 16. Unfortunately, Vance could be as wild as he was fast in those early years, and in that debut game he had walked five and hit a batter by the third inning and was removed. One week later, before he got a chance to pitch in another game, the Pirates sold him to the minor league St. Joseph, Missouri, team of the Western League. In his first game with that squad, he pitched a three-hit 1-0 complete-game shutout against Omaha.

Vance remained in the St. Joseph rotation for most of the summer until the Yankees purchased the phenom on August 23, 1915. He reported to manager "Wild" Bill Donovan, who had compiled an impressive pitching career of his own, and had managed Babe Ruth with Providence the season before. Donovan inserted Vance into his first Yankee game on August 28 against Ty Cobb's Tigers in Detroit in relief of Ray Fisher, one of the team's top starters. Dazzy pitched the final two innings and allowed only one hit and no runs. He faced Hall of Fame outfielder Sam Crawford with the bases loaded, partially due to errors, and induced him to pop up.

Vance's next two appearances came in relief in both games of a double-header against Washington on September 9 at New York. He would showcase his blinding speed to New York fans for the first time that day, pitching the final inning of each game and giving up no hits or runs.

Without even a day of rest, Donovan then gave Vance his first starting assignment the next day, September 10 against St. Louis at New York. He made a good impression overall, despite coming up short in the 3-1 loss. Vance pitched all nine innings, gave up only two earned runs and six hits while striking out six. He even got his bat into the act by slugging a double. New York beat writer Harry Dix Cole wrote "his work was quite impressive."

Eight days later, Vance was given another starting assignment at the Polo Grounds, this time with the unenviable task of facing Shoeless Joe Jackson, Eddie Collins, and the Chicago White Sox. The rookie hurler had his hands full and was tagged with the 7-3 loss. After one more relief appearance at home versus the Browns, he was given what would be his final start of the season on September 24 against Nap Lajoie's Indians in New York. In his eight innings of work he allowed seven hits but also sent seven batters down on strikes. With little support he lost the game 4-1, and it was written that he "got a bad start but pitched fairly well."

Vance's final appearance of the season came in the last game of the year, facing the pennant-winning Boston Red Sox. This may have been his finest performance in a major league uniform to this point. Coming on in relief to start the fourth inning he pitched four scoreless innings, giving up only one hit and issuing no walks. He also managed to retire the great Tris Speaker. Observers at the Polo Grounds were duly impressed, and Yankee fans had every reason to believe that his scorching fastball might be a fixture in the New York rotation the following season.

Over the winter Vance suffered an injury to his pitching elbow while boxing that would set his progress back for some time. He was with the Yankees in training camp in Macon, Georgia, in the spring of 1916, but was having serious problems with the elbow. Manager Donovan, recognizing his potential, gave him many chances, but it was clear Vance would not be ready. The team sent him to several specialists to be examined, and few gave him much hope of coming back 100 percent. Yet the Yankees stuck with him and eventually assigned him to Columbus of the American Association, where he was only able to appear in 14 games.

For 1917 the Yankees had Vance split time between Toledo and Memphis. He started off the 1918 season back with Memphis, but got the call in late June to return to the Yankees. He rejoined the team, now managed by Miller Huggins and featuring the great third baseman Frank Baker. Vance got into his first game on July 2 at Philadelphia, coming on in relief late in the game and

pitching scoreless ball. Back at the Polo Grounds two weeks later, he did mop-up work in relief in a lopsided Detroit victory. In *The Sporting News*'s July 25 issue that season there was a photo of him in his Yankee uniform, along with those of several other young major league hopefuls, and he was called "a pitcher of considerable natural ability."

By early August he was transferred to Rochester of the International League, as the minor league team had lost several players to World War I and was desperate for pitching.

In early 1919 Vance received a good offer to pitch for Sacramento of the Pacific Coast League and opted to sign. Had the Yankees been able to retain him a bit longer, Dazzy may well have become a key member of the pitching staff of several championship teams. Instead, after starting to improve his control he blossomed not far away in Brooklyn with the Dodgers. He dominated his league in the 1920s, leading in strikeouts for seven straight seasons. By the time he had thrown his last fastball in 1935, only seven pitchers in the history of baseball had struck out more batters. Dazzy would never forget that the first several of those strikeouts came while wearing the New York Yankee uniform, and the years he spent with the organization were essential building blocks to his future success.

In 1955 the Hall of Fame's Veterans Committee made Vance the fourth man to have pitched for the Yankees to be enshrined in Cooperstown. On July 25 of that year, he was formally inducted, along with ex-Yankee teammate Frank Baker.

Vance passed away in Homosassa Springs, Florida, in 1961, two weeks before his 70th birthday.

WILLIAM MALCOLM DICKEY
NEW YORK A.L. 1928-1946

SET RECORD BY CATCHING 100 OR MORE
GAMES 13 SUCCESSIVE SEASONS. PLAYED
WITH YANKEES, CHAMPIONS OF 1932-36-37-
38-39-41-42-43, WHEN CLUB WON 7 WORLD
SERIES TITLES. HOLDS NUMEROUS WORLD
SERIES RECORDS FOR CATCHERS, INCLUDING
MOST GAMES, 38. PLAYED ON 8 ALL-STAR
TEAMS FROM 1932 TO 1946. LIFETIME
BATTING AVERAGE OF .313 IN 1789 GAMES.

Bill Dickey

(Elected 1954)

I n the tradition of great Yankee catchers, working backward from Thurman Munson to Elston Howard to Yogi Berra and beyond, it is Bill Dickey who stands as the original model. His excellent combination of potent offense and his particularly outstanding handling of pitchers prompted Bob Feller to say after having him as a batterymate in the All-Star Game, "If I could pitch to Bill Dickey I believe I could win 35 games a year."

A native of Louisiana who spent much of his youth in Arkansas, Dickey was spotted by Yankee scout Johnny Nee while catching for Jackson of the Cotton State League in 1927. Nee wired back to Yankee management of the 20-year-old prospect, "I'll quit scouting if this boy does not make good." By early September of that season, Dickey's name was on a Yankee contract.

The young catcher attended Spring Training with the Yankees in 1928 and made a big impression on manager Miller Huggins, particularly with his deadly accurate throwing arm. It was decided however that he would benefit from just a bit more seasoning as he did stints that season with Little Rock and Buffalo. Dickey was recalled by New York in August and saw his first action in a major league game on the 15th of that month versus the White Sox in front of the Yankee Stadium fans. It was in the third game that he appeared for the Yankees, August 28 against St. Louis, that he struck his first big-league hit, a triple off George Blaeholder. The following day versus the Tigers he doubled and scored his first run. In all in that 1928 season, Dickey appeared in just 10 games for the Yankees, who had captured their third straight A.L. pennant and would be meeting the St. Louis Cardinals in the World Series. Though he was placed on the Series roster, Dickey saw no playing time behind regular catcher Benny Bengough and his backup, Pat Collins, as New York swept St. Louis in four games. But Bill had gotten his feet wet at the major league level and was now poised to serve as the Yankees primary catcher for well over the next decade.

In the spring of 1929, Dickey not only took over as the staring catcher, he established himself as a star in the American League at 21 years old. Aside from his noteworthy defensive work, which included leading all A.L. catchers with 95 assists and 13 double plays, the lanky 6-foot 1-inch left-handed hitting southerner contributed 10 home runs, 65 RBIs, and an impressive .324 batting average. It was also this year, 1929, in which Dickey first donned his uniform number 8, which became a trademark that he much later passed on to a young Yogi Berra.

Dickey followed up his fine rookie season with another equally fine season in 1930, matching his RBI output of 65, and hitting at a .329 clip. He was beginning to be viewed by some as approaching the same class of backstop overall as Philadelphia Athletics superstar Mickey Cochrane. In 1931, Dickey achieved quite a distinction behind the plate by not allowing a single passed ball in his 125 games caught, in addition to leading all A.L. catchers in putouts (670) and fielding percentage (.996).

After having watched Cochrane's Athletics dominate the A.L. for the previous three seasons, Dickey finally had a chance to see postseason action in 1932. He had contributed to the pennant-winning cause with what had been to that point career highs in home runs (15) and RBIs (84). In what turned out to be an eventful four-game sweep over the Chicago Cubs, Dickey was not only flawless behind the plate, he was second to only his roommate Lou Gehrig with the bat in going 7 for 16 for a .438 clip. Like many of his noteworthy teammates had already done, Dickey could now wear the title of World Champion.

As the 1933 Yankees set out to defend their crown, Dickey played a big part of a very memorable game early in the season. On May 27 in New York the White Sox were leading the Yankees 11-3 going into the bottom of the eighth inning. New York came back with a 12-run rally in the bottom of the inning, which included a grand slam by Dickey as the Yankees ended up winning 15-11. By this time, Bill was generally regarded as the best overall catcher in the American League. He clearly had a knack for clutch hitting and was considered the heart of the Yankee defense. Dickey was extremely well respected by his pitchers and almost like having another coach on the field. He virtually ran the game from behind the plate.

When the first All-Star Game was organized and ultimately played on July 6, 1933, he had been selected as an A.L. representative. Although A.L. manager Connie Mack curiously left him on the bench the entire game,

Dickey would see plenty of All-Star Game action in years to come. In his first
All-Star at-bat the following year, Dickey had the distinction of breaking Carl
Hubbell's legendary act of striking out five future Hall of Famers by stroking
a single.

The Yankees finished second in the A.L. behind the Washington Senators
in 1933, though Dickey had a typically productive season. One of the unusual
highlights of the season came in the final game as Dickey witnessed a complete-
game victory thrown by the mighty Babe Ruth himself. It was the fifth and
final game Ruth had pitched for New York in his 14 seasons with the team.
Dickey had become close with his teammate Ruth, and often engaged in
games of bridge with him, Gehrig, and others on long train rides.

In both 1934 and 1935 the Yankees were bridesmaids again in the
American League, finishing second to Detroit each year. This merely allowed
Bill to get back to Arkansas a bit earlier to go quail hunting, which was one of
his favorite hobbies. But the arrival of young Joe DiMaggio in the spring of
1936 along with a jump in offensive production from Dickey helped to put the
Yankees on an unprecedented run of success. They gained revenge on the
Tigers by beating Detroit out for the pennant in 1936 by 18½ games. Dickey's
noticeable improvement at bat yielded 22 home runs, 99 runs scored, 107 RBIs,
a .362 batting average (third best in A.L.), and a very powerful .617 slugging
percentage. The Yankees were to be meeting the nearby rival Giants in what
would be Dickey's second Fall Classic.

In Game Two at the Polo Grounds, with the Yankees having lost Game
One, Dickey came through as one of their big offensive weapons. Batting fifth
in the order, he went three for five with five RBIs and three runs scored,
including a three-run home run in the ninth inning as the Yanks evened the
Series with a 16-4 blowout. Heading to the Bronx for the next three games the
Yankees captured two of three, then clinched the Series in Game Six across the
river at the Polo Grounds. Bill Dickey's Yanks reigned as World Champions for
the first time since 1932.

In 1937 Dickey achieved possibly his most impressive season in terms of
durability plus production. He appeared in a career-high 140 games and his
530 at-bats was 50 more than any other season. He compiled his best figures
in home runs (29), RBIs (133), and doubles (35, fourth best in the A.L), and
again he was a major component in the Yankees topping second-place Detroit
by 13 games. Again the Yanks were to face the Giants in the World Series, but
this time the road to the title seemed a bit smoother.

Doing some fine pitch-calling, Dickey sat behind the plate and collected
Lefty Gomez's six-hit, 8-1 win in Game One; Red Ruffing's 8-1 win in Game

Two; Monte Pearson's 5-1 win in Game Three; and Gomez's 4-2 Series-clincher in Game Five at the Polo Grounds. The Yankees were not only champions of New York City, they were champions of the world, and it was not a title they were ready to relinquish any time soon.

Dickey's typically spectacular performance in 1938 impressed MVP voters enough that he was deemed the second-most valuable player in the entire league behind only Red Sox slugger supreme Jimmie Foxx, who muscled out 50 home runs and 175 RBIs. But when it came to team accomplishments, Dickey's Yankees came out on top of surprising second-place Boston by a considerable margin. Next up on New York's Fall Classic schedule would be the Chicago Cubs, the team against whom Dickey saw his first World Series action six years prior.

The Series opened at Wrigley Field on October 5, 1938, and apparently it wasn't enough that Dickey called the pitches for Ruffing's 3-1, no-walk victory. He also managed to go four for four with an RBI, run scored, and even stole a base. New York prevailed again the next day and the Series shifted to the Stadium with a 2-0 lead. That day, Dickey caught Monte Pearson's complete-game, five-hitter, and Bill's solo home run in the eighth inning tacked on an insurance run in the 3-1 win. And without further ado, the Yankees completed the sweep the following day, October 9, as Ruffing worked a complete-game 8-3 victory for the Yankees' third straight title.

Unbeknownst to anyone at the time, Dickey's great friend and road roommate Lou Gehrig had just played his last World Series game. Come early May 1939, an unknown illness removed the great first baseman from the lineup, and when he received the official diagnosis weeks later, it was Dickey who was the first of the Yankees teammates to learn of the extent of the tragedy. Though it will forever remain the most enduring and heartfelt story from baseball that year, the Yankees went on to achieve an unprecedented feat on the field.

Again they beat out second-place Boston for the A.L. flag, this time by a full 17 games. Dickey contributed with what could be considered his last truly great season, hitting .302 with 24 home runs, 105 RBIs, and 98 runs scored. On July 26 he had one of his biggest days at the plate hitting three home runs against the St. Louis Browns. Dickey was thought of as a "catcher without peer" in the decade of the 1930s. And the Yankees of 1939 may well have been a team without peer. Many baseball historians now regard the 1939 edition as very possibly the greatest, most dominating team of all time.

The team was slated to face a new opponent in the Series, the Cincinnati Reds, and it turned out to be a mismatch. Game One in New York was the most closely contested, with the score tied at one going into the bottom of the ninth. With one out, Dickey singled up the middle to bring in Charlie Keller with the winning run. He also had an RBI single in Game Two in which the Yankees shut out the Reds 4-0.

Two days later, the two teams met for the first World Series game held in Cincinnati since the infamous Black Sox scandal of 1919. With New York leading 6-3 in the fifth inning, Dickey drilled a solo homer deep to right field to finish the scoring and give the Yankees a commanding 3-0 Series lead. The following day, the game remained scoreless until the top of the seventh when Charlie Keller led off the inning with a solo home run. Two batters later, Dickey added his second solo homer of the Series. The Reds managed to put off the inevitable by coming back later to tie the game at four, forcing extra innings. The Yankees put across three in the top of the tenth, however, and prevailed 7-4 for the Series sweep. They had now accomplished what no team had before them—four consecutive World Series titles.

Dickey had just come off a four-year span during which he had batted a combined .326, while averaging nearly 26 home runs and 115 RBIs per season. Turning 33 in 1940 he began to experience a decline in both his playing time and offensive production. The Yankees as a team in 1940 experienced a drop as well, perhaps not coincidentally, winning 88 games and finishing in third place, yet only two games behind pennant-winning Detroit. New York's impressive World Series string was broken temporarily, but they returned to the Fall Classic the following year after dominating the A.L. once more, this time by a margin of 17 games. Dickey's offensive numbers improved slightly over 1940, and for the 13th straight season he caught over 100 games, which stood as a major league record until equaled by Johnny Bench in 1980.

The surprising Brooklyn Dodgers won the 1941 N.L. pennant and would be meeting the Yankees in the Series for the first of numerous October matchups. In Game One at the Stadium, Ruffing threw Dickey a six-hit beauty, and Bill contributed an RBI double to help edge Brooklyn 3-2. One of the major highlights of the Series came in the ninth inning of Game Four with the Dodgers on the verge of going up two games to one. With two out, Tommy Henrich struck out but reached on Mickey Owen's passed ball. The Yankees' rally included Dickey walking and eventually scoring as New York won the game, and in Game Five the Series, to return to the top of the baseball world.

Dickey's playing time was further reduced in 1942, as he appeared in only 80 games behind the plate. His ability to handle pitchers and call a game were still top-notch, however. Ernie Bonham, who led the Yankee staff with 21 victories said, "I never have to shake Dickey off. I just let him pitch my game for me." At 35, Bill was still an important part of a team that totaled 103 wins, earning yet another Series invitation, this time versus the St. Louis Cardinals. And despite his part-time status during the 1942 season, manager Joe McCarthy saw to it that Dickey caught every inning of every Series game.

The Cardinals were the youngest team in the majors and were considerable underdogs to the far more experienced Yankees. In Game One at St. Louis, Ruffing went 8⅓ innings before he gave up his first hit, and though he faltered late, New York still hung on for a 7-4 win. The young Cardinals then shocked the Yankees by winning the next four games and Bill Dickey experienced his first World Series defeat. One year later, New York would have the chance to gain revenge on St. Louis, and as it turned out, veteran Dickey would come through as a significant part of the attack.

In Game One the teams were tied at two in the sixth inning when a wild pitch scored Frankie Crosetti and Dickey then singled home another run as the score stood 4-2 in the Yankees favor. The Cardinals bounced back to win Game Two, but heading into Game Five New York pulled out to a three-games-to-one advantage. Spud Chandler and Mort Cooper became locked in a pitchers duel in Game Five with no score heading into the sixth inning. With Charlie Keller on base, old Bill Dickey came up in what would be his final World Series game and deposited the ball over the right field wall for a 2-0 score that ultimately clinched the Series. Dickey had added to his many Fall Classic highlights with likely the most memorable of all. He had now appeared in eight World Series and been on the winning side a remarkable seven times.

After the Series ended, with the country fully engaged in World War II, Dickey enlisted in the U.S. Navy at 36 years of age. He enrolled in an officer's program and went on to serve two years in the Pacific. He rejoined the Yankees in the spring of 1946, and when longtime manager Joe McCarthy stepped down in mid-May, it was Dickey who was installed as his replacement. Bill had actually been offered managerial jobs with the Braves and Phillies earlier in the spring, but passed on them.

Dickey served as a player/manager through the summer of 1946, but stepped down as field boss on September 12. He simply felt the job wasn't for him and ended with a major league managerial record of 57-48. With his playing career concluded as of 1946, he left behind a resume worthy of the greatest catchers to have pulled on a mask: a .313 lifetime batting average; 202 home runs; 1,209 RBIs; a spot on 10 A.L. All-Star teams, even though the game was not created until his fifth full season; and helping to lead his team to eight World Series, seven of which resulted in Yankee victories. His Yankee career spanned two distinct eras of team greatness, from the Babe Ruth, Lou Gehrig, Tony Lazzeri days, to the Joe DiMaggio, Phil Rizzuto, Joe Gordon days.

Dickey had a positive impact on the future of Yankee catching when he came to Spring Training in 1949 and 1950 to tutor Yogi Berra, and also worked closely with Elston Howard in the spring of 1954. Berra thanked Dickey during his speech at the Hall of Fame when he was inducted in 1972 for "giving [me] pointers on catching that put me on the right track." Howard said humbly "Without Bill, I'm nobody, Nobody at all. He made me a catcher." Dickey stayed on as a coach through most of the 1950s, calling his return to the Yankees "one of the most satisfying moments of my life." He left the coaching staff in 1957, but returned as bullpen coach in 1960, staying on only until July.

In 1954, in what was surely a foregone conclusion, Dickey received 13 more than the required amount of votes from the baseball writers to solidify his place in the Baseball Hall of Fame. The Yankees honored Dickey along with Berra at the same time in 1972 by retiring uniform number 8 that both men wore while achieving so much.

Dickey passed away on November 12, 1993, at the age of 86 in Little Rock, Arkansas.

EDWARD GRANT BARROW

CLUB EXECUTIVE, MANAGER, LEAGUE
PRESIDENT IN MINORS AND MAJORS FROM
1894 TO 1945. CONVERTED BABE RUTH FROM
PITCHER TO OUTFIELDER AS MANAGER BOSTON
A.L. IN 1918. DISCOVERED HONUS WAGNER
AND MANY OTHER GREAT STARS. WON WORLD
SERIES IN 1918. BUILT NEW YORK YANKEES INTO
OUTSTANDING ORGANIZATION IN BASEBALL
AS BUSINESS MANAGER FROM 1920 TO 1945,
WINNING 14 PENNANTS, 10 WORLD SERIES.

Ed Barrow

(Elected 1953)

While Yankee Stadium is known as "The House that Ruth Built," the Yankees of the 1920s, 1930s, and 1940s could just as easily be known as "The Dynasty that Barrow Built."

The one constant in the team's success over the quarter of a century beginning in 1921 was its top-ranking executive Edward Grant Barrow. Hired late in 1920 by owners Jacob Ruppert and Tillinghast Huston as the Yankees business manager and secretary, Barrow essentially performed the duties of a general manager and was the architect of their original dynasty.

Barrow's rise to the distinction of being the most powerful front office man of his era in baseball began back in Ohio in the 1890s. He himself had never played above the semipro level, but displayed his organizational skills by forming a small league in that state. It was during this period that he is credited with discovering future all-time great shortstop Honus Wagner, who was playing for the circuit's Steubenville team. Barrow went on to become the president of the Atlantic League in 1896, remaining in that position for four years. He made his first foray into major league baseball when he was appointed manager of the Detroit Tigers in 1903. He was replaced in the midst of a mediocre 1904 season.

Barrow returned to the minor leagues, managing in Indianapolis in 1906, and winning a pennant with Toronto in 1907. A few years later, he became president of the Eastern League, which eventually changed its name to the International League. In 1914, he saw a young Babe Ruth make his debut in the league with Baltimore, and playing later that season with Providence of the same circuit. Barrow stepped down from the league presidency in 1917 when he was hired by Boston Red Sox owner Harry Frazee as the team's field manager. He found success immediately as his team, featuring a 23-year-old Ruth, beat the

Chicago Cubs to win the World Series. It was also under Barrow's watch in 1918 that Ruth began to make the transition from pitching to the outfield.

Barrow was a rough, tough, fearless, burly man with an explosive temper, and an oft-told incident with Ruth during 1918 helps to illustrate the point. The young Ruth, 27 years Barrow's junior, got into a verbal altercation with the manager and suggested that a fistfight might ensue. Barrow then called Babe into the clubhouse where he removed his jacket and gave him the opportunity to settle it right then and there. The young slugger wisely declined the chance at a physical altercation, sensing he might be overmatched. There were many that would admit however that while Barrow certainly had a gruff exterior, he also had a softer side as well. He could alternately be referred to as "Simon," as in Simon Legree, or to some, simply "Cousin Ed."

It was a year after Ruth had joined the Yankees that Barrow followed him to New York. Ruppert lured him away from the Red Sox and hired him as the Yankees' business manager on October 29, 1920. Assuming what were largely duties of a general manager, he immediately assured field manager Miller Huggins, whose job some felt was in jeopardy, that he would give him complete backing as field boss. Barrow was quoted in the *New York Times* as saying to Huggins, "You're the manager. You will get no second guessing from me. Your job is to win and my job is to see that you have players to win with. You tell me what you need and I'll make the deals. And I'll take full responsibility for every deal I make." Barrow also made it a point in the spring of 1921 to inform Yankee players in no uncertain terms that Huggins was the boss on and off the field. It is not a complete coincidence that New York won its first American League Championship in Barrow's first season with the team.

That first year he began to make personnel moves that helped shape the coming dynasty. His first major acquisition came just six weeks after joining the organization, as he brought future Hall of Fame pitcher Waite Hoyt along from the Red Sox. Hoyt paid dividends right away by winning 19 games in his first season with New York.

After the 1921 season, he brought more of his ex-Red Sox players in, trading for pitchers Joe Bush and Sam Jones, along with shortstop Everett Scott. Third baseman "Jumpin" Joe Dugan came from Boston after the 1922 season, and pitcher Herb Pennock from the Red Sox a few months later, as the nucleus of the Yankees first World Championship team was now in place. Along with helping to create a winning tradition on the field at that time, Barrow also had his hand in many aspects of the building of Yankee Stadium, which was set to open in the spring of 1923.

Barrow's standing within the baseball world was such that when A.L. president Ban Johnson stepped down in 1927 after nearly a three-decade reign, he was mentioned as a possible successor. "Cousin Ed," however, still had many championships to preside over. At the conclusion of the 1928 World Series, the Yankees had won six A.L. titles and three World Championships in Barrow's eight seasons at the helm. An editorial cartoon in *The Sporting News* in 1928 featured a caricature of him that stated, "Ed Barrow is the man who made the Yankees, though he receives no cheers from the fans." The accompanying article hailed him for assembling such a magnificent team. An interesting sidenote from this period is that in 1929 Barrow became the first major league executive to have numbers put on the back of his team's uniform. Within two years this would become the standard.

Barrow made a very shrewd move when he hired Joe McCarthy to take over as field manager before the 1931 season. McCarthy had been let go as manager of the Cubs by owner William Veeck after failing to bring his team back to the World Series in 1930 as he had in 1929. He had the chance to gain a measure of revenge against Chicago in 1932 as the Yankees triumphed over the Cubs in that year's Fall Classic in a four-game sweep. Barrow went on record many years later as saying that McCarthy was the greatest manager who ever lived, evidenced by seven World Championships in 15 years in the Yankee dugout.

In 1934, Barrow wisely took the advice of his staff and took a chance on a young Joe DiMaggio, despite a troublesome knee, and before long it was yet another feather in his cap. A decade earlier he had guessed correctly on another San Francisco native, infielder Tony Lazzeri, who had been known to suffer seizures.

By the mid-1930s, Barrow had helped to organize a productive minor league system for the team, having placed George Weiss in charge of that aspect. Owner Colonel Ruppert always wanted the best players he could buy or develop, and Weiss and Barrow were extremely adept at locating them. At the major league level, the Yankees were set to embark on their most successful period to that point, winning the first of an unprecedented four straight World Championships in 1936. It is an unfortunate consequence that a team that consisted of names such as Gehrig, DiMaggio, Lazzeri, Dickey, Gomez, and Ruffing would tend to obscure the name of its chief architect.

Ruppert had passed away a couple of months after the Yankees victory in the 1938 World Series, and on January 17, 1939, the board of directors elected Barrow as the team's president. He also continued his general manager duties, and New York went on to capture its fourth consecutive title that season. Titles were also added in 1941 and 1943, with a loss to St. Louis in the 1942 Series.

In January 1945, when Larry MacPhail, Dan Topping, and Del Webb purchased the Yankees from the Ruppert estate, Barrow stepped down as head of the team and became the chairman of the Board of Directors and acted primarily in an advisory capacity. His remarkable 24-year reign had come to a close, but the effect he had on the franchise is best defined by the 14 American League pennants, which resulted in 10 World Championships. It is arguable that no single player who wore the Yankee uniform had as much of an impact on the overall success of the team.

Barrow was still so highly thought of in baseball circles that when it came time to select a new commissioner in April 1945 to succeed the deceased Judge Landis, his name was mentioned. The 78-year-old Barrow turned down the offer, however, and finally fully retired from the game at the end of 1946. He wrote his autobiography in 1952 entitled *My Fifty Years in Baseball*.

Barrow was elected to the Hall of Fame by the Veterans Committee in September of 1953, just two-and-a-half months before his death in Port Chester, New York.

PAUL GLEE WANER
(BIG POISON)
PITTSBURGH-BROOKLYN-BOSTON, N.L.
NEW YORK, A.L.
1926-1945

LEFT HANDED HITTING OUTFIELDER BATTED
.300 OR BETTER 14 TIMES IN NATIONAL
LEAGUE. ONE OF SEVEN PLAYERS EVER TO
COMPILE 3,000 OR MORE HITS. SET MODERN
N.L. RECORD BY COLLECTING 200 OR MORE
HITS EIGHT SEASONS. MOST VALUABLE PLAYER
IN 1927 AND FOUR TIMES SELECTED FOR
ALL STAR GAME.

Paul Waner

(Elected 1952)

As the 1944 American League pennant race was coming down the homestretch with the Yankees battling for first place with the Browns and Tigers, manager Joe McCarthy was looking for any addition that might put them over the top. At the same time, longtime National League star Paul Waner became available after being placed on waivers in late August by the crosstown Brooklyn Dodgers. Unclaimed and subsequently released, the Yankees, seeking a left-handed hitter off the bench, signed Waner as a free agent on September 1, 1944. As pitcher and former teammate Burleigh Grimes had done 10 years earlier, Waner would be joining the Yankees after a very long and distinguished career spent exclusively in the N.L.

Forty-one years old at the time, Waner brought with him an extremely impressive resume. In 1942 he had stroked his 3,000th hit, becoming only the seventh player in history to reach the figure. By the time he had hooked on with the Yankees, only one player in the history of the National League, Honus Wagner, had accumulated more base hits than Waner's 3,151. He had won three N.L. batting titles and had amassed a whopping 603 doubles and 190 triples. In becoming a Yankee and an American Leaguer for the first time in his long career, he had hopes of one more trip to the World Series. His only appearance in the Fall Classic to that point was back in 1927 when the Yankees' famed "Murderer's Row" swept Waner's Pirates in four straight.

The 1944 A.L. pennant race was said at the time to be one of the most dramatic in history, and Waner wasted no time seeing action upon being signed. That day, McCarthy sent him up wearing number 24 on his home white uniform to pinch-hit for pitcher Steve Roser in the sixth inning versus Washington at the Stadium. The hitting master promptly delivered his first American League

single and RBI. On September 10, he batted for Frank Crosetti and subsequently scored a run that helped narrowly edge the Red Sox 4-3.

On September 18 in Detroit, fans that arrived at the ballpark early witnessed a rather unusual sight involving Waner. With southpaw Hal Newhouser set to pitch for the Tigers, manager McCarthy had the lefty-throwing Waner pitch batting practice to the Yankee hitters to help them adjust to the portside delivery.

By season's end, Waner had been used exclusively as a pinch hitter on nine occasions, though he was considered a competent backup outfielder if needed. Waner would not get a crack at the World Series in 1944, as the Browns went on to what would be their only A.L. pennant in their history.

After the conclusion of the season, Waner volunteered to do his part for the war effort by joining a small group of ballplayers that would go overseas to entertain U.S. troops. He then spent the winter at his home in Sarasota, Florida, still very much in the Yankee plans for 1945. Waner was late reporting to Spring Training, which was held in Atlantic City, New Jersey, as he had to tend to his 16-year-old daughter who was confined to bed with a serious hip injury. He finally saw his first training camp action on March 29 against the Red Sox and went on to pinch-hit several more times.

Opening Day for New York was scheduled to take place in Washington on April 16, Waner's 42nd birthday, but was postponed due to bad weather. Once the season commenced, six games went by without Paul seeing action. Finally on April 26, he pinch-hit in Philadelphia for pitcher Al Gettel and drew a base on balls in what would be his final appearance in a major league game. Another week would pass before McCarthy came to the conclusion that with Tucker Stainback and Bud Metheny on the bench, he simply couldn't give Waner enough at-bats to justify keeping him on the roster. On May 3 he was given his unconditional release. Many of his Yankee teammates were very sorry to see Waner go. His experienced batting eye and keen observations helped many hitters on the team to whom he had given advice. Two weeks later, a photo of Waner in *The Sporting News* showed him laboring at a burial vault company in Pittsburgh.

Though his time in a Yankee uniform was brief, it was while wearing the pinstripes that he managed to record the final hit, RBI, run scored, stolen base, and at-bat of his illustrious career.

Waner was rewarded with his rightful place in Cooperstown by the baseball writers in 1952. He was enshrined that summer in what would be his only trip to the tiny village of baseball immortality. Waner passed away 13 years later in Sarasota at the age of 62.

HERBERT J.(HERB) PENNOCK
OUTSTANDING LEFT HANDED PITCHER IN
THE A.L.AND EXECUTIVE OF PHILADELPHIA
N.L.CLUB.AMONG RARE FEW WHO MADE
JUMP FROM PREP SCHOOL TO MAJORS.SAW
22 YEARS SERVICE WITH PHILADELPHIA,
BOSTON AND NEW YORK TEAMS IN A.L.
RECORDED 240 VICTORIES,161 DEFEATS.
NEVER LOST A WORLD SERIES GAME,
WINNING FIVE.IN 1927,PITCHED 7¹/₃
INNINGS WITHOUT ALLOWING HIT IN
THIRD GAME OF SERIES.

Herb Pennock
(Elected 1948)

When Lefty Gomez first saw Herb Pennock pitch in 1930 he said, "If that guy can win 25 games in this league I can win 50." Not an overpowering pitcher, Pennock, who usually gave up more hits than innings pitched, relied instead on a smooth, slow delivery and great control. His soft curves created the illusion that he was easy to hit. Easy to hit maybe, easy to beat, hardly.

Pennock was dubbed "the Knight of Kennent Square" because he raised thoroughbreds and fox hounds in his home town of Kennent Square, Pennsylvania. He came to the majors directly from Wenonnah Military Academy and debuted with the Philadelphia Athletics in 1912. After showing some promise and having a brief appearance in the 1914 World Series against the "Miracle Braves," he was sold to the Red Sox in 1915 in a Connie Mack fire sale for $1,500. Mack stated at the time that he thought Pennock would eventually become a good pitcher but that he had pitchers who could help right away. It's a safe bet that Mack didn't realize just how good he would become.

After two mediocre seasons with the Red Sox Pennock went into the Navy for a year and missed the 1918 season. He returned in 1919 and pitched through the 1922 season for the lowly Red Sox, compiling a respectable 76-72 record for bad teams. Fortunately for Pennock he followed the footsteps of many of his teammates when he was sold to the Yankees. Harry Frazee, who by this time was so popular in New York City that he could have run for mayor, got rid of Pennock for three players and $50,000. Greatness for Pennock, a 29-year-old veteran with 10 years experience, was only a train ride away.

The 1923 season signaled the dawn of a new era for both Pennock and the Yankees, who welcomed the opening of their new stadium. Pennock's memories of their previous home, the Polo Grounds, included two forgettable moments. The previous September 4 he had yielded Babe Ruth's last regular season home run of the 1922 season, while a few years earlier he had given up Ruth's first home run as a Yankee, also at the Polo Grounds.

After losing the previous two World Series Championships to their crosstown rivals the New York Giants, Pennock was just what the Yankees needed to put them over the top. He didn't disappoint as he went 19-6 in 1923 and led the league in winning percentage at .760. More importantly, Pennock led the Yankees in the Series as he made three pitching appearances in five days, a feat unheard of for starters today. After dropping the first game, the Yankees' Series woes seem to have carried over from the previous season. Pennock would have none of it as he started and threw a complete-game 4-2 victory in Game Two as Ruth homered twice. He entered Game Four in the eighth inning and retired four of the five batters he faced to save the game. In Game Six Pennock was once again on the mound as he struck out six and walked none in seven innings. The 6-4 victory clinched the Series over the Giants and gave the Yankees their first ever World Championship.

Jack Conway of the *New York Daily Mirror* noted, "The Yankees can get along without Herb Pennock like an automobile without its gasoline, like a hunk of liver without its rasher of bacon, like a mud-turtle without it's shell. Pennock is the best left-hander in the business."

The 1924 season brought much of the same for Pennock as he posted a 21-9 record and finished fourth in the MVP voting. Pennock was among the league leaders as he finished second in wins and winning percentage, third in innings pitched, shutouts and complete games, and fourth in lowest opponent's on-base percentage. Unfortunately it was not enough as Washington nipped the Yankees for the pennant.

Pennock, who led the league in innings pitched with 277, finished 16-17 in 1925. Although his record wouldn't indicate it, his year was still respectable as the Yankees once again failed to win the pennant. Pennock finished second in ERA and third in lowest opponent's on-base percentage and complete games. He also finished fourth in games and fewest hits allowed per game and fifth in fewest walks per game. Pennock also finished 12th in the MVP voting in 1925—a testament to his effectiveness, considering his record was below .500.

The highlight of the season came on July 4, 1925, as he battled Lefty Grove in a 15-inning pitchers duel. Pennock yielded no walks and only four hits yet lost 1-0. He would later say that this game was his greatest thrill in baseball.

Pennock's record rebounded in 1926 as he posted a 23-11 mark and carried the Yankees to their first pennant in three years. While finishing fourth in the

MVP voting, Pennock led the league in lowest opponent's on-base percentage and fewest walks per game. He was also second in wins and winning percentage, third in innings pitched, and fifth in complete games. In the World Series Pennock was 2-0 with a 1.23 ERA. In Game One he was on the mound as 23-year-old Lou Gehrig made his Fall Classic debut. Pennock didn't disappoint the youngster as he picked up where he had left off in 1923 and threw a complete-game, three-hit masterpiece for the 2-1 victory. After allowing a run on a double and single in the first, Pennock settled down and allowed only four base runners and one hit the rest of the way. Although not playing in Game Four, Pennock sat and watched his good friend Babe Ruth swat three home runs to even the Series at two games apiece. Pennock was again on the hill for Game Five and after his Game One performance—though it is hard to believe he could equal it—he did. Pennock struck out four en route to a 10-inning, complete-game 3-2 victory. He also helped his cause at the plate. While trailing 1-0 in the sixth he doubled and later scored to tie the game. The Yankees won it in the tenth and held a seemingly insurmountable 3-2 Series lead. Unfortunately for the Yankees, Pennock could not pitch every game. After losing Game Six and trailing Game Seven 3-2 through six innings, they once again tried riding the arm of Herb Pennock to victory. Pennock performed admirably holding the Cardinals in check the rest of the way. Fortunately for the Cardinals the Yankees were unable to score again and the Series was theirs. Pennock's valiant effort went for naught.

While earning $20,000 as the game's highest-paid left-hander in 1927, Pennock went 19-8 for what most consider the greatest team of all time. His 19 victories equaled the number of games by which the Yankees won the pennant. As they faced off against the Pirates in the World Series, Pennock outdid himself once again in Game Three, his only Series appearance. He took a perfect game into the eighth, retiring the first 22 batters he faced. His perfect game was broken up by Pie Traynor who, ironically, would be elected to the Hall of Fame with Pennock some 21 years later. Pennock allowed only three hits and went on to another complete-game World Series victory, this time by an 8-1 score. His greatest World Series victory ever would also be his last. The Yankees would turn the trick the next day as they swept Pittsburgh and treated their fans to the first World Series Championship captured at Yankee Stadium and their second overall.

Although the first Mid-Summer Classic was still six years away, the Baseball Writers Association of America voted Pennock to the major league All-Star team in 1927 as its left-handed pitcher.

His 17-6 record in 1928 ended a three-year run which resulted in a 59-25 record and helped the Yankees once again capture the pennant, their fourth in six years. Pennock was once again amongst the league leaders as he finished second in ERA and fifth in shutouts. As luck would have it, a bad arm would prevent Pennock from pitching in the Series, thus not allowing him to continue his mastery in the Fall Classic. This year it wouldn't matter, as he sat back and enjoyed the show, the Yankees rolling over the Cardinals once again with a four-game sweep. Not only was this their second consecutive sweep of the World Series, it was payback for the 1926 Series loss to this same St. Louis team.

Pennock attempted to cure his sore arm through "bee sting therapy" as he exposed his arm to a swarm of bees, but after it swelled painfully there were no signs of improvement. He later told reporters, "All I can say is that nature intended self-respecting bees to spend their time getting honey out of flowers and not go drilling into a pitcher's arm." Pennock never again returned to his past glory following his injury. Over the next five years (1929–1933), he had a mediocre 47-33 record and never won more than 11 games again. As went Herb Pennock so went the Yankees; they failed to win the pennant from 1929 to 1931.

In 1932 the Yankees were on top once again. They won the pennant and swept the Series 4-0 over the Cubs. Although he didn't win any games in the Series, Pennock was still an integral part of the championship. He saved both Game Three and the clinching Game Four. In Game Three he witnessed both Ruth and Gehrig hit two home runs each (It was in this game that Ruth is said to have called his shot.) In a total of four innings pitched, Pennock allowed only one earned run on two hits while striking out four and walking one. His final World Series appearance came 18 years after his first in 1914.

In January 1933 when asked by some veteran baseball writers, "What do you think were the outstanding spots in the World Series?," Manager Joe McCarthy replied, "Babe Ruth calling his shot when he made his second homer in the third game and Herb Pennock's relief pitching."

Pennock finished out his Yankee career with a 7-4 record in 1933 as the Yankees lost the pennant to Washington by seven games. Pennock was released from the team with fellow Yankee and future Hall of Famer Joe Sewell.

At the time of his retirement Pennock owned or shared nine World Series records and arguably was the greatest World Series pitcher up to that point. He led the Yankees to their first World Series title in 1923 and went on to win three others with them. His career World Series mark is 5-0 with two saves and an enviable 1.95 ERA. All his Series wins and saves came as a Yankee.

Pennock is considered by many to be one of the great Yankees of all time. Miller Huggins referred to him as "the greatest left-hander of all-time." While with the team, he posted a 164-90 record en route to a career mark of 240-162.

This included a six-year span from 1923 through 1928 in which he went 115-57. In 1945, Yankee great and future Hall of Famer Bill Dickey was quoted as saying, "Pennock was so easy to catch I didn't give signals, I just sat there and caught the ball and threw it back." Pennock was named the greatest left-handed pitcher (an award he shares with Lefty Gomez) on the all-time Yankee team selected for its 50th anniversary.

After many years with the Red Sox in a variety of capacities, Pennock became the general manager of the Philadelphia Phillies. He held this post until his death, at the age of 53, from a cerebral hemorrhage on January 30, 1948, the 25th anniversary of his acquisition by the Yankees from the Red Sox.

Upon hearing about the death of his friend, Babe Ruth, who was only months away from his own passing, was quoted as saying, "He was a honey as a pitcher and a regular guy in every way, everybody was crazy about him. I bet Herb never made an enemy in all his life, he was tops." Years earlier Pennock had provided Ruth as well as others such as Gehrig, Lazzeri, and Combs with hitting advice when they were in slumps. His pitcher's insight provided an invaluable tool for his teammates.

Herbert Jefferies Pennock was elected to the baseball Hall of Fame on February 27, 1948, less than a month following his death.

CLARK C. GRIFFITH

ASSOCIATED WITH MAJOR LEAGUE BASEBALL
FOR MORE THAN 50 YEARS AS A PITCHER,
MANAGER AND EXECUTIVE. SERVED AS A
MEMBER OF THE CHICAGO AND CINCINNATI
TEAMS IN THE N.L. AND THE CHICAGO,
NEW YORK AND WASHINGTON CLUBS
IN THE A.L. COMPILED MORE THAN 200
VICTORIES AS A PITCHER, MANAGER OF THE
CINCINNATI N.L. AND CHICAGO, NEW YORK
AND WASHINGTON A.L. TEAMS FOR 20 YEARS.

Clark Griffith
(Elected 1946)

Not only did Clark Griffith help start the American League in 1901, he was instrumental in bringing success to the newly founded New York American League Baseball Club in 1903.

Born in a log cabin in 1869, he would spend 67 of his 85 years in baseball. After his parents moved to Bloomington, Indiana, from Clear Creek, Missouri, the young Griffith, who once held Jesse James's horse and trapped furs with his father, a commercial hunter, discovered his life's work.

After pitching a game for $10 in Hoopeston, Illinois, Griffith began his professional career with Bloomington of the Central-Interstate League. He earned $50 a month before he was sold to the Milwaukee Brewers of the Western League for $700.

In 1891, having made it to the majors, Griffith split time between St. Louis and Boston before he was released due to arm trouble. After a year and a half back in the minors playing for Oakland of the Pacific Coast League, Griffith landed in Chicago. Cap Anson had signed Griffith to pitch for the Colts, as the Cubs were known at that time.

From 1894 to 1899 Griffith won no fewer than 21 games per season as his six-pitch arsenal earned him the nickname "Old Fox." He claimed to have invented the screwball and regularly scuffed up the ball. Decades later Griffith helped lead the charge to ban all such pitches.

The ambitious Griffith learned under Anson's tutelage and served as the vice-president of the League Protective Players Association. In 1900, as players demanded a $3,000 minimum salary and uniform allowances from owners, Clark led the troops out on strike. Griffith convinced 39 players to jump ship and sign with the new upstart American League that was being formed by his good friend Ban Johnson.

266 THE PROUDEST YANKEES OF ALL

Griffith was awarded for his efforts and sent to Chicago to serve as the new team's player/manager. He led the team to the first ever pennant in the new league's history in 1901 as he posted a 24-7 mark.

On August 25, 1902, Ban Johnson announced that the A.L. intended to have a team in New York in 1903. After completing the 1902 season Griffith was once again called upon by Johnson, this time to lead the new A.L. presence in New York.

Griffith opened with his team in their inaugural season on April 23 in Washington, unfortunately the team fell 3-1. The home opener a week later produced different results as ace Jack Chesbro, who had lost a week earlier against the Senators, won 6-2.

On May 17, 1903, Griffith lost a 9-2 decision against Cleveland. The game was played in Columbus due to the Sunday ban on baseball in Cleveland. On June 3 he pitched what was described as a masterful six-hit shutout in a 2-1 win over St. Louis.

On June 16, Griffith recorded a 1-0 shutout over his old White Sox team. It was the first shutout for New York, and Clark finished the season at 14-11 with a 2.70 ERA. The *Sporting Life* issue of October 17, 1903, praised Griffith for having put the team together from scratch and finishing as high as fourth place, with a 72-62 record.

In the spring of 1904 Griffith declared that the team was 25 percent stronger than it had been the year before. In mid-April he said the pennant race would be the fiercest ever.

Opening Day was April 14 and the Highlanders beat Boston, the defending champs, 8-2, as Jack Chesbro posted the first of his record 41 wins. Griffith, who had been shelved with a sore wrist early in 1904, made his first appearance of the season on May 23. Serving in a relief role, he was given a huge ovation by the fans in Chicago as he still remained very popular there. Griffith recorded his only shutout of the season on June 12 as he blanked the White Sox 2-0. Offensively he contributed a double and a sacrifice.

While New York held onto first place in August, Boston and Chicago trailed close behind. As September rolled around the race began to heat up. Playing in St. Louis with a week to go in the season, Griffith came in to relieve Al Orth who had hurt his arm. He pitched 2⅔ scoreless innings to keep the Highlanders within one game of Boston. The final series of the season was in New York against Boston, with the pennant at stake. Their hopes were dashed when Jack Chesbro uncorked his infamous wild pitch and the team finished 1½ games out. After the season the New York papers praised Griffith for gallantly fighting until the last day.

Griffith's major strategic contribution to the game started to develop in 1905. While pitching his two stars Jack Chesbro and Jack Powell a staggering 845 innings, Clark made a career high 18 relief appearances. Griffith's reliance on the bullpen would revolutionize baseball. The 1905 season marked the last time Griffith would pitch on a regular basis.

The New York press reported that the 1904 team had encountered more than its share fair share of injuries. They expected the Highlanders to be in the thick of things in 1905. In late March Griffith brought Hal Chase into camp. Chase, who is regarded as one of the best defensive first basemen of all time, would go on to manage the Highlanders in 1910–1911 before being banned in late 1919.

Griffith's first game of 1905 was on April 27 as he threw a five-hit shutout over Philadelphia. It temporarily put New York into first place. The Highlanders were riddled with injuries and by late May they were floundering around last place. The situation was so bad that at one point New York had to borrow a catcher from the Athletics.

On July 14 Griffith filled in for left fielder Patsy Dougherty after he hurt his hand. It was the only time Griffith had played anywhere other than pitcher for the team. In late July and early August New York went on a 12-game winning streak which got the Highlanders back over .500 for the season. Griffith's final career shutout came in Washington on September 6 as he won 2-0. A week and a half later on September 16 he took a shutout into the tenth inning before yielding three runs to lose the game. The Highlanders faded late to finish 21½ games out. The most successful part of the season came when many players bet and made money on team owner Frank Farrell's horse that was named "Clark Griffith."

Griffith liked New York's chances in 1906, and in early April said that it was one of the finest teams he had yet managed. Wm. F. H. Koelsch wrote in *Sporting Life* on April 7 that "Griffith is deserving of much praise for his efforts since he came to New York, more than has yet been accorded him."

Griffith was involved in an interesting incident during a game on May 7. Umpire Tim Hurst punched Griffith in the mouth and subsequently received a five-game suspension. New York moved into second place on May 31 as Griffith won a 7-3 complete game over the A's. New York won their 11th straight game the next day to move into first place. This would be their second longest streak of the year as they would also win 15 straight at one point. On July 20, Griffith relieved for the final 3⅔ innings in a 5-4 win over Cleveland. It was the last victory of Clark Griffith's major league career. Koelsch wrote on

July 22 that ". . . his work against (Nap Lajoie's) sluggers again demonstrated that he is still a master of the art of crafty pitching."

The Highlanders finished the season in second place, three games out.

As the Highlanders finished a distant 21 games out in 1907, Griffith pitched in only four games, which resulted in no decisions. The lowlight of the season came on June 12 after New York committed 11 errors in a 14-6 loss at Detroit. Griffith got into a donnybrook with a fan after the game and was later charged with assault, but claimed self-defense and received only a fine.

The Highlanders got off to a good start in 1908 but skidded badly in June. Griffith was disheartened and discouraged by the team's slump, which saw them drop from first place on June 1 to fifth place on June 24. After the loss in Philadelphia on that day Griffith sent his resignation in writing to team owner Frank Farrell. Farrell immediately went to Philadelphia in an ultimately unsuccessful attempt to change his mind. Griffith took losing extremely hard and was beginning to wear down physically and mentally. He felt he should step aside and allow Farrell the chance to try another manager. Griffith had kind words for his replacement, Kid Elberfeld, and asked the team to give him their full support. After resigning, Griffith went to Europe for a much-needed rest.

Griffith went to the Reds and spent the next 47 years in a variety of capacities, most noteworthy the owner of the Washington Senators. Clark Griffith was considered one of the most respected player/managers of all time. Honus Wagner named him as one of the five best pitchers he ever faced and Ban Johnson said it was Griffith who picked most of the New York players in the franchise's infancy.

Noted New York sportswriter Dan Daniel wrote an impassioned plea in *The Sporting News* on February 17, 1944, in support of Griffiths' consideration for the Hall of Fame. This may have opened the eye of the Old-Timers Committee as they elected the "Old Fox" two years later.

On October 27, 1955, the Senators owner died of a massive stomach hemorrhage in Washington, D.C.

JOHN DWIGHT CHESBRO
"HAPPY JACK"
FAMED PITCHER WHO LED BOTH LEAGUES
IN PERCENTAGE-NATIONAL LEAGUE IN
1902; AMERICAN LEAGUE IN 1904. SERVED
WITH PITTSBURGH N.L. AND THE NEW YORK
AND BOSTON A.L. WON 41 GAMES, TOPS
IN MAJORS, IN 1904 AND DURING BIG
LEAGUE CAREER COMPILED 192 VICTORIES
WHILE LOSING ONLY 128.

Jack Chesbro

(Elected 1946)

While growing up in the small Massachusetts town of North Adams, little did Jack Chesbro know that Cooperstown, New York, a small village 100 miles west, would play a significant role in his future both before and after his death.

In 1896 Chesbro played semipro ball for Roanoke of the Virginia League until it folded on August 20. Jack then finished the year playing in Cooperstown, perhaps becoming the first Hall of Famer to pitch there on a regular basis. Fifty years later and 15 years after his death Chesbro would once again come to Cooperstown, this time embossed in bronze, and he would remain a permanent fixture.

He may also be the only Hall of Famer to get his nickname from a patient in an insane asylum. In 1894 while working for a state mental hospital in Middletown, New York, he was called "Happy Jack" by one of the patients. Chesbro worked with patients as he honed his skills on the hospital baseball team.

Chesbro, who had developed the spitball in 1902, was one of the first players signed by the newly formed New York American League club in 1903. Having led Pittsburgh to the pennant in 1901 and 1902, Chesbro was just what the Highlanders needed to compete with the rival New York Giants. Chesbro brought with him two consecutive 20-win seasons, with a league-leading 28 in 1902 as he won 12 consecutive games. He also had led the league in winning percentage and shutouts the last two years.

Chesbro also witnessed Pirates teammate Honus Wagner become the first player to steal home twice in a game in the new century on June 20, 1901. Earlier in his career Chesbro was traded to Louisville in a multiplayer deal which included Wagner and another future Hall of Famer, Rube Waddell, who went to

Pittsburgh. Almost half a century later Chesbro and Waddell were posthumously inducted into the Hall of Fame together.

Chesbro had the honor of pitching not only the first game in the history of the Highlanders, but also their first home game a week later. On April 23, 1903, Chesbro opened the inaugural season with a 3-1 loss at Washington. Eight days later on April 30, Chesbro returned the favor as he beat Washington 6-2. Chesbro finished 1903 with a 21-15 record as the team finished 17 games out.

On April 14, 1904, Jack Chesbro won the season opener on the way to a monumental season. During the 8-2 victory Chesbro had two hits, including a home run. On June 25 he won his 12th consecutive game (to tie his personal best) as he beat Cy Young and Boston 5-3. On the fourth of July Chesbro set an American League record as he won his 14th straight game, a record that stood until Walter Johnson broke it with 16 consecutive wins in 1912. Twelve days later Chesbro stole home in the bottom of the tenth inning to win his own game 9-8. After completing 30 games in a row, en route to 48 complete games, Chesbro was knocked out of a game by the White Sox on August 10.

Late in the season, the Highlanders were in a tight pennant race with the Boston Pilgrims (not yet known as the Red Sox). Chesbro beat Boston three times from mid-September to early October to give the Highlanders a half-game lead.

The two teams played a doubleheader on the last day of the season that would decide the pennant. Although Chesbro recorded one of the greatest pitching seasons ever, it would be all but forgotten with one pitch. With the score tied 2-2 in the top of the ninth and a man on third, Chesbro threw what may have been the most infamous pitch in history prior to Ralph Branca's "shot heard 'round the world" pitch to Bobby Thompson in 1951. The pitch, thought to be a spitball, sailed over the head of Highlander catcher Red Kleinow. It was scored a wild pitch but Chesbro and others thought it should have been a passed ball, as the catcher had made a half-hearted attempt to catch it. The runner on third scored and Boston won the game and the pennant. New York finished 1½ games out. This was the closest they would come to a pennant until they finally broke through in 1921. Long after his death in 1931 Chesbro's wife continued her efforts to try and overturn the official ruling, contesting that the "wild pitch" was actually a passed ball.

The New York press labeled Chesbro a goat and never let him forget it. Forgotten was the fact that Chesbro had one of, if not the greatest, seasons

ever by a pitcher. He finished with a 41-12 mark, leading the league in wins, winning percentage (.774), games (55), innings pitched (455), and complete games (48). Chesbro also led in fewest hits per game (6.7), lowest opponents batting average (.208), and lowest opponent's on-base percentage (.249). He was also second in strikeouts (239) and fourth in ERA (1.82).

Total Baseball stated that if the Cy Young and MVP Awards had existed in 1904 "Happy Jack" Chesbro would have won them both. To this day Chesbro still holds the modern major league record for wins (41) and complete games in a season (48). He also holds the modern American League record for innings pitched (455).

For the third consecutive Opening Day Chesbro was on the mound as he beat Washington to start the 1905 season. He would finish the season with a 19-15 record as the Highlanders finished 21½ games out. A noteworthy event occurred on August 30 as Ty Cobb made his major league debut. Chesbro was on the mound as Cobb got the first of his 4,191 hits.

Opening Day 1906 found Chesbro and Cy Young locked in a pitchers duel through eleven innings. New York pushed across an unearned run in the twelfth for the win. Future Hall of Famer John Montgomery Ward, a major New York baseball star in the nineteenth century, was on hand and threw out the first pitch. Jack would finish the season 23-17 as the Yankees finished three games out. He led the league in games with 49 and finished second in wins and fourth in innings pitched.

Chesbro pitched 1,407 innings (nearly half his career total) between 1903 and 1906, an average of approximately 350 per year. Fatigue and an ankle injury slowed him considerably in 1907 as he finished 10-10.

The next year wasn't any better as he finished 14-20 for a winning percentage of .412. However, this was much better than his team, which achieved a .313 winning percentage while finishing in last place. On July 25, 1908, Chesbro was involved in an odd event. During the eighth inning of a game with Detroit, New York manager Kid Elberfeld moved Chesbro from the mound to first base and brought first baseman Hal Chase in to pitch against left-handed batter Claude Rossman. Rossman flied out and Chesbro returned to the mound. This marked the only game that Chesbro ever played at first base and the first and last time Chase ever pitched. In August 1908 Chesbro and Chase were part of an All-Star team that played in Boston to celebrate "Cy Young Day." Years later Chase would be banned permanently from baseball for gambling, having played a role in the "Black Sox" World Series scandal of 1919.

Chesbro went 0-4 in 1909 before the team released him. Boston picked him up off of waivers on September 11, 1909. He would pitch and lose his only game with them before calling it quits.

Jack Chesbro retired to Conway, Massachusetts, where he became a chicken farmer. He also coached at Amherst College and played some semi-pro ball. In 1912 he attempted what would ultimately be an unsuccessful comeback with New York.

"Happy Jack" Chesbro was inducted into the Hall of Fame in 1946.

FRANK LEROY CHANCE

FAMOUS LEADER OF CHICAGO CUBS. WON
PENNANT WITH CUBS IN FIRST FULL SEASON
AS MANAGER IN 1906-THAT TEAM COMPILED
116 VICTORIES UNEQUALLED IN MAJOR
LEAGUE HISTORY-ALSO WON PENNANTS
IN 1907, 08 AND 1910 AND WORLD SERIES
WINNER IN 07 AND 08. STARTED WITH
CHICAGO IN 1898. ALSO MANAGER
NEW YORK A.L. AND BOSTON A.L.

Frank Chance

(Elected 1946)

eading the Cubs to pennants in 1906, 1907, 1908, and 1910 as player/manager earned Frank Chance the nickname "The Peerless Leader." Anchoring the famed "Tinker-to-Evers-to-Chance" double play combination, he was immortalized in Franklin Adams's poem "Baseball's Sad Lexicon" in 1908.

After initially attending the University of California to pursue dentistry, Chance transferred to Washington College in Irvington, California. After Cubs outfielder Bill Lange spotted Chance in a summer league he urged the club to sign him. They did, and Frank never spent a day in the minors.

Early in his career he was nicknamed "Husk" due to his husky build and aggressive play. Chance reached the majors in 1898 as an outfielder and part-time catcher and batted .279 in 53 games.

Chance continued in that role through the 1902 season and after Bill Hanlon left the team in the spring of 1903, Frank was installed as the Cubs new first baseman. Manager Frank Selee's intention to use Chance only until he could find a regular became unnecessary, as he proved to be up to the task. In addition to his defense, Chance's offensive production markedly increased. He batted .327 with 83 runs scored and 81 RBIs. In his first year as a full-time player he also led the National League with 67 stolen bases.

Chance's production remained consistent in 1904 and 1905. Due to illness, manager Selee left the team and Chance took over the role after winning a narrow vote by the players. Just 27 years old, Chance had been serving as road manager because Selee, who was suffering from tuberculosis, didn't make the trips. Under Chance's tutelage the Cubs were able to move up to third place by the end of the season.

In 1906, his first year as manager, Chance led the Cubs all the way to the pennant as they won a record 116 games. He had his most productive offensive season as he batted .319 while leading the league in runs (103) and stolen bases (57). In the World Series they lost to their crosstown rivals, the White Sox, in six games.

The Cubs returned to the World Series in 1907, this time finishing the deal as they stopped the Tigers. Chicago won its third straight pennant in 1908 and repeated as World Champs, once again sending the Tigers packing.

After finishing third in 1909 the Cubs captured their fourth pennant in five years in 1910. Unfortunately for Chance and the Cubs they fell to Connie Mack's A's in five games in the World Series.

On July 11, 1911, Chance left a game after suffering a blood clot in his brain. Despite 13 more appearances in his career his full-time playing days were over.

Chance had a talent for getting the most out of his players, as evidenced by his final two years as Cubs manager. In 1911 and 1912 he led his aging team to a second and third place finish respectively. Frustrated, during the 1912 campaign Chance quarreled with Cubs owner Charles Murphy about obtaining players.

After recovering from surgery to cure headaches caused by the blood clot, Chance was released by the Cubs on September 28, 1912. On November 9 Chance signed with the Reds but was later waived so he could pursue the New York manager's job. The Highlanders paid the Reds $1,500 for him on December 14, 1912, and he signed to manage the team on January 8, 1913. Receiving $12,000 per year for three years, Chance stated at the time that he would give New York a team worthy of its name. He inherited a team that had finished dead last in the A.L. the previous year, and the New York papers reported, "The coming of Chance to the Highlanders will stir up renewed interest in the A.L. here." Adding a figure like Chance to the A.L. was considered a great coup for the league.

In addition to the change in managers, the team also permanently changed its name, now officially known as the Yankees, and would be playing in the Giants' Polo Grounds after the lease expired on Hilltop Park. Frank Farrell's plans to build a new park eventually fell through and the Yankees remained at the Polo Grounds until 1923 when Yankee Stadium opened.

The team returned from Spring Training in Bermuda on April 3, 1913, and the Yankee players were very enthusiastic about Chance managing the club. On April 10, 1913, President Woodrow Wilson threw out the first pitch on opening day at Washington's National Park. Playing their first game under

their new moniker the Yankees lost 2-1 in Chance's managerial debut. In this game Walter Johnson began a string of what would become a record 55⅔ shutout innings. Seven days later before 25,000 at the Polo Grounds it was Washington who spoiled the Yankees home opener as they lost 9-3.

Chance played his first game in a New York uniform on April 22 against the A's in Philadelphia and went one for three. He played the next several days and hit safely in his first four games. On May 17 the White Sox held "Frank Chance Day" at Comiskey Park, and the guest of honor played one inning for his old hometown crowd. The Illinois governor and Chicago mayor were on hand and there was a tremendous outpouring from the fans, who still admired him greatly. On May 19 he singled, drove in two runs, and scored as the Yankees came from behind to win 8-6. This was his last major league hit.

In May he made two significant personnel changes. He acquired shortstop Roger Peckinpaugh from Cleveland and the new infielder would one day replace him as Yankee manager. On May 31 he accused Hal Chase of playing below his capability and traded him to the White Sox for Rollie Zeider and Babe Borton. Chase, who was known to be a gambler, remained on the scene for another six years before he was banned from baseball. Many felt Chance had rid the team of an unsavory character.

Without the right players to make a run in the standings the *Sporting Life* of September 13, 1913, noted that "Credit must be given manager Frank Chance for the great work he has accomplished in one season with the New York A.L. team. As a matter of fact he has entirely reconstructed the team and now has a really formidable aggregation. If anyone has taken the trouble to carefully watch Chance's work this season they have noticed the systematic manner in which he has built up the ball club."

The Yankees held their 1914 Spring Training in Houston as Chance felt that the Bermuda climate wasn't good for his players. On April 14, the Yankees beat the World Champion A's at the Polo Grounds on Opening Day. New York also won the next game on April 17 by a score of 4-0, which prompted Walter Johnson to report about a week later that he never saw such improvement in a team from one year to the next. Chance played his last game on April 21 versus Washington in New York, a 3-2 Yankee win.

In late April Chance was delighted with the spirit of his players and thought the team would really come around by season's end. In May, Ban Johnson expressed his extreme satisfaction with Chance and the job he was doing. The team remained above .500 until late May before floundering.

Chance, frustrated with owner Frank Farrell for not spending more money on better players so the team could compete, resigned on September 15.

Chance and Farrell had a conversation that day and after the owner paid him the balance of his 1914 salary they parted on friendly terms. Farrell said he was sad to see him go as he appointed Roger Peckinpaugh to replace him.

After that day's game, Chance said goodbye to his players and asked them to support Peckinpaugh. The last thing he said was "Work hard boys, and always remember that I'll be rooting for you."

Chance returned to California and operated an orange grove before returning to the majors with the Red Sox in 1923. He was slated to take over the White Sox when his health failed—he died on September 24, 1924.

Chance is regarded as one of the most successful player/managers of all time and in 1946 he was elected to the Hall of Fame alongside his former teammates Joe Tinker and Johnny Evers.

The old double play combination would be together forever.

WILLIE KEELER
"HIT 'EM WHERE THEY AINT!"
BASEBALL'S GREATEST PLACE-HITTER;
BEST BUNTER. BIG LEAGUE CAREER
1892 TO 1910 WITH N.Y. GIANTS,
BALTIMORE ORIOLES, BROOKLYN SUPERBAS,
N.Y. HIGHLANDERS. NATIONAL LEAGUE
BATTING CHAMPION '97-'98.

Willie Keeler

(Elected 1939)

S tanding only 5-foot 4-inches tall and weighing only 140 pounds, the diminutive "Wee" Willie Keeler was more than a giant on the baseball diamond—he was king. Dubbed the "King of the Place-Hitters," Keeler will forever be known for "hitting them where they ain't."

Born in Brooklyn on March 3, 1872, he was the son of a horse-drawn trolley car conductor. As a boy he was interested in little else but baseball and his teachers at Primary School 26 in Brooklyn told him that he would not amount to much. However, Keeler thought that earning a living playing baseball was a spectacular idea and he quit school in 1888 to pursue his goal.

Playing pitcher and third base for the semipro Brooklyn Acmes he made $1.50 per day. After an injury sidelined the regular third baseman of the Eastern Leagues Binghamton team, Keeler was recruited and began his professional career in 1892.

After hitting .373 in 93 games Wee Willie was acquired by the New York Giants for $800. After an ankle injury in 1893 he was again sold for $800, this time to Brooklyn. Imagine the thrill Keller must have felt, as he would be playing not only in New York but for his very own hometown team.

When he returned from his injury Keeler split time between Brooklyn and Binghamton for the rest of the season. That winter he was traded to Baltimore along with veteran Dan Brouthers who himself was also a future Hall of Famer. Baltimore manager Ned Hanlon moved the left-handed third baseman to right field and Keeler became a star. Despite his size, Keeler had a strong arm, possessed terrific speed, and was a brilliant defensive player. Former National League and American Association manager Theodore Sullivan once called Keeler "the greatest right fielder in the history of baseball."

As good as he was in the field it was his offensive skills that received the greatest raves. Willie choked up so much on his bat that Hall of Famer Sam Crawford once said, "He only used half his bat." As he pecked at the ball he used one of the smallest bats in major league history, a 29-ounce, 30-inch splinter. It was in Baltimore where Keeler and John McGraw perfected the hit-and-run play.

With his perfect bat control he would either slap the ball over the infielders heads if they played in close or lay down a bunt if they were back. Never a power threat, almost all of Keeler's home runs were the inside-the-park variety and as the ultimate slap hitter, 2,536 of his 2,932 hits were for singles. Keeler would also chop down on the ball and as it bounced off the hard infield dirt in Baltimore he would leg out a hit. This "Baltimore Chop," as it was called, is still referred to today. The great Honus Wagner was quoted as saying:

> Keeler could bunt any time he chose. If the third baseman came in for a tap, he invariably pushed the ball past the fielder. If he stayed back, he bunted. Also, he had a trick of hitting a high hopper to an infielder. The ball would bound so high that he was across the bag before he could be stopped.

In 1894 Keeler hit .371 with 165 runs scored, 94 RBIs, and 219 hits. This began a string of eight consecutive years in which he had at least 200 hits. Over the nine-year span from 1894 to 1902, Keeler batted .378, averaged 215 hits, and 134 runs per season as he played on five pennant-winning and three runner-up teams.

Playing for Baltimore in 1897 he enjoyed his finest season at the age of 25. Keeler hit .424, which was the fourth-highest batting average ever at that time and remains the fifth-best single season average in major league history. Playing in only 128 games he led the league with 239 hits and his 44-game hitting streak, since equaled by Pete Rose, stills stands as the National League record. Willie won a second batting title in 1898 as he hit .385 and again led the league with 216 hits.

After the Baltimore owners obtained control of the Brooklyn franchise, the manager and many of the star players left to play in New York. The combination of Baltimore and Brooklyn stars was just the right mix as they won the pennant in 1899 and again in 1900. In 1899 Willie led the league with 140 runs scored as his average fell to .379 and in 1900 he led the league in hits with 204 as he batted .362. When Abe Yager, a reporter for the *Brooklyn Eagle*, asked him to explain how he hit, Keeler replied, "Keep a clean eye and hit 'em where they ain't."

Rule changes in 1901 (which now called foul balls strikes) and 1902 (counting bunted third strikes as outs) hurt Keeler and the other "scientific" hitters. These changes, compounded with the fact that pitchers were using spitballs and the like, contributed to the drop in batting averages throughout the league. Keeler's average dropped to .339 in 1901 and .333 in 1902.

After the American League declared itself a major league in 1901, many National League stars were lured away with better pay. Although the N.L. salary cap was $2,400 per year, Keeler resisted all initial offers to jump ship. In 1903, however, the lure became too great, as the new A.L. franchise in New York came calling. Needing an immediate drawing card the Highlanders offered Keeler $10,000 per year and made him the highest-paid player in baseball. Keeler remains one of the few players to have played for all three New York professional baseball teams.

Although 31 at the time, the Highlanders were hoping Keeler still possessed some of the abilities he displayed for so many years in Baltimore and Brooklyn. Unlike many future stars who are obtained to secure a pennant, Keeler was obtained to help secure and build a franchise. The team knew what they were getting in Willie and paid him as much for his reputation and career .377 batting average as they did for his current abilities. "If you get him they will come" was the philosophy used by the Highlander management in obtaining the National League star.

In January 1903, Hall of Fame outfielder Joe Kelley said that he considered Keeler a better all-around player than Nap Lajoie, and thought he was the best player in baseball at that time.

The team opened their first season on the road in Washington on April 23, 1903. Keeler batted second and achieved two franchise firsts as he walked and later scored the team's first ever run. A week later on April 30 during the team's first home opener, it was Keeler who got the first hit and scored the first run at Hilltop Park.

The column "A.L. Notes" in the May 16, 1903, issue of *Sporting Life* stated that "Billy Keeler is the idol of the New York fans, and why not? One of the greatest ballplayers the game has ever produced is Wee Willie."

In 1903 the Highlanders held their own, although they finished 17 games out in their inaugural season. Keeler was worth the price of admission as he led the team with a .318 average, good enough for fifth in the league and finished third in runs scored with 95. The left-hander also came in from the outfield and played four games at third base. Keeler's highlight in 1903 came on July 29 as he connected for four hits off of the great Cy Young in a 15-14 New York win.

The 1904 season brought substantial improvements for Keeler and the Highlanders as the team finished only three games back. Willie's .343 average led the team and was good enough for second in the league. His 186 hits, of which 162 were singles—a then-American League record—also placed him second in the league. Although he didn't win a batting title in 1904, his average was 84 points higher than the team average and 98 points higher than the league average. On August 24, in a 9-1 Highlander win over the St. Louis Browns, Keeler hit two inside-the-park home runs to lead the way.

New York slipped to sixth place in 1905 as Keeler hit over .300 for the 14th consecutive season, batting .302. Although this was 41 points lower than a year earlier, it was still good enough for the team lead and runner-up status in the league. His 169 hits placed fourth in the league and only eight players hit more than his four home runs. The team led the league with 200 stolen bases as Keeler contributed with 19, and his 42 sacrifices set a still-unbroken major league record. On September 16 the Highlanders, who were playing a doubleheader, found themselves short-handed on infielders. The left-handed Keeler stepped in and played second base in both games. He would end the year having played 12 games at second base and three games at third.

Keeler batted .304 in 1906 as the Highlanders finished three games out for the second time in three years. It was the 15th consecutive year he had hit at least .300 and the last time as a full-time player. Keeler once again set the American League singles record for a single season with 167 as he surpassed the 162 he hit in 1904. This record would stand until Ty Cobb broke it with 169 singles in 1911. Willie's 96 runs scored were good enough for third in the league. On August 18 Keeler struck out for only the second time all year as he was once again the victim of spitballer Big Ed Walsh.

In June, over a two-game span, Keeler connected for eight hits, which may have prompted *Sporting Life* to report on June 16 that "Willie Keeler goes along getting two and three hits each day, and that's what he has been doing for some time."

On September 3 New York set a record by sweeping a doubleheader on consecutive days for the fifth straight time. In Game One, Kid Elberfield assaulted umpire Silk O'Laughlin and was removed by the police. In Game Two Keeler collided with shortstop Lave Cross as he was trying to field a ground ball, which allowed two runs to score. The A's first baseman and

Captain Harry Davis was so enraged he argued with the umpires. After eight minutes the umpires forfeited the game to the Highlanders.

Age began to catch up with Keller in 1907 as the 35 year old hit just .234 in 107 games. This didn't help the team as they slipped to fifth, finishing 21 games back. The Wee Willie Keeler era as the team's first big star was starting to come to an end.

The 1908 season was not much better for Keeler as he batted .263 in 91 games. It was rumored that Highlander owner Frank Farrell wanted to talk to Keeler about becoming the team's manager. Not a commanding type, Keeler led by example on the field and had no aspirations to be a manager. While in Philadelphia for a series with the Athletics, he actually ducked out of the hotel lobby as Farrell was looking for him to discuss the job. On August 13 Keeler played on an All-Star team in Boston to celebrate "Cy Young Day." Over 20,000 fans turned out to witness the game and to celebrate the multiple presentations made to Young, including a great loving cup from the American League. Cy pitched briefly against a team that in addition to Keeler included Jack Chesbro, Hal Chase, Harry Davis, and George Mullin.

The 1909 season marked the last time Keeler played for the Highlanders as he batted .264 in 99 games. He finished his major league career in 1910, playing in 19 games for the New York Giants. He officially retired from baseball after playing 39 games with Toronto of the International League.

All in all, the boy from Primary School 26 in Brooklyn who teachers said wouldn't amount to much, had played 19 years in the major leagues. He finished with 2,932 hits, 1,727 runs scored, 810 RBIs, and a remarkable .341 average—still good for 12th all time in major league history. His .372 National League batting average still stands as the best of all time in that league. He also had five hits in a game four times in one season, a record he still shares with Ty Cobb, Stan Musial, and Tony Gwynn. He and Lou Gehrig remain the only two players to have had 200 hits and 100 walks in a season eight different times.

Having retired from baseball with a reported $100,000 saved, Keeler was referred to as the "Brooklyn Millionaire." Over the next few years many unwise real estate investments resulted in Keeler being literally broke near the end of his life. So broke was Keeler that in 1921 Major League Baseball gave him a gift of $5,500. Although the money was greatly appreciated, it was too little too late for Willie, as he had become an all but forgotten man. In 1922 when George Sisler was making his assault on Keeler's 44-game hitting streak, no one came calling to interview him. Sisler's quest ultimately failed as he hit safely in 41 games.

In December 1922 Keeler was bedridden with a bad heart. In fading health, Willie told his brother that he wanted to live to see the new year. On

January 1, 1923, Keeler passed quietly at his home in Brooklyn; he was 50 years old. Wee Willie Keeler is interred at Calvary Cemetery in Brooklyn.

Upon hearing of Keeler's death, Walter Trumball of the *New York Herald* wrote:

> Wee Willie Keeler you have journeyed west;
> Just an old Oriole Flown to his nest.
> Wee Willie Keeler smallest of them all;
> But in height and manhood you were mountains tall.

An editorial in the *New York Tribune*, which described Keeler's batting prowess, also noted his "swiftness and accuracy of observation, a poise permitting of instant allocation of plan and execution."

The Sporting News named Keeler to their all-decade team for the 1900s and ranked him the 75th greatest player of all time.

William Henry Keeler was elected to the Hall of Fame in 1939, the same year the museum opened, as one of the first dozen men so honored.

HENRY LOUIS GEHRIG
NEW YORK YANKEES · 1923 - 1939
HOLDER OF MORE THAN A SCORE OF
MAJOR AND AMERICAN LEAGUE RECORDS,
INCLUDING THAT OF PLAYING 2130
CONSECUTIVE GAMES. WHEN HE RETIRED
IN 1939, HE HAD A LIFE TIME BATTING
AVERAGE OF 340.

Lou Gehrig

(Elected 1939)

I t was June 19, 1903, and it would produce one of the more noteworthy events in Yankee history.

It was not because the team, in their first season of existence and still known as the "Highlanders," unceremoniously lost to the Tigers in Detroit 7-0. It was because back home in New York City, the greatest first baseman in team history, Henry Louis Gehrig, was born.

He was born to German immigrant parents at an apartment on Second Ave. in the Yorkville section. When Lou was about five years old, they moved to a tenement house on upper Eighth Ave. in Washington Heights. Living very near Hilltop Park where the Highlanders played, he soon developed an interest in the game. In 1917 he began attending Manhattan's High School of Commerce on West 65th St., where he starred on both the baseball and football teams. On the diamond, young Lou pitched, played first base, and the outfield. During his junior season his coach had arranged a trip for the team to Chicago to play a local high school team at Wrigley Field. Gehrig created quite a bit of attention for himself when he hit a home run in the game that was estimated at 450 feet.

Upon graduating from Commerce High in the spring of 1921, he was accepted into Columbia University. That summer, however, Gehrig signed to play with the Hartford Senators of the Eastern League. He had received bad advice and was unaware that he was jeopardizing his college athletic career by playing pro ball. When this was explained to him by a friend who worked at Columbia, he left Hartford after having played only 12 games. Gehrig then threw himself on the mercy of the school's athletic board, and was granted leniency by being assessed only a one-year sanction of ineligibility for the baseball team.

By 1923, Gehrig was finally pitching, playing first base, and outfield for the Lions of Columbia, and slugging prodigious home runs. Just around the time that Yankee Stadium was hosting its first games in its inaugural season, scout Paul Krichell had the occasion to witness a Columbia–Rutgers game. Playing right field in that game, the muscular young Gehrig, just shy of his 20th birthday, hit two long home runs. Krichell called Ed Barrow shortly after and excitedly exclaimed that he'd "found another Babe Ruth."

Within days, the Yankees made Gehrig an offer of a $1,000 signing bonus and a $2,000 salary for the duration of the 1923 season. Lou's father was out of work often due to ill health, while his mother worked as a cleaning woman. With an unstable financial situation, he felt the offer was just too tempting and signed. He reported to Miller Huggins at Yankee Stadium, and after weeks on the bench he finally got into a game on June 15, replacing Wally Pipp at first base late in the game. In need of seasoning, Gehrig was optioned to Hartford, the team for whom he had played briefly two years prior.

He adjusted quickly to pitching at that level, and in 59 games he hit 24 home runs with a batting average of .304. At the conclusion of Hartford's Eastern League season, Lou was brought back to the Yankees to finish out the major league season. On September 27, 1923, he connected for his first major league home run, off Boston's Bill Piercy at Fenway Park.

Gehrig attended his first training camp with the Yankees in New Orleans in the spring of 1924. He went north with the team as the regular season opened, but with Pipp a fixture at first base and no openings in the outfield, Huggins thought it best to have him playing regularly in Hartford. He built upon his good performance there the year before by hitting 37 homers and batting at a .369 clip in 504 at-bats. Lou celebrated his 21st birthday with Hartford on June 19 by hitting a home run, a triple, and a double. He returned to the Yankees in September, and would total only 12 major league at-bats for 1924.

In 1925 the Yankees held Spring Training in St. Petersburg, Florida, for the first time. Lou was again taken north by manager Huggins with the team, but this year there would be no demotion. Gehrig was in the majors to stay. In the first six weeks of the season he pinch-hit several times, and even played a handful of games in right field. He was helping to fill in for Babe Ruth, who had missed all of the season to that point because of abdominal surgery. Ruth finally returned to the lineup on June 1. On that same day, Gehrig was sent in to pinch-hit for shortstop Pee Wee Wanninger. A few weeks prior, Wanninger had been the player who had replaced Everett Scott in the Yankee lineup, breaking his consecutive game streak at 1,307. Eight years later, it was Scott's record that Gehrig would surpass in establishing his own streak.

Then on June 2, one day after Gehrig's appearance as a pinch hitter, a twist of fate would change the course of his career forever. During batting practice, first baseman Pipp was struck on the temple with a pitch that caused him to spend time in the hospital. Huggins then informed Gehrig that he would be the first baseman for the immediate future. No one, least of all a slightly insecure young Lou, could imagine that mishap would lead to 14 seasons without missing a game.

When Pipp returned from his head injury, he barely saw any action at all and was shuttled off to the Cincinnati Reds after the season. Gehrig would admit later, however, that Pipp had been kind enough to help him in learning the finer points of playing first base at the major league level.

Gehrig finished off his first full season in the majors with respectable numbers. In 126 games he batted .295 with 20 home runs and 68 RBIs. On July 23 he hit the first of what would be a career-record 23 grand slam home runs, a record that would still be standing on the centennial of his birth

Come 1926, Gehrig was unquestionably the incumbent first baseman, and the Yankees were on the verge of rebounding in a big way from their disastrous seventh-place finish the year before. Lou continued to show improvement both at the plate and in the field. He was becoming a big part of the Yankee offense, leading the team in runs scored with 135, and driving in 107. Though he only managed to hit 16 home runs, he showed a bit of power and speed by leading the league in triples with 20. The local boy would be getting a chance to represent his city in the World Series against St. Louis as the Yankees finished three games better than the Cleveland Indians for the A.L. crown.

In front of the home crowd on October 2 in the opener, Gehrig was a significant factor in New York's victory. In the first inning with the bases loaded, he hit a grounder to score Earle Combs and also made it to first before the double play could be turned. In the sixth with the score tied 1-1, Lou singled home Ruth from second base, and the game ended that way with Gehrig driving in both runs.

In Game Four in St. Louis with New York needing a win to even the Series, Lou again played a role. In five trips to the plate, he doubled, singled, walked with the bases loaded, and laid down a successful sacrifice bunt as the Yankees doubled up the Cardinals 10-5. The next day, Lou doubled in the ninth inning and scored the tying run in a game they would win in the tenth 3-2.

It all came down to Game Seven, and St. Louis edged out New York 3-2 to take the title. But the 23-year-old Gehrig had shown that he was undaunted by World Series pressure, as evidenced by his .348 Series average and his four runs scored, only topped on the Yankees by Ruth's five. But Gehrig would not have to wait long to experience the thrill of reaching the top of the baseball mountain.

The 1927 season would be a most memorable one for the Yankee franchise and Lou also as he elevated himself to superstar status. With his tremendous upper body strength, he began to produce truly gargantuan power numbers seen previously only by the likes of Ruth. Babe and Lou became locked in a race for the home run title that by mid-August had thrust Gehrig into the national spotlight. Lou was now hitting in the cleanup spot behind Ruth as they formed a deadly one-two combo. In the August 18, 1927, issue of *The Sporting News*, Gehrig's photo appeared along with Ruth's in an ad for Louisville Slugger bats for the first time. Lou was being referred to often by the sporting press as "Buster," though the nickname wouldn't stick. Gehrig, with his $7,500 salary was being paid nearly 10 times less by the Yankees than Ruth, yet was slugging with nearly as much proficiency. The two were tied in home runs at 44 until Ruth pulled away for good at the beginning of the second week of September on his way to 60.

Gehrig had an extraordinary season however, ending with 47 home runs and setting a new single-season record for RBIs with 175. The baseball writers bestowed upon the 24 year old the honor of being the Most Valuable Player in the American League. His enormous value was especially meaningful, as the Yankees had a season for the ages with 110 wins, finishing a full 19 games ahead of second-place Philadelphia.

Lou would be making his second trip to the World Series, this time against the Pittsburgh Pirates. His bat had an impact right away in Game One at Forbes Field on October 5. He came up in the first inning with Ruth on base and tripled to drive in the first run. In the third, Lou walked and eventually scored, and later in the fifth he hit a sacrifice fly scoring Mark Koenig. The Yankees went on to win 5-4, and Gehrig had either driven in or scored three of the runs.

The Series moved to New York for Game Three on October 7, with the Yankees having won the first two games. In his first at-bat he hit a towering drive that bounced off the left-center field wall, driving in the first two New York runs. He was out at the plate trying to stretch it to an inside-the-park home run and was credited with a triple. He also doubled later, but his triple already had provided the team with all the runs they needed as they won 8-1. The Yankees were able to dispose of the Pirates the following day as Lou got to celebrate his first of numerous championships. After the Series concluded, Gehrig and Ruth went on a 20-city barnstorming tour across the country. Lou captained a team called the "Larrupin' Lous," while Ruth's squad was dubbed the "Bustin' Babes." They played to many fans, particularly in the western part of the country, who had never gotten to see them before.

Lou was beginning to reap the financial rewards that came with baseball stardom. Aside from his World Series share and barnstorming money, his Yankee salary for 1928 was increased to $25,000. He set out to prove he was well worth it as he ranked among the very top of the league in numerous batting categories. Though his home run total had dropped to 27, he was still second in that department to only Ruth. He managed to tie Babe for the lead in RBIs with 142, as well as leading the A.L. in doubles with 47. Lou was the runner-up in hits, runs, slugging percentage, and home run percentage, and had the league's third-best batting average at .374.

The Yankees of 1928, beset with injuries, held off a late surge by the improving Athletics and copped the flag by a margin of 2½ games. They would have the opportunity to face the St. Louis Cardinals in the Series and atone for their loss of two years prior. As he did the year before, Gehrig stepped right up in his first at-bat in the first game and put the Yankees on the scoreboard. He pounded a double to drive in Ruth, and they would not trail after that. Later on in the eighth Lou singled to drive in Koenig with the final run in the 4-1 win.

The next day at the Stadium, Gehrig hit the first pitch he saw into the right field bleachers for a three-run home run. In the third inning he walked and scored, and New York cruised on to a 9-3 win. It was then on to St. Louis for Game Three with a 2-0 lead. The change of scenery didn't bother Gehrig a bit as he hit a towering solo home run to right field in his first at-bat, and a two-run inside-the-park drive in his second. The 7-3 win put the Yankees in the position to sweep the Cardinals the next day.

After walking in his first three times up, Gehrig rocked his fourth home run of the Series, tying Ruth's record for homers in a single Series. His ninth RBI also broke Bob Meusel's record of eight in one Series set in the 1923 Fall Classic. In this game, Ruth hit three home runs, and as was so often the case, he somewhat overshadowed his younger slugging teammate. The 7-3 New York win finalized the sweep, however, and it would be hard to overlook that it was Gehrig who was the overall offensive star of the 1928 Series.

Lou would don what would become his familiar uniform number 4 for the first time in the spring of 1929 when the Yankees introduced the innovation. Signifying his spot in the batting order, he was a fixture in the cleanup position behind Ruth. Gehrig had one very noteworthy day early in the season when he hit three home runs in a game for the first time. The Yankees could not sustain their dominance of the previous two years, finishing well behind the powerful

Philadelphia Athletics. The A's were embarking on a three-year span of dominance of their own in the A.L.

Gehrig and the Yankees suffered a tragic blow at the end of the 1929 season when longtime manager Miller Huggins died of a skin disease. Gehrig was devastated by the news and told reporters how much Huggins had helped him early on. He considered the little manager a true friend and was stunned by his death. He went along with the funeral procession to Cincinnati where Huggins was buried.

While Lou's offensive production in 1929 had dropped off slightly from the previous years, he was still one of the top sluggers in the A.L., finishing second in home runs with 35, behind only Ruth. He bounced back considerably in 1930, increasing his batting average 79 points from 1929 to .379, narrowly missing the batting title by two points. He drove in 48 more runs for a league-leading 174. And his 41-homer total was once again second to only Babe. Lou hit three home runs again on May 22 to help beat Philadelphia 20-13. But New York's 86 victories under Huggins's replacement Bob Shawkey was way off the pace set by the Athletics, and they had to settle for third place.

Lou kept in shape over the winter of 1930–1931 by ice skating regularly and exercising at a local gymnasium. He was regarded at this time as the best physical specimen in the game. He had signed a three-year contract in early 1931 that called for him to make $30,000 per year, making him one of the top-paid players in the game. Arriving at Spring Training in St. Petersburg in early March he met new manager Joe McCarthy, and the two men developed a mutual respect very early on. McCarthy was all business, and he admired Lou for his discipline and work ethic.

Gehrig had several big days with his bat in 1931 that contributed to his extremely bulky numbers. On his 28th birthday he celebrated with a home run, two doubles, and a single to beat the Browns. On September 1 he hit his third grand slam in four days, which was also his sixth home run in the same span. Lou broke his own A.L. record for RBIs in a season with 184, a figure that was still the circuit mark at the turn of the twenty-first century. His league-leading 163 runs scored had only been exceeded twice in the twentieth century, both times by Ruth in 1921 and 1928. His 211 hits also topped the league, and his 46 homers tied Babe for the most, with an unusual incident preventing Gehrig from being the sole leader.

Late in the season Lou hit a home run with two outs and shortstop Lyn Lary on second base. The ball went over the fence and bounced back into the outfielder's glove. As Lary was running to third he looked up and saw the ball in the glove and assumed it was caught for an out and ran off the field. Lou, running with his head down, passed third base and was called out for passing the runner. He was credited with a triple, and missed out on a chance to beat the Babe that season by one home run.

The Yankees were set to break with their postseason drought by turning the tables on Philadelphia in 1932, winning a lofty 107 games and topping the A's by nearly the same margin they had lost to them in 1931. On the way to capturing the pennant Gehrig had an amazing day on June 3 that landed him in the record books once again. At Shibe Park in Philadelphia, Lou hit home runs in his first four at-bats to make him the first player in the twentieth century, and only the third player ever, to hit four homers in a game. Amazingly, later in the game he missed a fifth home run by less than a couple of feet.

Come September 28, the Yankees were set to host the Chicago Cubs in Game One of the 1932 Series, and Joe McCarthy would have the opportunity for a bit of payback against his former team. For Lou it was his first World Series in four years, and he was about to make up for lost time. He picked up where he left off in the 1928 Series, slugging at a tremendous clip.

In the fourth inning of the opener at Yankee Stadium, Gehrig hit a line-drive home run to right with Ruth on to put New York ahead 3-2. He later walked and scored in a big five-run sixth inning, singled in the seventh, and narrowly missed a home run in the eighth. Lou and the Yankees got off to a rousing start in the Series, dominating Chicago 12-6.

Gehrig started right in again the next day by stroking a single in the first to drive in the first Yankee run. He singled twice more and scored two runs as New York went up two games to none with a 5-2 win. It was then off to Chicago's Wrigley Field where Lou had homered so many years before as a 17-year-old high school boy. It is only speculation to think that returning to the scene for the first time, the 29-year-old slugger pondered the memory and hoped that he could duplicate it. If so, it would turn out even better than he hoped.

The game produced an incident so memorable it would be debated and discussed for decades. Ruth homered in the first, and later in the fifth, in the midst of incredible taunting from the Cubs bench, he hit what was to forever be known as his "called shot." Somewhat lost in all the resulting hoopla was the fact that Gehrig hit two home runs of his own in the 7-5 Yankees win. Lou was again overshadowed by his far more flamboyant teammate.

The next day in Game Four Gehrig had his fourth straight multihit game, stroking a double and a two-run single in the Yankees 13-6 clincher. For the Series, he had led the team in batting average, slugging average, home runs, RBIs, runs, and hits. But Lou was not one to seek headlines. He was content in knowing that his immense contributions had put the Yankees on top of the baseball world for the third time in his career.

The 1933 season was the first time that serious attention was paid to Gehrig's consecutive-games-played streak. Come August 17 in St. Louis, Lou appeared in his 1,308th consecutive game since his pinch hit for Pee Wee Wanninger back on June 1, 1925. He had broken the record set by his former teammate Everett Scott, and was recognized for his feat with a small ceremony at home plate that day at Sportsman's Park.

When the All-Star Game was conceived and held for the first time in July 1933, Lou was the starter at first base. He would be a fixture there for the following five years.

The Yankees couldn't quite catch up to the pennant-winning Senators in 1933, settling for second place. Though Lou was very slightly off his pace of 1932, he still led the league in runs scored and finished either second or third in home runs, RBIs, batting average, slugging average, and total bases.

There was one other important event for Lou that occurred during the last week of the baseball season. The shy bachelor made Eleanor Twitchell of Chicago the new Mrs. Lou Gehrig.

As the 1934 season proceeded, it appeared that marriage had a positive effect on Gehrig's performance on the field. His first home run of the season was the 300th of his career on his way to a season-high 49. In the end, he reigned as the American League's triple crown winner. He had a couple of close calls with his consecutive-games-played streak in 1934. On June 29 he was struck with a pitched ball in an exhibition game in Norfolk, Virginia. His streak had reached 1,414 games at that point, and it was thought that he had sustained a concussion. The next day's game was in Washington, and not only was he able to play, he hit triples in his first three at-bats. This would have tied a major league record, but the game was rained out before it became official. A couple of weeks later while in Detroit, he was experiencing severe pain in his back and was sure he couldn't play. McCarthy allowed him to lead off the game, and after getting a single, he came out for a pinch runner.

Ruth having left the Yankees after the 1934 season, Lou could now escape from under his considerable shadow. Though never one to be very vocal, Gehrig was considered a fine choice as team captain when appointed by McCarthy in the spring of 1935. He would remain as Yankee captain until the end of his career.

Gehrig led the A.L. in walks in 1935 for the first time in his career and also was the leader in runs scored with 125. The Yankees however finished as runner-up to Detroit for the second year in a row.

No sooner had Gehrig emerged as the focal point of the team when young up-and-coming superstar Joe DiMaggio came in 1936 and attracted an enormous amount of attention. Lou was certainly pleased with any addition that would help put the Yankees back in the World Series, and young Joe D. treated his boyhood idol Gehrig with nothing but respect. With Joe generally batting third just ahead of Lou, the two formed an outstanding power combination. The veteran first baseman, now in his 14th season with the Yankees, flourished in 1936. He matched his career high in home runs with a league-high 49, connecting for his 400th that season. He batted at an impressive .354 clip, led the circuit in slugging percentage and, like he had the year before, topped the A.L. in runs and walks. For his efforts, Gehrig was again presented with the league's MVP Award, as he had been in 1927. When the Yankees swept a doubleheader from Cleveland on September 9, they had clinched the pennant earlier than any team in a 154-game schedule. The Series would pit them against the rival Giants from across the river.

After dropping the opener at the Polo Grounds, the Yankees exploded the next day for an 18-4 win. Gehrig hit a sacrifice fly with the bases loaded in the first inning to begin the scoring. When the carnage was over, Lou had contributed three RBIs to the cause. Moving over to Yankee Stadium for Game Three, Gehrig got the Yankees on the board in the second inning with a solo home run. The clout would turn out to be very meaningful as the A.L. champs won the contest by the slim margin of 2-1.

Lou was a big factor in the 5-2 victory in Game Four, hitting a two-run home run, and scoring after ripping a double. The home run came off Carl Hubbell, who had made Lou one of his famous five-consecutive-strikeout victims in the 1934 All-Star Game.

The Giants came back to narrowly win Game Five 5-4, but Game Six was all Yankees, 13-6. Gehrig's two homers and seven RBIs in the six games tied for team leads.

Lou's performance over the years had created certain expectations by the fans, and he delivered just what they had come to expect in 1937. His .351 average, 37 homers, 159 RBIs, and 138 runs all blend in well with what he had done in seasons past. But no one could know that it would be the last of these typically productive seasons.

The Yankees again beat out the second-place Tigers by a wide margin and were set for a rematch with the Giants in the Series. While Lou's bat was fairly quiet he did have a noteworthy at-bat in Game Four at the Polo Grounds, homering off great lefty Hubbell as he had done the year before. The next day Gehrig struck a double to drive in the fourth and final run in the Yankees 4-2 win that clinched their second consecutive World Series.

As Gehrig entered the 1938 season, there appeared to be a few significant attainable milestones to be reached. If he could post numbers similar to those

of the previous year, he could just barely reach 500 career home runs and 2,000 RBIs. Two thousand consecutive games was also well within reach, and he passed the mark on May 31.

But somehow, 1938 was not quite the same for Lou. He seemed to battle prolonged batting slumps all season. There was continued speculation in the press as to the reasons, and some openly wondered if it was the end of the line. But he kept gamely battling on, trying everything he could to turn things around. He surged slightly toward the end of the season, and many players would be thrilled to compile the numbers he ended with—a .295 batting average, 29 home runs, 114 RBIs, and 115 runs scored. In hindsight, there is little doubt that he was already suffering the effects of the disease that would end his career the following spring.

With about a week to go in the 1938 season, Gehrig hit his 493rd career home run. It was 15 years to the day of his first homer, and this would be his last.

The Yankees had captured their third straight pennant in 1938 and were to be opposed in the Fall Classic by the Chicago Cubs. But while the Yanks rolled over the N.L. champs with relative ease in four games, Gehrig played a conspicuously small role in the victory. He uncharacteristically managed only four singles in his 14 at-bats, and didn't drive in a run.

Lou was determined to work hard over the winter to return to form, but come Spring Training in St. Petersburg in 1939, he seemed to decline even further. He was not only having extreme difficulty hitting with any consistency, he was also having a hard time in the field, struggling to even cover first base on routine plays. McCarthy stuck with him and allowed him to start the season right where he had spent the previous 14 seasons.

Finally, after eight games, getting only four singles in 28 at-bats, Lou had come to a painful decision. He approached McCarthy and informed him that he would not be in the lineup for the May 2 game in Detroit. His incredible streak was now over at 2,130 games. The Yankee captain continued his duties of bringing the lineup card out and meeting with the umpires before the start of each game, then he would watch the game from the bench.

A few weeks later he traveled to the Mayo Clinic in Rochester, Minnesota, to undergo a battery of tests. A short time later, the grim news came out. Lou was diagnosed with amyotrophic lateral sclerosis, a degenerative disease that attacked the central nervous system. Many did not understand the specifics of the affliction, but it was clear that he would never play ball again.

The Yankees decided to hold "Lou Gehrig Appreciation Day" on July 4, 1939. It was, of course, on this day that Lou courageously spoke the poignant line, "Today . . . I consider myself . . . the luckiest man . . . on the face of the earth." It is a moment that endures as one of the most famous in the history of not only baseball, but all of sports. A little less than two years later, on June 2, 1941, the great and humble man succumbed to the illness that would come to bear his name.

December 8, 1939, just a little more than seven months after his final game, the Baseball Hall of Fame held a special election that saw Gehrig unanimously elected to the shrine. It was also at that time that the Yankees made his number 4 the first uniform number to be retired in the history of professional sports.

On July 4, 1941, a month after his premature passing, the Yankees erected a monument in his honor in center field that read:

HENRY LOUIS GEHRIG
JUNE 19, 1903–JUNE 2, 1941
A MAN, A GENTLEMAN, AND A GREAT BALL PLAYER
WHOSE AMAZING RECORD OF 2,130 CONSECUTIVE
GAMES SHOULD STAND FOR ALL TIME
THIS MEMORIAL IS A TRIBUTE FROM THE YANKEE
PLAYERS TO THEIR BELOVED CAPTAIN AND
TEAMMATE
JULY THE FOURTH 1941

GEORGE HERMAN (BABE) RUTH
BOSTON-NEW YORK, A.L.; BOSTON, N.L.
1915 - 1935
GREATEST DRAWING CARD IN HISTORY OF
BASEBALL. HOLDER OF MANY HOME RUN
AND OTHER BATTING RECORDS. GATHERED
714 HOME RUNS IN ADDITION TO FIFTEEN
IN WORLD SERIES.

Babe Ruth

(Elected 1936)

I t is difficult to imagine a public figure from the twentieth century who was more recognized, idolized, influential, and photographed than Babe Ruth, the most popular baseball player of all time. While the memories of those who achieved worldwide acclaim as the best at their chosen profession tend to slightly fade over time, Ruth's standing as his game's greatest seems secure nearly 70 years after his exit.

Never has a player, a team, and a city seemed so suited to each other than when 25-year-old George Ruth first donned the Yankee pinstripes in the spring of 1920. Already having established himself as a top notch left-handed pitcher-turned-slugger and one of the biggest drawing cards in the game by age 23, his persona was suited to display his abundantly growing talents on the grand stage that only New York could provide. With his transfer to the Yankees, there is little doubt that he himself, the team, and the game of baseball benefited immeasurably.

Babe had captured the attention of the sports world in a big way with his breaking of the home run record with his 29 in 1919. Within weeks of his sale to New York, he boldly predicted he would exceed that figure with the Yankees. What he didn't say was that he would do it by July 16, or that he would post the most gaudy, bloated batting figures that had ever been seen in a single season. A shocking 54 home runs (more than any other entire A.L. team), 158 runs scored, 138 RBIs, 148 walks, and a .376 batting average were combinations that left mouths agape. He even managed to lead his team in stolen bases with 14. George Ruth was plainly treading on territory that was unfamiliar to anyone in or around the game.

As phenomenal as Ruth's batting feats were in his inaugural campaign with the Yankees, he somehow managed to improve on most of them in 1921.

Hitting at a .378 clip (third best in the A.L.) he further pushed his home run record up to 59 and established new marks in RBIs, walks, and total bases. Now, early in the twenty-first century, it would likely take a player hitting 100 home runs and driving in 200 runs to have similar shock value as what Babe was accomplishing. Not to be overlooked is that Ruth set the career record for home runs in that 1921 season. It was a performance that is widely regarded as the most productive offensive year of the twentieth century.

Polo Grounds turnstiles were spinning at an unprecedented rate as New Yorkers from all walks of life wanted to get a close-up look at the slugging phenom. The 1921 season was a great time to watch the Yankees, with Ruth's efforts contributing greatly to the team's first A.L. pennant.

Ruth and the Yankees were set to face John McGraw's New York Giants for the title in October 1921. The feisty McGraw was an old-school baseball man and had been critical of Ruth's power hitting. Whether he liked it or not, McGraw would see Ruth's influence spread throughout the game in the 1920s, with more and more players swinging for the fences. Ruth would only homer once in this Series, and with an abscess on his elbow he was unable to start the final three games and had to watch the Giants walk away with the title. Ruth would have other chances to gain revenge on McGraw and many other chances to shine in October.

His earnings were increasing rapidly, as he was far and away the highest paid player in the game. By 1922 he realized his dream of earning $1,000 a week by signing a contract for an even $52,000 for the year. With so many decades of inflation, it is difficult to fathom the spending power of $1,000 a week in 1922, and Babe was never known to pass up on a good time. He was no doubt finding out just how far it would go. If there was deprivation in his childhood, there would be little of it in adulthood. Of course, he was further supplementing his princely income by being a forerunner among athletes endorsing products, putting his name on several men's items from shaving products to shirts to socks. The name Babe Ruth had become extremely hot property on Madison Avenue as well as in American League ballparks. Ruth's income was a source of fascination with the public throughout his career, adding further to his mystique.

As powerful as he was becoming in the game, he came across one man who was able to neutralize him temporarily. When Ruth engaged in an unauthorized barnstorming tour after the 1921 World Series, commissioner Kenesaw "Mountain" Landis levied a suspension that caused Ruth to miss the first month of the 1922 season, likely costing him the home run title that year. Babe's total of 35 was just 4 shy of the league lead. He did provide enough offensive clout to help the Yankees back to the World Series in a rematch with the Giants. McGraw's pitchers were able to hold Ruth in check however, as the Giants prevailed again, this time in five games.

But plans were in the works for a new stage for Ruth and the Yankees to showcase their talents, allowing them to say goodbye to the old Polo Grounds as a home venue. In April 1923, finishing touches were being put on spectacular new Yankee Stadium, a state-of-the-art baseball facility just across the Harlem River. A week before the new ballpark was to hold its grand opening, Ruth was brought in for a tour and took a few swings in street clothes. He launched several into the right field seats and instantly knew he had found a home. It was only natural that on Opening Day, April 18, Ruth hit the first home run in the park as New York beat the Red Sox 4-1.

Playing in every Yankee game in 1923, Ruth posted what would be for him a typical performance, leading the A.L. in home runs, runs scored, RBIs, walks, and slugging percentage. He recorded what would be the highest batting average of his career at .393, and surprisingly even led his team in stolen bases with 17. It is often overlooked how good of a base runner Ruth was early in his career, or how competent he was as an outfielder. But much more importantly in 1923, the team captured the pennant by a wide margin, and would get yet one more chance against McGraw's Giants in October. This time, Ruth showed his critic McGraw that the slugging game not only could be an effective style, but that it was here to stay.

With two solo homers in Game Two at the Polo Grounds, Ruth supplied the margin of victory in the 4-2 win that tied the Series at one game apiece. One unusual occurrence this game had Ruth seeing his only action at first base he would ever see in World Series play, replacing Wally Pipp late in the game.

His third home run of the Series, a prodigious blast into the upper deck of the Polo Grounds' right field bleachers came in Game Six to help the Yankees finally capture the title. Ruth had hit safely in all six games and had led his team in runs scored with eight. For the first time in their history, the Yankees, largely on the sheer power of the Babe, now clearly were the darlings of New York City baseball.

Ruth proved that he was more than just a home run slugger in 1924 as he captured the league batting title with a lofty .378 average. He also missed the triple crown by just eight RBIs. There would be no World Series for Babe's Yanks in 1924, as they finished three games behind the Washington Senators.

As the team was working its way north in April 1925, Ruth suffered an abdominal attack that required surgery. As a result of that and a suspension for what manager Miller Huggins felt was bad behavior, he was limited to just 98 games that season. It was one of the true low points of his career. One of his few highlights of the dismal season came on September 24 when he hit a game-ending grand slam, something that no Yankee did again until Jason Giambi performed the feat in 2002.

But without their most potent bat in the lineup much of that 1925 season, the Yankees underachieved woefully, finishing a dismal seventh. In the off-season Ruth decided to employ a personal trainer to get himself back into shape. He was thought to be the only ballplayer at that time to have ever done such a thing, as he faithfully reported to Art McGovern's gym on 42nd St. Come the spring, a svelte Babe weighing roughly 30 pounds less came to camp as he and the team were ready to put 1925 behind them and embark on a new period of dominance. For the first time Ruth had young players like Lou Gehrig and Tony Lazzeri with him in the lineup every day, and the team's offense benefited greatly as they led the league in runs scored, slugging percentage, and home runs by wide margins. Ruth led the way by posting the type of numbers that were now expected: 47 home runs (Al Simmons, in second place had 19); 145 RBIs (Lazzeri was second with 114); 139 runs scored; and a .372 batting average (six points higher would have earned Ruth the triple crown).

New York was set to take on St. Louis in the 1926 World Series in what would prove to be a back-and-forth, down-to-the wire affair. Though Ruth only had one single in Game One, he managed to score what would be the winning run in the sixth inning on a Gehrig single in Herb Pennock's 2-1 three-hitter. Babe's bat then went fairly silent until Game Four with the Yankees down two games to one, as he exploded with the most impressive display seen to that point in Series play.

In the first inning he sent the first pitch he saw over the right field bleacher roof of Sportsman's Park to give the Yankees a 1-0 lead. In his next at-bat in the third inning he slugged it over the right-center field bleacher roof to give New York a 2-1 lead. Babe walked in the fifth and ended up scoring on a sacrifice fly as the Yanks put across four to take a 7-4 lead. The next inning, with one out and Earle Combs on base, Ruth struck his historic third home run of the game, this time to deep center field. He had now scored four runs in the game as New York held a commanding 9-4 lead. St. Louis wanted no part of Babe in his next at-bat, walking him on four pitches, and New York's 10-5 win evened the Series at two.

Ultimately, it would all be settled back in New York on October 10. Ruth started the scoring in the third inning with yet another home run, his fourth of the Series. The solo blast represented his only official at-bat of the game. In his other four trips to the plate the Cardinals took the bat out of his hands by issuing him a free pass for what would be a Series record of 11.

When Ruth was walked with two out in the bottom of the ninth inning trailing 3-2, a most unusual thing occurred. With Bob Meusel at the plate, Babe took off for second base and was caught stealing as Rogers Hornsby applied the tag. Shock spread throughout the Stadium. Babe apparently thought that in such an unexpected moment the Cardinals might be caught by surprise, but the surprise was that the Yankees had just lost the Series. Ruth would wear the goat horns for a time, but phenomenal success and exclusive numbers lay just ahead.

It was that magical, marvelous season of 1927 that Babe and young Lou Gehrig really first combined as a spectacular and unprecedented power duo. The two were battling for the home run title early on, but come September Babe began to pull away. He hit three home runs in a doubleheader on September 6, and two the next day to lead Gehrig 49 to 45. His 52nd home run, which came on September 13, helped to clinch the pennant a full two-and-a-half weeks before the end of the season. And his legendary 60th on the next-to-last day of the season, September 30, still stands as one of baseball's biggest highlights. In all, Ruth had added 14 home runs in the month of September.

The Yankees made quick work of Pittsburgh in the World Series, dispatching them in four games. Ruth socked a three-run homer in Game Three, and a towering two-run shot in the clincher at the Stadium on October 8. *The Sporting News* editorialized on Ruth at that time, "His class is his own, and it begins with Babe and ends with Babe." He was at the height of his popularity and personified the Jazz Age and all its excesses. Large, fancy automobiles, floor-length raccoon coats, big cigars, fancy women, fine restaurants, and an abundance of drink to wash it all down. He was possibly the most famous, most recognizable man in America, but he was not the type of celebrity to be reclusive or to hide himself behind an entourage. Babe seemed at his most comfortable in the middle of a crowd. He was a major attraction on the postseason barnstorming tours through the hinterlands of America, particularly in the smaller cities located far away from major league venues. The local folk in these smaller towns treated an exhibition visit by Babe as if it were a national holiday.

Ruth continued his relentless assault on American League pitchers in 1928, pounding 54 homers, driving in 142, scoring a whopping 163 runs, drawing 135 walks, all of which were league leads. It was widely accepted by this point that as a hitter, Ruth simply did not have a weakness, and pitchers were largely at a loss as to how to deal with him.

There is an interesting story from July 1928 that illustrates Babe's ability to almost hit a home run at will. An elderly priest known as Father Van der Schueren came to Yankee Stadium to see Ruth play for the first time. As a young man the priest had played college baseball in the New York area, but later left to do missionary work in India, where he remained for 42 years. He had heard of Ruth from newspapers and when he finally returned to the United States he wanted to see him play. The priest got to meet Babe just before the game he attended and he put his hand on Ruth's shoulder and said, "Now my boy, I have come all the way from India to see you hit a home run. If you do not I will leave a disappointed man." Babe replied, "Father, orders are orders. I'll hit one or break my back."

The priest left happy, as the request was fulfilled.

There was another incident that occurred in May 1928 that demonstrates Babe's willingness to reach out to fans, no matter what their place in society. While in Philadelphia, he visited the state penitentiary and talked to inmates, even signing autographs for them.

It was not surprising that the juggernaut Yankees finished on top of the A.L. in 1928. They would have a chance at revenge against St. Louis, who had shocked them two Octobers prior. Ruth came right out in Game One with two doubles, a single, and two runs scored to gain the early advantage with a 4-1 win. Two more singles and two more runs for Babe the next day and the 9-3 win put New York up 2-0. Moving on to St. Louis, he yet again stroked two singles and crossed the plate twice as the 7-3 victory put their first ever back-to-back titles just one win away.

Lest anyone thought that Ruth had lost his power stroke, he saved his best for last in Game Four on October 9. For the second time in three years, he managed to pound out three home runs in one World Series game, hitting solo shots in the fourth, seventh, and eighth innings. New York topped St. Louis 7-3 and had now administered two consecutive Fall Classic sweeps. Ruth was hailed not only for his three homers, but also his brilliant running catches, including the one in foul territory to end the final game.

Ruth was in the headlines for a different reason in the spring of 1929. On the morning of the season's opening day, April 17, Babe wed his longtime girlfriend Claire Hodgson. Most observers would agree that the new Mrs. Ruth brought stability and had a positive influence on the manner in which he took care of himself and his overall financial situation.

The Yankees were unseated from the spot as defending A.L. champs in 1929 by Connie Mack's powerful Athletics, though Babe had a fairly typical year at the plate. His big bat accounted for 46 home runs as he again won what almost could be considered the "Ruth triple crown"—leading the league in home runs, slugging percentage, and home run percentage.

Ruth's stature caused him to make headlines for something that occurred off the field again in the spring of 1930. During training camp he and the Yankees agreed on a record-setting contract that would pay him an incredible $80,000 per year for the coming three seasons. He would continue to maintain his distinction as the highest-paid ballplayer as he had throughout the decade of the 1920s.

Babe had two prominent highlights regarding home runs during the 1930 campaign. On May 21 he battered World Champion Philadelphia for three homers in a game, a feat he had achieved only once previously in the regular season. On August 11 he reached a plateau no one would have dreamed remotely possible just a few years before with his 500th career home run, which came in Cleveland. Showing a sentimental side, he made it known that he would like to save the milestone ball as a keepsake, and when park officials were able to track down the young boy who retrieved it outside the park, Ruth bought it for $20.

As a home run hitter, Babe never lacked confidence, and long before his famous "called shot" he occasionally would predict the destination of an upcoming pitch. The first known incident was way back in 1918, and Ruth was reported to have pulled it off in the spring of 1930. The story goes that the Yankees were in San Antonio in late March to play an exhibition against that city's minor league team. When Babe came up for his first at-bat he asked the San Antonio catcher where Giant slugger Mel Ott had hit his home run there not long before. When the catcher informed him it was "this side of the scoreboard," Ruth stated, "Well I'm going to smash one over the other side," and proceeded to do exactly that.

Later during the 1930 season, Babe had an amusing exchange during batting practice one day with St. Louis Browns manager Bill Killefer. Upon seeing Ruth, the manager said to him, "Your face is certainly getting fatter and fatter," to which Ruth responded, "Yeah, well I don't hit, run, or slide with my face!"

Two items in particular appeared in *The Sporting News* in 1930 that tend to illustrate Ruth's generosity of both his time and spirit. In the March 30 issue the following item appeared:

> Babe Ruth has offered to give 1,000 autographed baseballs to sell or auction as a means of raising funds to rebuild an orphanage in Omaha which was destroyed by fire last week.

And Boston sportswriter Burt Whitman's column in early August included:

> Ruth, as usual was busy in errands of mercy while in Boston. The big lad really and truly acts as if he gets a big kick out of visiting hospitals and chatting with the wee shut-ins among boys.

Ruth was said to have rededicated himself to the game going into 1931, taking everything much more seriously. He had returned to McGovern's gym over the winter and reported to training camp at about 225 pounds, which was lighter than he had been in some time. Now 36 years old, he went on to have what many consider his last truly Ruth-like season in 1931 with 46 home runs, a .373 batting average (second best in the A.L.), 128 walks, and a hefty .700 slugging percentage. Yet the Yankees still saw Philadelphia walk away with their third consecutive A.L. flag by a considerable margin. But as always with Babe, there were highlights. He was given a day in his honor at Yankee Stadium on June 7, and he reached another out-of-this-world milestone on August 21 when he slugged his 600th home run. As with his 500th, he paid a young fan for the souvenir for his personal collection.

There was no shortage of baseball writers penning superlatives of Ruth and his legend around this time. In late May, Sid Keener wrote in his *Sporting News* column:

> Besides developing into baseball's greatest individual attraction, the Babe is a salesman and a showman. He receives all visitors with a smile whether he's on the bench, in the clubhouse, or hotel suite.

Keener also relayed in his column that Ruth said once before batting practice, "Gotta get up and hit a few for the cash customers. They're here expecting to see me hit a couple and I gotta give 'em what they want."

An editorial in the March 19 issue of *The Sporting News* stated:

> Babe Ruth may be one of the best batters of home runs who has ever lived, but he has also been one of the greatest and most willing producers of courtesy to everybody who attends a ball game from the smallest of boys to the grownest up of men, and there are times when this bit of human decency on his part seems to us to be greater than all of his home runs put together.

And Bud Shaver of the *Detroit Evening Times* added:

> There is a warm, human element about the big fellow which will strike a responsive chord in the baseball public, even when he is too feeble to mace a bat or chase a fly.

The general belief seemed to be that Ruth had entered a level that few if any athletes had ever occupied. And yet there were still big moments in the sun left for Babe on the field. Though his power numbers dropped slightly in 1932, he was still one of the major offensive weapons along with Lou Gehrig on a team that won 107 games and coasted to the pennant. Entering the World Series against the Cubs, Babe was set to add another chapter to his legend.

In the first two games, which were played in New York, Ruth had only two singles but had managed to score four runs in the two Yankee wins. Going to Chicago for Game Three on October 1, he was set to do what he did best. Right away in the first inning, after Earle Combs and Joe Sewell reached base, he drove a home run deep into right-center field. He came very close to another home run in his next at-bat in the second inning, but Kiki Cuyler caught it right up against the right field bleachers.

By this time the verbal sparring between the two teams had become unmerciful. The war of words seemed to have started earlier, when the Yankees had been critical of Cubs players for failing to vote ex-Yankee Mark Koenig a full share of the pennant-winning money. The shortstop had been picked up by the Cubs in August and had hit well over the final month of the season.

When Ruth came up with no one on base in the fifth inning, the taunting from the Cubs dugout was intense and Babe was giving it right back. The facts are that Ruth let two strikes go by and made some type of hand motion after each. He then deposited the next pitch in the center field bleachers and was still giving it to the Cubs bench as he rounded the bases. This famous "called shot" would be Ruth's 15th and final home run in World Series play, a record that would stand until broken by Mickey Mantle in 1964.

The legend of this home run and whether or not Babe really pointed to where he was going to hit the ball survived the decades. Many historians believe that Ruth was merely gesturing that "it only takes one pitch . . ." while holding up a finger on his right hand. Home plate umpire George Magerkurth repeated over the years that he heard Ruth say just prior to the pitch that he was going to "knock it over the fence."

Given Ruth's history and his confidence and desire to hit home runs, is there any doubt that he did exactly what he wanted to do?

The Yankees of course went on to win the game and sweep the Series as Babe was part of his final World Championship team.

Come 1933, it was fairly apparent that at 38 years old, Babe's extraordinary skills were beginning to diminish. His bat was starting to slow down and he was striking out at a rate higher than ever before. His legs were bothering him and making it harder for him to field his position. But he was still "the Babe" and finished second in the league in home runs with 34, was third in slugging percentage, and once again led the league in walks. And when the first

annual All-Star Game took place at Comiskey Park, it was inconceivable that Ruth wouldn't occupy a spot on the A.L. squad. Fittingly, it was Babe who hit the game's first home run. He also surprised everyone by making a great catch on a long fly ball in the eighth inning.

There would be no more postseason for world titles, but Babe ended the 1933 season in rather memorable fashion. In the final game of the schedule, Ruth returned to the pitcher's mound one final time, starting against the Boston Red Sox. Having only pitched in one major league game in the previous 12 years, Babe pitched a complete game, helping his own cause with a home run in his 6-5 win.

It was expected by many that 1934 would be Ruth's last year as an active player. That season he often started in the outfield but was replaced part way through the game, and also saw more duty as a pinch hitter than ever before. Ruth did reach one last major milestone when he socked his 700th career home run on July 13 against the Tigers.

Come September the Yankees were lagging behind Detroit in the pennant chase. On the very day that Ruth made his last appearance in a game at Yankee Stadium, New York was eliminated from the race and relegated to a second-place finish. The scene was anticlimactic, with none of the heroics that had come to be associated with the legendary performer. Noticeably limping, he caught a routine fly in the first inning, and in his first at-bat in the bottom of the inning he walked. He was then replaced by a pinch runner. As he sorely trudged off the Yankee Stadium turf for the last official time, the tiny crowd of only 2,000 cheered him on.

The team headed out on the road for the final five games of the 1934 season, wrapping up in Washington on September 30. A pregame ceremony was held at Griffith Stadium that day at which Babe was presented with gifts and his old school, St. Mary's of Baltimore, had sent their band to play at the occasion. Babe reached base once via walk, was sent to third on a Gehrig single, and scored on a George Selkirk slow roller. Ruth had now appeared in a Yankee uniform in an official capacity for the final time.

Ruth approached team management to inquire if there might be an opening for him as Yankee skipper. He was informed that they were satisfied with Joe McCarthy and had no plans to replace him. While there was strong sentiment in some quarters to bring Babe back as a pinch hitter and part-time player, he himself was most interested in a major league managerial job. Finally, in February 1935, the struggling Boston Braves worked out a deal in which they would sign Ruth as a player and assistant manager, giving him hope that it would soon lead to the job he coveted. Paving the way for the deal to be made, Jacob Ruppert gave Ruth his unconditional release on February 26. That officially closed the book on Babe Ruth as a New York Yankee.

Ruth would make countless appearances over the next decade-plus as a spectator at Yankee games, in old-timers games, at ceremonies, and at special events. None, however, created the lifelong happy memories that he made in the 15 glorious seasons he spent in New York changing the face of baseball. He put his indelible stamp upon the sport and defined himself as unquestionably the greatest figure in a century and a half of the great game.

But to merely focus on his professional life alone is to miss much of George Ruth. Teammate Tony Lazzeri called him "one of the nicest guys who ever lived." Jimmy Reese, a teammate who had roomed with him briefly in the early 1930s recalled, "He wasn't a choirboy, but he was the nicest man in the world." And Mark Koenig summed him up this way: "He was just a big kid at heart . . . he was just interested in girls, drinking, eating, and hitting home runs."

Few men were as dedicated to their favorite hobbies as Babe Ruth.

Future Yankee Additions to Cooperstown

With the parade of ex-Yankee personnel that has marched into the Hall of Fame on a fairly regular basis since the institution was founded, there is no reason to believe that the tradition will not continue for the foreseeable future. As the team has continually strove for excellence, trying to maintain the standard of success that was established in the early decades of the twentieth century, they have virtually always included players, managers, or executives who were worthy of a high standing in the game's history. The process got underway with the Yankees first team in 1903, which contained three men destined for baseball immortality—Clark Griffith, Willie Keeler, and Jack Chesbro—and will certainly not end with the induction to the Hall of Fame of Dave Winfield in 2001.

In the early years of the twenty-first century it is only natural to wonder, speculate, or even debate just who may be the next members of the Yankee family to take their places in Cooperstown over the next several years. After careful review, the following individuals appear to be the most likely choices, to varying degrees.

The Sure Things

Rickey Henderson. Regarded by most as the greatest leadoff hitter of all time. Not only has he put the career stolen base record seemingly out of reach, he owns the career record for runs scored and walks, and is a member of the exclusive 3,000-hit club.

Henderson spent five seasons with the Yankees from 1985 to 1989, leading the major leagues in runs the first two seasons, and topping the A.L. in stolen bases four of the five seasons. Henderson is the Yankees' twentieth-century team leader in stolen bases with 326.

Roger Clemens. Has reigned as the most dominant pitcher overall from the period of the mid-1980s through the very early twenty-first century, and is arguably one of the five greatest pitchers of all time. Having proven his greatness on an individual basis, he came to the Yankees and added two World Championships to his resume. Clemens was the winner of the Series-clinching game in the 1999 Series over Atlanta, his first year with the team.

In 2001 he became the fifth Yankee pitcher to win the Cy Young Award, his record sixth, with his spectacular 20-3 record.

Wade Boggs. By the late 1980s, the third baseman was widely regarded as the best pure hitter in the game, having had seven straight 200-hit seasons and five batting titles. The perennial All-Star came to the Yankees in 1993 and remained for five seasons, through 1997. In his second season with New York he added his first Gold Glove for fielding excellence to his crowded trophy case, following it up with another the next year.

One of the main highlights of his fabulous career came when he was part of the 1996 World Championship Yankee team. Boggs retired after the 1999 season with 3,000-plus hits and a .320-plus career batting average.

Joe Torre. Brooklyn native Torre authored an extremely noteworthy 18-season playing career between 1960 and 1977 that saw him compile a .297 batting average and 252 home runs. Primarily a catcher but also seeing significant time at first and third base, he had his finest season in 1971 when he copped N.L. MVP honors. Upon retirement as a player, he immediately embarked on a managerial career that included stints with the Mets, Braves, and Cardinals.

But taking over the Yankees in 1996 proved to be a near-perfect baseball marriage. Joe's temperament and managerial style were just right for the team and he played a major role in four World Championships over the next five seasons. Winning four world titles as a manager puts Torre in an exclusive club that includes only Connie Mack, Joe McCarthy, Casey Stengel, and Walter Alston.

Other Noteworthy Candidates

Rich "Goose" Gossage. The big, hard-throwing, intimidating right-hander was one of the game's dominant closers in the decade from the mid-1970s to the mid-1980s. A contemporary of Hall of Fame reliever Rollie Fingers, many of his 310 saves came in an era when closers were expected to work two innings rather than just one.

Gossage joined the Yankees in 1978 and was a big part of two pennant-winning teams.

Don Mattingly. A Yankee for his entire 14-year career, "Donnie Baseball" displayed an outstanding ability to hit for a combination of power and average. His 1985 season serves as a great example as he earned MVP honors for hitting .324 with 35 home runs and 145 RBIs.

Mattingly shined equally bright with his glove, as his spectacular fielding at first base earned him nine Gold Gloves. He retired at only 34 years old due to back problems, and had compiled a .307 lifetime batting average with 1,099 RBIs.

Joe Gordon. One of the slickest-fielding second baseman of his time, "Flash" was outstanding at turning the double play. A productive hitter as well, he hit over 20 home runs five times and drove in over 100 runs four times.

Gordon was a key part of three Yankee World Championship teams, 1938, 1939, and 1941, and missed two years to the military during World War II.

Ron Guidry. Many have compared Guidry's career stats to those of fellow lefty Sandy Koufax. Guidry's 1978 season at 25-3 with a 1.74 ERA ranks with Koufax's best, and "Louisiana Lightning" also had the disadvantage of facing designated hitters throughout his entire career.

Guidry had three 20-win seasons; led the league in ERA in back-to-back years; and was the ace on two World Championship teams.

Thurman Munson. The tough-as-nails Yankee captain was likely the best overall catcher in the A.L. in the 1970s. The six-time All-Star won three Gold Gloves, and also drove in 100 or more runs in three straight years. He helped lead the Yankees to appearances in the World Series from 1976 through 1978. His tragic death in 1979 was one of the saddest events in Yankee history.

* * *

Decades from now, Yankee fans may walk through the Hall of Fame's hallowed gallery of legends and also gaze upon the bronze plaques of Derek Jeter, Bernie Williams, Mariano Rivera, and Alfonso Soriano.

As the years go on, the New York Yankees will continue to strive to attain additional championships and provide a significant presence in Cooperstown.

Bibliography

Books

Allen, Bob, with Bill Gilbert. *The 500 Home Run Club: Baseball's 15 Greatest Home Run Hitters from Aaron to Williams*. Champaign, Ill.: Sports Publishing, 1999.

Blake, Mike. *Baseball Chronicles—An Oral History of Baseball through the Decades*. Cincinnati, Ohio: Betterway Books, 1994.

Cohen, Richard, and David Neft. *The Sports Encyclopedia: Baseball*. 6th ed. New York: St. Martin's Press, 1985.

Gutman, Bill. *The Golden Age of Baseball, 1941–1964*. New York: Gallery, 1989.

Halberstam, David. *October 1964*. New York: Villard Books, 1994.

Honig, Donald. *The All-Star Game: A Pictorial History, 1933 to Present*. St. Louis, Mo.: Sporting News Pub. Co., 1987.

———. *The American League: An Illustrated History*. New York: Crown, 1987.

Honig, Donald, and Lawrence Ritter. *The Image of Their Greatness: An Illustrated History of Baseball from 1900 to the Present*. New York: Crown, 1992.

Jackson, Reggie, with Mike Lupica. *Reggie: The Autobiography*. New York: Villard Books, 1984.

James, Bill. *The Bill James Historical Baseball Abstract*. New York: Villard Books, 1988.

Johnson, Dick, ed., with text by Glenn Stout. *DiMaggio: An Illustrated Life*. New York: Walker & Co., 1995.

Keene, Kerry. *1951: When Giants Played the Game*. Champaign, Ill.: Sports Publishing, 2001.

———. *1960: The Last Pure Season*. Champaign, Ill.: Sports Publishing, 2000.

Keene, Kerry, Ray Sinibaldi, and David Hickey. *The Babe in Red Stockings: An In-Depth Chronicle of Babe Ruth with the Boston Red Sox, 1914–1919*. Champaign, Ill.: Sagamore Publishing, 1997.

Lowry, Philip J. *Green Cathedrals: The Ultimate Celebration of All 271 Major League and Negro League Ballparks Past and Present.* Reading, Mass.: Addison Wesley, 1992.

Luciano, Ron. *The Umpire Strikes Back.* Toronto; New York: Bantam Books, 1982.

MacPhail, Lee. *My 9 Innings: An Autobiography of 50 Years of Baseball.* Westport, Conn.: Meckler Books, 1989.

Mantle, Mickey, with Lewis Early. *Mickey Mantle: An American Dream Comes to Life.* Champaign, Ill.: Sagamore Publishing, 1996.

Mantle, Mickey, with Herb Glick. *The Mick.* Garden City, N.Y.: Doubleday, 1985.

Marazzi, Rich, and Len Fiorito. *Aaron to Zuverink.* New York: Stein and Day, 1982.

The National Baseball Hall of Fame and Museum, The National Baseball Library, and Gerald Astor. *The Baseball Hall of Fame 50th Anniversary Book.* New York: Prentice Hall Press, 1988.

Neft, David S., and Richard M. Cohen. *The World Series: Complete Play-by-Play of Every Game, 1903–1989.* New York: St Martin's Press, 1990.

Okrent, Daniel, and Harris Lewine. *The Ultimate Baseball Book.* Boston: Houghton Mifflin, 1988.

Perry, Gaylord, with Bob Sudyk. *Me and the Spitter: An Autobiographical Confession.* New York: Saturday Review Press, 1974.

Prebenna, David. *The Baseball Encyclopedia: The Complete and Definitive Record of Major League Baseball.* 10th ed. New York: Macmillian, 1996.

Reidenbaugh, Lowell. *Baseball's Hall of Fame: Cooperstown, Where the Legends Live Forever.* New York: Arlington House, 1986.

Rizzuto, Phil, with Tom Horton. *The October Twelve: Five Years of Yankee Glory—1949–1953.* New York: Forge, 1994.

Seymour, Harold. *Baseball: The Golden Age.* New York: Oxford University Press, 1989.

Thorn, John, Pete Palmer, with David Reuther; with historical text by David Nemec. *Total Baseball.* New York: Warner Books, 1989.

Werber, Bill, and C. Paul Rogers III. *Memories of a Ballplayer: Bill Werber and Baseball in the 1930s.* Cleveland, Ohio: Society for American Baseball Research, 2001.

Williams, Ted, with John Underwood. *My Turn at Bat: The Story of My Life.* New York: Simon & Schuster, 1988.

Magazines

The Baseball Digest
Sport Magazine
Sporting Life
The Sporting News
Time
USA Today Baseball Weekly

Newspapers

Detroit Evening News
Durham Morning Herald
New York American
New York Daily News
New York Evening Sun
New York Herald
New York Post
New York Times
New York Tribune
Philadelphia Public Ledger

Web sites

www.baseballlibrary.com
www.baseball-reference.com
www.baseballhalloffame.org
www.mlb.com
www.yankees.com
www.retrosheet.org

Photo Credits

The following photos were provided by the National Baseball Hall of Fame: 3, 10, 13, 16, 24, 29, 30, 36, 46, 54, 60, 62, 66, 70, 73, 76, 82, 86, 89, 92, 95, 98, 109, 112, 124, 136, 142, 144, 150, 154, 156, 161, 164, 167, 170, 177, 178, 188, 194, 196, 198, 200, 208, 224, 226, 230, 233, 236, 246, 249, 252, 254, 256, 261, 264, 267, 270, 273, 276, 279, 282, 287, 290, and 304.

The following photos were provided by the New York Yankees: 21, 33, 42, 50, 64, 69, 79, 84, 120, 133, 147, 186, 206, 223, 243, and 300

The photo on page 314 was provided by the Babe Ruth Museum.

Index

Frohman, Al, 18
Fultz, Dave, 8

Galbreath, John, 27
Garagiola, Joe, 125
Gavin, Joe, 9
Gehrig, Lou, 55–58, 88, 110, 141, 151–52,
    155, 162, 168, 173–75, 192–93, 199, 201,
    204, 213, 238–40, 242, 258, 262, 288,
    290–302, 309; salary of, 294–96
Gehring, Hank, 197
Gentile, Jim, 27
Gettel, Al, 255
Giambi, Jason, 308
Gibson, Bob, 63, 108, 121, 132
Gilliam, Jim, 115
Gionfriddo, Al, 217
Gomez, Lefty, 38, 58, 61, 88, 136–43, 172,
    174–75, 202, 239, 257, 262
Gonzalez, Mike, 72
Gordon, Joe "Flash," 96, 146, 204, 216, 242, 318
Gordon, Joseph, 9, 11
Gorman, Tom, 78, 115
Goslin, Goose, 56, 94
Gossage, Goose, 32, 68, 317
Greater New York Base Ball Association, 9
Greenberg, Hank, 80, 212
Griffith, Clark, 6, 7, 9, 11, 12, 14, 15, 93, 189,
    264–69
Grimes, Burleigh, 196–99, 253
Grove, Lefty, 88, 137, 174, 258
Guidry, Ron, 28, 63, 318
Gwynn, Tony, 288

Hadley, Bump, 141, 203
Haines, Jesse, 56
Haller, Tom, 119
Haney, Fred, 71
Hanlon, Bill, 277
Hanlon, Ned, 8, 283
Harris, Bucky, 39, 92–97, 126–27, 146, 180
Havlicek, John, 31
Healy, Francis, 197
Henderson, Rickey, 316–17
Henrich, Tommy, 100, 146, 205, 215, 241
Hilltop Park, 10, 11
Hodges, Gil, 127
Hodgson, Claire (Mrs. Babe Ruth), 310

Hooten, Burt, 49
Hornsby, Rogers, 56, 159, 189, 309
House of David, 58
Howard, Elston, 26, 28, 108, 131–32, 146,
    237, 244
Howser, Dick, 51
Hoyt, Waite, 69, 156–62, 168, 193, 248
Hubbell, Carl, 140, 173, 203, 211, 239, 299
Huggins, Miller, 55, 57, 151, 157–59, 162,
    166, 171, 172, 188–95, 201, 232, 237,
    248, 260, 292, 293, 296, 307
Hughes, Tom, 173
Hunter, Catfish, 48, 66–69
Hurst, Tim, 268
Hurst, William, 9
Huston, Tillinghast, 190, 247

Jackson, Reggie, 18–20, 46–53, 69
Jackson, Shoeless Joe, 232
Jenkins, Ferguson, 65
Jennings, Hughie, 93
Jeter, Derek, 318
Johnson, Ban, 1–8, 11, 12, 14, 189–90, 250,
    265–66, 280
Johnson, Randy, 63
Johnson, Walter, 93, 172, 191, 272, 280
Jones, Sam, 248

Kansas City Athletics, 47, 67, 74, 101
Kansas City Monarchs, 26
Keane, Johnnie, 108, 110, 132
Keeler, Willie, 7, 8, 12, 14, 15, 214, 282–89
Keener, Sid, 312
Keller, Charlie, 146, 215–16, 241
Kelley, Joe, 4, 6, 8, 285
Kelly, George, 158
Keltner, Ken, 215
Killefer, Bill, 311
Kiner, Ralph, 59, 80
Kleinow, Red, 272
Koelsch, F. H., 5, 268
Koenig, Mark, 192, 244, 313, 315
Koufax, Sandy, 107, 121, 132
Krichell, Paul, 37, 113, 202, 292
Kubek, Tony, 132, 146
Kucks, Johnny, 183
Kunitz, Al, 37
Kurowski, Whitey, 176, 216

About the Authors

Author and entrepreneur **David Hickey** lives with his wife, Corey, and three children in Whitman, Massachusetts, where he manages his son's Little League team. He coauthored *The Babe in Red Stockings* in 1997 and recently completed a history on the town in which he lives. He is a member of the Society for American Baseball Research and the Whitman Historical Society. He received a bachelor of science degree from Bridgewater State College in 1989 and has owned and operated two companies since 1995.

A longtime member of the Society for American Baseball Research, **Kerry Keene** contributed dozens of articles on the game's history to newspapers in southern New England throughout the 1990s. He coauthored *The Babe in Red Stockings* in 1997, followed by two solo efforts, *1960: The Last Pure Season* in 2000 and *1951: When Giants Played the Game* in 2001. He is married with two children and lives in Raynham, Massachusetts.